Praise for *The Light Work*

"One of the most down-to-earth books on spirituality."
—Terri Cole, psychotherapist, author, and podcast host

"A heartfelt reminder of our inner power. . . . Read it, and you're not just changing your life—you're helping to shift the entire world."
—Amy Porterfield, *New York Times* bestselling author of *Two Weeks Notice*

"A spiritual empowerment book, here to wake you up to the truth of what your body is truly capable of: to heal itself so you can heal the world."
—Dr. Will Cole, leading functional medicine expert and *New York Times* bestselling author of *Intuitive Fasting*

"The ultimate guide on what it means to be a Lightworker today. . . . Reading it will unlock your light."   —Shaman Durek, bestselling author

"This book feels like it's been written by my best friend who loves me dearly and confides her deepest thoughts, experiences, and tales through raw and honest magnetic storytelling."
—Sah D'Simone, bestselling author of *Spiritually Sassy*

"Powerfully taps into energetics, the future of wellness, and will guide you step-by-step to unlock your full energetic potential."
—Mastin Kipp, bestselling author and creator of Functional Life Coaching™

"A divinely guided road map for how to succeed in the Age of Aquarius."
—Ophira Edut, The AstroTwins and astrologer for *Elle*

"A one-of-a-kind guide to wake you up and remember just how powerful, brilliant, and needed you are. Each chapter is a key to unlock the truth of who you really are. Devour this book. . . . The world is waiting for you to shine."   —Heather Dubrow, Real Housewife of Orange County

"Powerful. . . . A spiritual blend of insight and entrepreneurial wisdom."
                                —Alyssa Rosenheck, author and photographer

"Jessica Zweig reminds us who we are, what goodness we are capable of, and *The Light Work* that moves us all toward a better way."
                                —Tara Stiles, cofounder of Strala Yoga

"Authentic . . . offering not only inspiration but a practical road map for those seeking to live in alignment with their cosmic truth."
                                —Julie Solomon, bestselling author and
                                founder of *The Influencer Podcast*

"Beautiful, raw . . . The authentic truth."
                                —Craig Siegel, bestselling author and global speaker

"This human experience doesn't have to have so much unnecessary suffering—it can be more magical and blissful. *The Light Work* shows you how."   —Emily Fletcher, *Wall Street Journal* bestselling author of *Stress Less, Accomplish More*, founder of Ziva, and podcast host

"A journey back home to ourselves, where the light shines the brightest, revealing that alignment will always be our most important assignment."
                                —Judi Holler, keynote speaker, author, and poetic voice

THE
LIGHT
WORK

ALSO BY JESSICA ZWEIG

*Be: A No-Bullsh*t Guide to Increasing Your Self Worth
and Net Worth by Simply Being Yourself*

THE
LIGHT
WORK

RECLAIM YOUR FEMININE POWER,
LIVE YOUR COSMIC TRUTH,
AND ILLUMINATE THE WORLD

JESSICA ZWEIG

ST. MARTIN'S
ESSENTIALS
NEW YORK

To Aleksa and Nora, the two other pieces of the triangle, the Holy Trinity, the most unbreakable shape in the Universe

◇◇◇◇◇◇◇◇◇◇◇◇◇◇◇◇

First published in the United States by St. Martin's Essentials,
an imprint of St. Martin's Publishing Group

THE LIGHT WORK. Copyright © 2024 by Jessica Zweig. All rights reserved.
Printed in the United States of America. For information, address
St. Martin's Publishing Group, 120 Broadway, New York, NY 10271.

www.stmartins.com

Interior art © Aleksa Narbutaitis

The Library of Congress Cataloging-in-Publication Data is available upon request.

ISBN 978-1-250-33296-7 (hardcover)
ISBN 978-1-250-33297-4 (ebook)

Our books may be purchased in bulk for promotional, educational, or business use. Please contact your local bookseller or the Macmillan Corporate and Premium Sales Department at 1-800-221-7945, extension 5442, or by email at MacmillanSpecialMarkets@macmillan.com.

First Edition: 2024

10 9 8 7 6 5 4 3 2 1

CONTENTS

Foreword by Michael Bernard Beckwith   ix

THE DAWN

Preface: But What Is Light, *Really*?   3

Introduction: I Am New   9

But First . . . A Word About the Dark   21

The Language of Light   26

PART I: INNER LIGHT

1. Source | *Finding Your Way Back*   33

2. Emotions | *The Keeper of Keys*   53

3. Body | *Your Sacred Vessel*   66

4. Power | *Claiming Radical Responsibility*   90

PART II: OUTER LIGHT

5. Soul Family | *Healing Yourself Heals the World*   109

6. Romantic Relationships | *Love's a Witch*   124

7. Female Friendships | *The Greatest Medicine of Them All*   141

8. Money | *Rewiring Your Abundance Codes*   155

PART III: FUTURE LIGHT

9. Mission | *Your Creation, Your Calling, Your Cause*   177

10. Mentorship | *Your Future You Needs You*   195

11. Gaia | *The Reason for Your (Light) Being*   210

12. Miracles | *Go Light Up the Fucking World*   227

YOUR LIGHTWORKER RESOURCES

The Radiance Realm: Reader's Guide   237

The Lightworker's Invocation   238

The Lightworker's Principles   239

The Lightworker's Playlist   242

The Lightworker's Toolkit   246

Symbols of Light   251

Acknowledgments   253

Notes   257

FOREWORD

Light is the agent, the energy that allows us to see and that makes all things visible.

We all understand this tangibly: we open our window curtains and blinds to allow in the sunlight during the day, and we turn on our lamps to illuminate a dark room at night. We understand this intellectually when we become enlightened on a topic or situation that we previously had less knowledge about. And of course, there's spiritual enlightenment, which is the conscious awareness of our nonphysical soul essence and identity, above and beyond our social conditioning and personality.

Every individual on this planet possesses Light. We're not just "one with" the Light, *we are the Light*. Our Light is the critical component, the foundation of our being. There is nothing more potent than our Light. It's life-giving, life-receiving, and life-sustaining. It stimulates growth and expansion. All organisms require, are drawn to, and thrive in Light. It's associated with ebullience. Goodness. Greatness. Peace. Joy. Love. Warmth. Everything that is the basis for who we are, why we are here, and the reason we chose to incarnate onto the planet is to bring more and expand the Light in our own unique ways.

This is why *The Light Work* is a critical and necessary book for this time, and Jessica Zweig, as the beautiful Light-bearer she is, has written an exceptional guide for all of us to step into our Light identity and be about our work in expanding humanity and the planet as never before. The Light allows us to perceive with the eye behind the eye to see what's Real, what's True, what's Eternal, and to create the conditions that align with that and move us forward.

But while our Light is innate, due to the limitations of our worldly, societal, cultural, and familial conditionings, in many respects, our Light has been greatly dimmed. Many of us have forgotten our power, our brilliance, our radiance, and our resilience, having fallen into the practiced vibrational habit of fear, lack, worry, doubt, limitation, guilt, anger, and a whole host of low-frequency thoughts and beliefs that not only hold us down but hold us back. We have no idea that everything we see and say about our lives and the world is just a reflection of the ideas we choose to focus on. It is our extreme attention to the conditions, situations, and circumstances we say we don't like or want that causes them to expand. The reason we're here is to evolve Life beyond our current paradigms. Thankfully—and by Universal design—these conditions, circumstances, and the thought-forms that create them are not fixed in time nor space, but can be transmuted when we remember and evoke our Light from within.

Jessica's offering is the literal light on the path back to that. This is because what we call darkness is not the *opposite* of the Light we might think, like it's an actual "thing," but because darkness is merely the *absence* of Light, which means we can access our Light anytime we choose to.

The Light Work reveals an illuminating, clearer way of seeing, being, and living that propels us toward our Light identity; a next-level awareness of ourselves, leading to a life of freedom, clarity, vision, and joy. Through the wisdom, insight, and inspiration borne out of her continuing, ever-evolving journey that has brought her through some of the darkest of human experiences into her Light, Jessica provides her readers with the powerful teachings and lessons of her lived experience, and the principles, tools, practices, and activations she utilizes to further expand and sustain her Light.

Jessica is an authentic disciple of Truth who lives on the edge of continual growth and expansion, and I truly admire and appreciate her passion and enthusiasm for not only her own adventure in conscious luminosity but for inspiring so many others to recognize their own Light and to fly with excellence.

If you are ready to discover, embrace, and reveal your own brilliance, absorb the pages of this book. Remember, you can only shine your light when you allow yourself to be the Light that you are. Shine on.

Michael Bernard Beckwith, founder and CEO
of Agape International Spiritual Center,
author of *Life Visioning* and *Spiritual Liberation*,
and host of *Take Back Your Mind Podcast*

THE DAWN

Step forward as a member of the Family of Light; have the
courage in all the days you walk this planet to live that light
and to share that light with all you encounter.

—BARBARA MARCINIAK

PREFACE

BUT WHAT IS LIGHT, *REALLY*?

You have most likely picked up this book based on your own unique perspective, opinion, or calling toward the word "light."

For as much as the savvy marketing entrepreneur in me would like it to be, the concept of light is not new.

Light is as old as eternity.

The Bible opens with the statement, "Let there be light"; the ancient Egyptians originally worshipped Ra, the sun god of light; the Jewish Kabbalah reflects that light is the manifestation of the metaphysical Divine, while quantum science is rooted in the study of light as energy.

Light has been studied, revered, and known since the dawn of humanity on this planet. Today, well, you'll hear the words "love" and "light" being tossed around like candy from every modern-day seeker and spread across every "woke" Instagram account you have most likely unfollowed by now.

These numerous perspectives, narratives, spiritual conversations, and cultural opinions around the word "light" can make your head spin. It sure does mine. Depending on where you look, "light" is deepening its potency at best, being misappropriated at worst, or potentially losing its gravity altogether.

When I originally pitched this book to publishers, I was told by one editor (clearly not the one who ended up publishing it) that the word "light" was "problematic."

I couldn't help but scratch my head. How could something so pure, so universal, so ancient, so undeniably available to each and every one of us and so necessary at this time on the planet, be . . . *a problem*?

Then it clicked.

You want to know what Light *really* is?

It's you.

It's you in the full embodiment of your power.

That, sadly, can be very threatening to people. Not because people are afraid of the Light that *you* are, but because they are afraid of their *own* Light often unexpressed within themselves.

I take that back. People aren't afraid.

People have just *forgotten*. Many of us have, but it's time to remember who we *really* are. It's time to turn the lock and realize you are the key.

For the last fifteen years, I have created a business, a brand, and a public platform as a leading entreprenuer in marketing and branding. I have also been on a deep spiritual journey during this exact time. When I launched my second business in 2017, the SimplyBe. Agency, an internationally recognized and award-winning personal branding firm that I would eventually exit seven years later, I combined my hard skills in marketing, branding, social media, and public relations with my passion for humanity. At the core, my job has been to help my thousands of clients "turn on their Light" in their businesses and brands in order to show up fully authentically online. The book you are holding in your hands is here to help you **activate that same Light in *every* aspect of your life so that you can *embody* authenticity (and empowerment, sovereignty, and joy) everywhere and anywhere.**

Professionally speaking, my philosophy has always been that there is no difference between your "personal brand" and your "professional brand." This integration is where your authenticity lives. **Spiritually speaking, there is no difference between *what you believe about yourself* and *how*** *you show up for the world,* **nor is there any difference between** *what you* **believe about the world** and *how you respond to it,* **and therefore how it responds to you.** This self-awareness is where your awakening lives. Through my own painful and transformative lessons, many of which I will share in this book, I have come to learn that your professional success will only grow to the extent that you grow as a human being and, ultimately, as a spiritual being.

This is not an easy task. This is why it's called *The Light Work,* and the operative word here is "work."

Please know you have not picked up this book by sheer coincidence. It is no accident you were called to it. You are here, reading this book, because you are a member of the Family of Light. This is a term I learned years ago myself from the Pleiadians, a group of higher dimensional beings, whom you will be learning much about in this book. For now, I want to honor you for being here. It means you are one of the select few who are awakening to the cellular memory, or *personal power,* in their DNA, and thereby helping the world around you wake up, too. It means you and I are family.

You have probably felt your whole life that you are here (not reading this book, but here on planet Earth, which I will refer to as Gaia) for a *reason,* a *mission.* Perhaps you have felt a bit like an outcast, a rebel, a revolutionary, a renegade. That's because you are, and you have been given an assignment to shift the frequency of the planet right now back to its original state of Love. Before you can complete this assignment, there are many steps to get there. There is *work to do.*

The way you help to restore the planet is by restoring yourself first. The way you heal the planet is by healing yourself first. The way you activate this planet into more Light is by activating yourself first. Buckle up.

To get the most out of this book, I strongly suggest you have a fresh journal by your side and entitle it *The Light Work* on the first page. As you go through the book, your journal will become your *own* sacred record. Perhaps find a friend (or a few), create your own collective of Lightworkers, and go through the material, exercises, and tools together. This book is intended to support raising the vibration on this planet, and there is power in numbers. Most importantly, the work here will no doubt bring up a lot of emotions, and it's always good to have someone by your side. Hold each other accountable, and be each other's reminders of the Light that you always are.

We cannot talk about Light Work without talking about Shadow Work. **While Light Work is about what you are here to consciously *express*, Shadow Work is looking at what you've unconsciously *repressed*.** Shadow Work involves diving into the unconscious material that shapes our thoughts, emotions, and behaviors based on our fears, then transforming, transmuting, and alchemizing them into the Light. The Light Work involves activating our conscious, integrated, whole, and authentic selves to embody our thoughts, emotions, and behaviors based on Love.

Light Work, at its core, is about *self-responsibility*. It's about turning on the proverbial light switch in every area of your life so you can finally, fully, *see* the truth of who you really are.

As I have come to understand from my studies of the Pleiadians, "Light is Information, and darkness is lack of information." "Light" will be used as a tool for personal transformation. This book is designed to challenge you to take *radical accountability* for how you show up in the world using your Inner Light (what you believe about yourself) and your Outer Light (what you believe about others and how you respond to the external world), so that you can step forward not only into a more empowered life for yourself but also a more inclusive, loving, and Light-filled world for future generations to inherit. This is the Future Light.

No individual can change the world and all of its atrocities. There is one thing we *can* change: *ourselves*. This, in turn, helps to change the world, one mind and one heart at a time. **You are *that* powerful. You are *that* important. You are *that* needed, *right now*.**

Perhaps you can't fully receive that. Based on your own unique life circumstances, you can't get past the darkness you see every day on the news, or you are consciously (or unconsciously) absorbing the dark energy of people around you at work, at home, or in your community. Darkness, because it lacks information, is the breeding ground for the most dangerous aspects of humanity: bigotry, racism, antisemitism, homophobia, bullying, and hate. While these characterizations are the most extreme offenders, the average woman possesses her own darkness: self-loathing, jealousy, scarcity, insecurity, competitiveness, and gossip, to name a few.

I have certainly been one of those women.

Please know that this is a journey. As you will learn from reading my personal stories in this book, this has not been a straight line for me. Oftentimes, I have had to go through the same lessons over and over again until I finally learned them, shifted my beliefs, and then integrated them into a new way of being.

There is no destination on the path to Light. We are infinite, after all, and this work belongs to all of us.

Speaking of belonging, the word "light," and therefore this book, is for *everyone*. While it is told through the lens of a cisgender, heterosexual white woman, my intention is that this book contains universal wisdom that supports all of your identities: whether you are woman, man, nonbinary, LGBTQIA+, BIPOC, disabled, neurodivergent, and/or of any religious or spiritual background, all are welcome here.

While this book is told from my perspective, as it is based on a deeply personal journey, my intention is to not only refine the word "light" with more personal responsibility but also to reunite us all. To remind us that just like light itself, it is exactly our beautiful, eclectic, multidimensional, and colorful differences that actually make up Light. We cannot exist in our full expression and in our full power without each other.

The world needs us so deeply right now.

It is *your* time to remember who you are and why you came here.

You are the Light.

We all are, in this great Family of Light.

Let us unlock the lock and remember we are the key.

Let us light the way.

I AM NEW

As I boarded a plane to Cairo, ready for my fifteen-day pilgrimage to Egypt, there was a part of me that was running on fumes. Burnout had hollowed me from the inside. I was tired to my bones, and in my mind, this trip was the only thing that might save me.

It was clear to me that I was trapped in a pattern: a painful rinse-and-repeat cycle of inspired enthusiasm, overexertion, and perpetual exhaustion. As the plane took off, I didn't feel an iota of my usual pretravel giddiness. All I felt was depleted and dark.

I was the opposite of Light.

You see, I had been sprinting up a mountain for the last five years, starting with the launch of my dream business in 2017. Just a few years prior, I had walked away from the first business I had built—a popular digital magazine for women—after failing to scale it. I was crawling my way out of a sea of credit card debt, newly married to a husband who was going through the scarcity of his own career dissolution, perpetually sick due to the onset of an autoimmune disorder from chronic stress and inflammation, and swimming in pervasive insecurity that came with, well, failing.

Upon my walking away from business number one, I desperately wanted to start another, the SimplyBe. Agency, inspired by a small tattoo on my wrist, a business that would help people build their authentic personal brands by teaching them how to *simply be* online and off.

Instead, I took a corporate job as a lifeline, which kept me golden-handcuffed (and on four airplanes a week) for two straight years of what felt to me like patriarchal corporate bureaucracy.

When I finally got enough courage to quit (and to face my husband's panic of leaving the six-figure salary, bonuses, and benefits that supported our family), I placed all bets on myself. I just couldn't stand to watch my dream of starting my next business sit on a shelf and rot for one more day. My husband and I fought for months leading up to it. I was only able to get him to concede by demonstrating that I could get enough clients in those first few months to pay half our rent plus groceries, which I did. It came out to $1,500 per month, which barely covered it. Nonetheless, I remember the exact feeling when I quit that corporate job to start my second company. It was the feeling of *leaping and knowing that the net would catch me.*

It did.

SimplyBe. Agency (the actual business this time, not the idea) exploded. Within less than eighteen months, I had hit seven figures in revenue, grew the agency to a multi-seven-figure business in the five short years following, and to my own astonishment became a bestselling author, a number-one-ranking podcast host, a sought-after speaker, and an award-winning CEO.

It wasn't all glamorous.

SimplyBe. started feeling less like a career and more like a rocket ship, and I got hooked on the dopamine hit of hustle. My addiction to work became insatiable. The highs I got from the money, the awards, the press, the success, and the attention became my favorite chase. I chased everything *fast.* I became a literal sprinter. Sprint! *Crash.* GET UP. Sprint! *Crash.* GET UP. Repeat.

I prided myself on my entrepreneurial tenacity, revered my professional grit, and would amaze myself at how much productivity I could cram into a single day. Unlike with my first business, I wasn't being driven by my ego.

I was being led by a purpose and a deep desire to serve. This can make the experience of hustling for your dreams a very complicated thing to reconcile within yourself.

After all, when you love what you do so much and are called to do it based on a clear understanding of your purpose, while being propelled from a higher source, how do you take your hands off the wheel?

You eventually crash the car, that's how.

In January 2022, a year after I had launched my first book, *Be.*, I crashed. You could call that year "the mountain's summit." Instead of pacing myself as one might do at the steepest, most intense vertical they have to climb, I turned up every circuit on the motherboard of my mind, body, and spirit to full blast and bolted.

It's no surprise that the burnout, physical depletion, and diagnosed depression that followed were insurmountable. I had hit burnout many times before while building my agency, but this was different. This was the first "Sprint! *Crash*" that I couldn't pick myself up off the floor from on my own. I needed help.

In that rock-bottom winter, I turned to my therapist, my astrologer, my meditation practice, my journaling, and a lot of solitude and inner reflection. As a spiritual person, I cognitively knew this was all part of my journey, but emotionally and physically I could not get myself out of the darkness. I lost all desire to shower or leave my house, let alone socialize. I isolated myself for months, and the few times I did leave to see only some of my closest friends, they remarked (gently) how I didn't look like myself. My husband felt helpless, and that's because he was. I had lost my "light," and I recall wondering with my therapist, session after session, if I'd ever get it back. She would hold my hand in compassion, smile into my swollen eyes, and not make any promises.

She recommended I explore medication. I was desperate to feel better and was ready to try a prescription drug for my mental health for the first time in my life. By the grace of God, I got a referral to a holistic psychiatrist, who definitively advised me against medication and instead helped me heal my physical body through sleep regulation and hormone rebalancing and who ultimately treated my depression with a series of ketamine IVs. Ketamine is a breakthrough therapy that restimulates neuroplasticity while reducing inflammation in the brain through its psychedelic properties, proven to drastically reduce symptoms of mental illness.

(Caveat: This is what worked for me, and by no means am I saying this is the path for everyone. Prescription medication for mental health diagnoses can save people's lives. There are various journeys one can take toward healing. You are a sovereign being. Find the right doctors, and ultimately, listen to yourself.)

I am grateful to say that my intensive two-week, six-treatment ketamine protocol was miraculously effective. It removed the dust that had been covering my eyes, so I could see my life clearly. While it absolutely healed my depression, it didn't heal my habits, my hustle, or my deep addiction to work. It certainly didn't banish the prolonged shadows that I'd been running from most of my life.

The rest of that year, with my brain technically healed and yet my life looking exactly the same as it had for years, I sank deeper into the overwhelm of my schedule, comparison to other women in my space, and resentment toward the monthly hamster wheel of sales I had to maintain in order to meet my gargantuan six-figure payroll every month. The feedback loop of the toxic, masculine hustle continued without end.

On my best days, I would talk to my therapist. This made me feel slightly better. On my worst days, I screamed into pillows, cried until my face was swollen, physically smashed things (even once, on a particularly low and shameful night, destroying a bag of makeup as I hurled it against the wall of my apartment amid guttural screams, scaring the living shit out of my husband and our two little dogs). If the tantrums didn't ease the misery, I would constantly complain to anyone close enough to me who would listen. This made me feel deeply validated.

When the day finally arrived to depart for my pilgrimage to Egypt from O'Hare Airport in the late fall of 2022, I had pretty much given up. The burnout from my business had turned into rage against the machine called my life. I was too fucking tired to fight anymore. My body hurt, my mind was fried, and my soul was cashed out. I wanted to quit. In my heart, I basically did.

As I stepped onto the United flight to Cairo, I collapsed into my seat, secured my seat belt, and took a short, contracted breath. As the plane began its ascent, my aching sobs rose with it.

The irony of my state of being wasn't lost on me, and I felt a sense of shame about it. I thought, *If only people knew that the girl from Instagram, the one with the sunny bright-yellow branding, who is always so positive and high vibe, pretty much hates her life right now as she's flying off to such a privileged experience.* The shame I felt was in large part due to the spiritual path I'd been on for decades. I should've known better. I should have turned to the tools that are *always* available to me to come back to my Light: breathwork, meditation, journaling, crystals, Reiki, acupuncture, plant medicine, chanting, ecstatic dance, somatic healing, and perhaps most significantly, connecting with my star family, the Pleiadians, who are the original teachers of Light on this planet.

Frankly, I had been too busy and too tired to reach for any of it. I just needed to get myself to Egypt, even though I had no idea what was waiting for me there.

At this point, I had no idea just how much I had forgotten.

I had no idea that Egypt would be my ultimate remembrance.

This trip had been booked a year prior, when the stars had aligned. My best friend, Megan, and I take an international trip every year, and we were considering Egypt. In that exact week we brought it into our awareness, we got news that one of our favorite healers was planning a pilgrimage for an intimate group the same month we were thinking of going. In hindsight, I have no other explanation for going to Egypt other than that I called it in as much as it called me.

Ten days into the trip, we finally reached Dendera, the Temple of the Goddess Hathor, in a town called Qena. It was there that everything changed. *I* changed.

From the Sphinx, to the Temple of Isis at Philae, to Sekhmet's chamber at Karnak, to Horus's Temple of Edfu, to the Kom Ombo Temple, my pilgrimage through Egypt was a compounding crescendo of recalling and recollecting my light codes. Stepping onto the grounds of Dendera, however, I felt a unique stir. It was a deep, quiet knowing: *I have been here before.*

Before reaching the temple doors, I was welcomed by a sprawling courtyard with a long pathway down its center. As I traversed the wide-open outdoor space, *massive* buzzing wasps began flying in circles around my body. Naturally, I felt a small panic that they would sting me, so I picked up my pace. I could not get away from them and inside Dendera fast enough.

Once our Egyptologist guided us through the grounds of the temple, explaining the historical facts of the structure itself, I was left to roam on my own for the next hour. This was my favorite part of this pilgrimage: when we were free to wander through these sacred sites alone.

As I made my way through Dendera's sprawling hallways, gorgeously engraved alcoves, and underground tunnels, I found myself at the foot of a tall ladder, ascending into a portal in the wall, about the size of a small closet, just tall enough to stand in. According to the guards, these were Hathor's music chambers, an especially powerful part of the temple, given that Hathor is the goddess of frequency.

It is believed that there are seven "Hathors" that stem from the constellation of Pleiades, approximately 444 light-years away from Earth. The Pleiades is one of the brightest star clusters in our galaxy, containing three thousand stars, with seven of its brightest stars representing what are called the Seven Sisters.

The second I entered Dendera's space, I felt a call to press my entire body against the wall. I wanted all my chakras, the seven major energy centers of my body, from my root to my belly to my heart to my third eye, pressed up as close to Dendera's vibration as I could get.

I closed my eyes, and within a matter of seconds, a huge, diamond-white flash of light poured through me, within me, and all around me. It felt exactly as though piercing white lightning had hit my physical body, and in an instant, my entire auric field expanded into one blindingly white energy bubble, reaching far beyond the music chamber, beyond Dendera, beyond the town Qena, beyond even Egypt itself, and into the infinite.

Then I started hearing voices.

They were speaking to me rapidly, in a chorus at times, then individually, talking over each other, eagerly clamoring for my attention. I knew immediately who they were: Hathor and the Seven Sisters of Pleiades, channeling through me from a higher dimension—the highest dimension I had ever been able to reach until that moment.

They pleaded with me:

Jessica, we want you to understand how lucky you are to be in a human body . . . and not just a human body but a woman's body. You could have incarnated as a man, but you didn't. You chose to be a woman, and you are therefore one with us, the Goddess.

We want you to remember just how lucky you are to have this human experience right now. It is meant for your enjoyment, for your pleasure, and for your bliss. You must stop apologizing for your beauty, inside and out. You must own your power. You must take responsibility for your mission.

And please, we beg you, you must take this Information to as many women as you can. The feminine frequency is here now, and this is the only way the planet will return to its natural state. You must help us. And the only way you can help is to reclaim this Information, live your Truth, and embody Love. These are the highest of frequencies, the Divine Laws of Light. This is the Light that belongs to you. This is the Light that belongs to everyone.

I peeled my body off Dendera's wall, and it was as though my entire physical and energetic bodies had expanded into an entirely new dimension of consciousness. I had never felt *that* awake, *that* alive, *that* present in my body, and *that* connected to Spirit all at once. Descending back down the ladder of the music chamber, I kept repeating to myself what I had just heard. I could not, and *would* not, forget it.

Making my way out of the grand entryway of the temple and back into the courtyard lush with the scent of ancient Earth, I saw the same dozens of massive wasps swirling around me.

Only a few hours prior, I had resisted them. Now, leaving Dendera with this new Information pulsing through my body, I possessed a new cosmic intelligence: the wasps were never going to sting me. These wasps were magic, an intrinsic piece of the interdependent spirit world with which I was now joined. The wasps were pieces of the Goddess. I felt profound love and reverence for them.

This is what it feels like to be embodied in my Divine Feminine frequency, I thought to myself. I had never felt so awake in my life. This feeling was new, but it wasn't unfamiliar. It was a homecoming; a return to Truth.

I boarded our bus back to the hotel, plopped down on a two-seater row by myself, and slid up against the window to feel the sun on my face. As soon as we started moving, my body began to ache. The aching grew into shivering, and suddenly I was freezing. I lay down in a fetal position and started to shake uncontrollably. I had no idea what was happening to me, so I didn't say anything; instead, I tried to breathe through it to stay calm. Three seemingly never-ending bumpy hours later, we arrived at our hotel in Abydos, Egypt. As I tried to stand, I found that it hurt to breathe; it hurt to move; it hurt to think.

We swiftly checked in and made our way to our rooms, and I immediately crawled into bed. I wrapped myself in as many blankets and towels as I could find. I couldn't get warm, and the shaking escalated. No matter what I did, I hurt.

Lying there in intense physical pain, with virtually no options to soothe myself, I had a conscious thought: to *hum*. For whatever reason, I intuitively knew the vibration of humming would help.

So I began. *"Hmmmmmmmmm."*

It wasn't strong enough. I had another conscious thought: to open my mouth as I hummed, to increase the vibration.

"Uuuuhhhhhhhhh," I moaned.

This resonance in my body began to comfort me from the inside out. With my mouth wide open, projecting this monotone sound, something involuntary and unexplainable started to happen.

I began speaking. It wasn't a language I knew. These were not words coming out of my mouth but intonations that rose and fell, quickening like staccato notes and then slowing down like rhythmic chants. The tone of my voice didn't even sound like my everyday voice; it had a higher, sweeter, and softer pitch. It sounded like babbling, but it was beautiful, symphonic, harmonic, and so incredibly pure.

My 3-D brain was conscious of what was happening and was a little freaked out by it, but something bigger encouraged me to release self-judgment and keep going. I lay in bed for an hour, allowing these beautiful soundscapes to come through and pour out of me. By the time they naturally subsided and I was done, I felt better. My body had stopped shaking, and I could move effortlessly without the ache.

I knew what had just happened: I had channeled Light Language.

I only knew this to be true because I had heard people speak Light Language in the past, either in ceremonies, healing sessions, or recorded talks and podcasts. **Light Language is the language of your soul.** It holds the unique frequency of your soul's essence, allowing you to create a two-way communication with Source. It is used as a modality for clearing low-vibrational densities in the body, healing traumas from current and past lives, activating dormant DNA, and transmitting direct guidance from Spirit. It comes *through you* versus *by you*. It has been said that your unique language can depend on your star family lineage. For many, hearing and/or speaking Light Language for the first time can feel like a cosmic homecoming.

I eventually fell asleep for fourteen hours, and when I woke up, I got dressed and went down to the restaurant, where our group was having breakfast. Still feeling a bit disoriented, I was eager to nonetheless share what had happened the previous night to make sense of it.

I scanned the restaurant and saw our two guides, our Egyptologist and our Egyptian tourism leader, enjoying hot coffee and shakshuka. I made a beeline to their table, greeted them quickly, and launched into the details of Dendera's temple, the sickness, the Light Language, the healing.

When I was done explaining, the two Egyptian men sat quietly. Their eyes slowly began to meet each other, and they softly, knowingly smiled. One of them finally spoke, as if I were not even standing there, and said directly to the other, "This is why people come to Egypt. So that they can *remember*. So that they can help to make this world a better place."

For the next few days, *I was fucking raw.*

While the shaking and aching had subsided, my body still felt physically off. I didn't have an appetite or much energy, and it was hard to stay warm. Up until Dendera, I had been sharing my trip on social media constantly, and I had a sudden urgent full-body desire to delete all my social apps off my phone, and so I did. The distraction of any outside activity was too much for my system to handle. I needed to just focus on the present moment. It was my only way to get through the day.

Most significantly, I was hypersensitive to everything and everyone. I was taking everything personally, from my roommate Megan's words, to the group of people on my trip and their insular conversations, to texts from my husband back home, who was supporting my international travels. Random childhood memories suddenly arose, and so did their subsequent sadness, hurt, anger, and loneliness. I saw stray dogs on the street, and my heart ached for them with an intensity I couldn't get past. I would lock myself in bathroom stalls to hide my incessant sobbing. I cried pretty much over everything, all day long.

Days went by as I processed these intense emotions, and the triggers finally subsided. I began to feel unexpectedly, remarkably, amazingly *open*. I was still *feeling* everything intensely, but it was no longer painful. It was exquisite. My heart was expanded, unblocked, and felt as vast as the infinite. My mind was quiet and clear as crystal. My body was grounded but so incredibly light. I was buzzing with a feeling I could only describe as euphoria.

It all started to make sense.

That moment in Dendera's temple when the Pleiadians spoke to me and through me was a "light activation." While it was a spectacular blessing, it was not something my human body was prepared for. You see, Egypt is a portal, a direct doorway to cosmic stargates. That day, standing directly inside of it in the goddess of frequency's frequency, I downloaded *lifetimes* of light codes, of quantum-level healing. I could easily see how it was far too much for my vessel of flesh, bone, and blood to hold. I needed to metabolize it and, ultimately, integrate it.

When I integrated it, something within me unlocked.

My DNA activated.

My light codes came online.

My cellular memory restored.

I remembered.

The previous version of me shed itself.

I upgraded.

I became new.

The version of myself that had stepped onto that plane *to* Cairo in November 2022 did not come home with me. She didn't just leave the proverbial building. She left this realm. I look back on that version of myself, that avatar, and I bless her. I thank her. I honor her. She is, after all, the woman who helped me to establish and create all the incredible things in my life up until that point: the loving marriage, wonderful friendships, a thriving business, published books, a platform, a healthy body, and a beautiful home. She was also the one who believed that in order to have those things, she had to hustle, grip, prove, convince, grind, compare, demand, fear, and sacrifice. She was the version who didn't trust that joy, pleasure, abundance, peace, rest, and bliss are her innate birthrights.

She is not the woman who is writing this book.

The woman writing this book found her own keys and unlocked her true power: her Light.

Now I am going to help you find the keys to unlock yours.

Please know: I am not here to be your inspiration. I am here to show you that you are your own inspiration.

As you embody this journey, it is going to take work: the *Light Work*.

I want to make it clear that I didn't expand because of Egypt. *I expanded because of all the work I did leading up to Egypt and all the work I have done after to transmute, alchemize, and integrate my darkness into the Light.* This book isn't here to convince you to buy a plane ticket. This book is here to help you claim radical responsibility for how you show up in every area of your life, starting now.

It's going to provide tools, frameworks, and prompts that will show you how to shed and transmute your dark, shadowy, self-limiting beliefs and programming. It's going to guide you back home to yourself, so that you can *remember* your birthright and *activate* your unique codes.

Ultimately, it's going to empower you to authentically, unapologetically live your Light, to shine and raise not just your own frequency but the world's.

Let's begin together, anew.

BUT FIRST ... A WORD ABOUT THE DARK

Before there was Dendera, there was Kom Ombo, which was described by my pilgrimage guides as "the Temple of Neutrality." The massive structure is divided into two equal but enormous halves, representing duality. One side represents the "light," dedicated to the falcon-headed god Horus, and the other side represents the "dark," dedicated to the crocodile-headed god Sobek, associated with the wicked god, the enemy of Horus. It is believed that if you step into the center, you can experience pure neutrality.

With my small group of friends by my side, I walked through the hieroglyphic-covered walls, encircling the two sides like a loop, as I allowed for the polarities to alchemize my energy body. After a few minutes, my intuition nudged me to step away and go off by myself. I made my way to the center of the temple, with one foot literally in each of the dark and light sides. I stretched my hands out in opposite directions. Reaching my right hand toward the dark side of the temple, I could viscerally feel all the heaviness, sadness, and rage that enveloped my life in the last few years. Most of all, I could feel the darkness inside me. Images of people I still harbored anger against, shame around my own behaviors, and guilt around my own dark feelings flooded me. I began to weep. Then I reached my left hand toward the light side of the temple, and I could feel sensations of innocence, purity, and joy. I saw my little-girl self in my childhood home, playing in my room. I wept some more.

Once our visit to Kom Ombo concluded, we returned to our dahabeah (an Egyptian riverboat we had been sailing down the Nile River on for days). I headed straight for my room, which had a small balcony peering over the water. I grabbed my journal and started writing down all the "dark" things I had seen and felt in Kom Ombo. I was ready to release them.

On a blank sheet of paper, I wrote them out:

My burnout. My scarcity. My bitchiness toward, well, everyone. My resentment toward my husband for not rescuing me. My jealousy of my friends who have seemingly easier lives. My imposter syndrome. My comparisonitis. My addiction to approval. My obsession with validation. My hypervigilance and perfectionism. My vanity. My father's meanness and my mother's victimhood, which I inherited. My business for crushing my soul and all my employees for breaking my heart. Zero fucking freedom. Zero fucking levity. Zero fucking space. Zero fucking joy. All my fucking hatred toward all of it.

I took in my words on the page and let the darkness, the pain, the anger arise in my body. I took a deep breath in and sighed it all out. When I felt complete, I ripped the piece of paper into tiny shreds, and with pride and satisfaction, I threw them into the Nile River to release everything.

I closed my eyes once more as I inhaled the misty, Egyptian dusk air. I sat back on the balcony's sofa and dropped into a state of silence, letting the small ritual settle.

As if out of nowhere, I heard a voice speak through me. It was the voice of my higher self. . . .

Jessica . . . these are not the pieces of you to drown, she said. *These are the pieces of you to love.*

◆ ◆ ◆

You are going to read a lot about Light in this book; however, I'm not here to tell you to mentally, emotionally, or spiritually bypass anything. It's easy to want to tear up all our dark shit and throw it in the proverbial river.

This is where we get in trouble. Remember that Light is simply *Information* and therefore darkness is *lack of Information*. Dark is not evil. It is necessary. It is an essential part of this dualistic, 3-D human experience to suffer sadness, anger, hurt, rage, jealousy, grief, shame, and despair. We all signed up for this. As members of the Family of Light, we are here on a mission to recall, remember, and literally wake up to the Light pulsing inside our cells. We cannot uncover it without polarity. Our darkness is our way-shower and our teacher. When the dark gets dangerous or lethal, putrefies, and becomes toxic, we ignore it, suppress it, deny it, avoid it, skip over it, and lock it away, because we forget that we hold the key to ending our own suffering. The darkness is not a nuisance; it's our gift. When we navigate the darkness with greater self-responsibility, personal empowerment, and support from our healers and guides, we awaken into becoming fully activated, integrated, authentic, powerful, and sovereign beings. We become Lightworkers.

The only way out of our darkness is to take the journey *through* it.

This book is a complete resource guide toward becoming a Lightworker. It is a manifesto of my own personal journey and, as such, is a mirror for you to see your own radiance through your own pain. Above all, it is an invitation to live, share, and embody your fully expressed power, Truth and Light. Should you accept this invitation, you will embark into a portal of transformation. Each chapter is a key, here to help you unlock your infinite power and remember who you really are. It is up to you to turn the key. It is for you to do the Light *Work*. I will, of course, be right by your side the whole time, step-by-step, imparting my own stories of walking through this portal myself.

While our unique journeys all do indeed look different, as there is only one "you," there are common threads we all share, and I have divided this book and its invitations accordingly.

In "Inner Light," we are going to unpack our relationships with our most inner selves: our connection to the Divine, or "Source," our emotions, our physical bodies, and our personal power.

In "Outer Light," we are going to adventure through the rocky terrain of relationships with others: our families of origin, our romantic partnerships, our friendships, and the relationships we have with the energy of money.

In "Future Light," we are going to examine our relationship to our true missions in this life and explore how those missions will impact future generations to come, as well as Mother Earth, or Gaia, as I will refer to her, through the power of mentorship and the everyday miracle of living our Light.

At the end of every chapter, there will be an "invitation," in the form of journaling prompts or a meditation, followed by a "key"—actions, embodiment practices, rituals, and integrations. Some of these exercises will be reflective, guiding you more deeply, quietly into yourself by simply owning, acknowledging, and accepting pieces of yourself. Others will encourage you to outwardly, loudly, and at times physically express yourself in order to move and clear density, so that you can transmute it into a higher vibration and reclaim your authentic frequency. All of them are designed to take you *in,* not around. This is how we remember. This is how we unlock.

I'm going to highly encourage you to truly be with these tools, and not rush them. Spend time with yourself, your Light Work journal, and a group of fellow Lightworkers, whom I call your "Radiance Realm." I encourage you to read this book together in community, and I have provided instructions as to how in "Your Lightworker Resources" at the back of the book. Just like my higher self told me in Egypt, the elements of your darkness are not the pieces of you to quickly rip up and discard. Each step in the book is a necessary, sacred step, and it requires your attention, your tenderness, your acceptance, and ultimately, your love. Be gentle, stay focused, and get comfortable being uncomfortable. This is how you transmute the dense shackles of your dark into the effervescent freedom of your Light. When you do the Light Work, deep resistance will most likely arise. This is good news, as this edge of discomfort is where you meet the next highest version of yourself. The deeper and darker you go *in,* the more Light you will find.

When we own our darkness through acknowledgment and self-responsibility, we become empowered. When we release our darkness through feeling it, moving it, and clearing it from our bodies and psyches, we become free. It is only when we learn to love our darkness that we truly heal. **This is the great transformation, transmutation, and ultimate alchemy of the dark into the Light.**

So let's start by diving *into* our Inner Light to call forth our cellular memory, so that we may shine our Outer Light onto the world around us as we create a ripple of awakening for all the Future Light to come after us.

That's what we members of the Family of Light came here to do, after all. To unlock the lock, let the darkness be seen, known, and felt, and ultimately *love* all of what we find. For as you will soon come to learn, there is nothing that Love cannot hold or heal. This includes your darkest of the dark.

Let's go all the way in.

THE LANGUAGE
OF LIGHT

You will come across various words and phrases in this book that might be familiar to you or entirely foreign. My desire for you, my dear reader, is for you to reclaim your feminine power, live your cosmic truth, and remember who you *really* are, without being distracted by what I mean when I write "starseed." And so I have compiled the official Language of Light as a frame of reference to give a contextualized understanding of how I, as the author, personally define these terms. You will no doubt find different definitions across other voices and, most definitely, the dictionary. As Lightworkers, we're creating our own reality *and* our own language. It is a free-will zone, after all. Enjoy.

1 + 1 = 11: A metaphor for "be a whole person" in the context of a romantic relationship.

3-D reality: The current reality human beings exist within on Earth by way of the mind, constructed by principles of duality and separatism, where primary motivations of the human species are predicated on survival and therefore fear.

5-D reality: An ascended reality that all human beings can access on Earth by way of the heart, founded upon the principles of Oneness, where the primary experience of the human species is guided by Love, which inspires a new, *truer* reality comprised of harmony, abundance, freedom, personal sovereignty, compassion, and peace.

cellular memory: The memory of all that has ever occurred in the universe, encoded with light inside the cells of your body; the truest expression of your DNA.

Dark Feminine: The holy, sacred, and transformative energy of the anger, rage, protective nature, and fury of the feminine.

Divine Feminine: The Goddess energy that lives within all beings, regardless of gender. The Divine Feminine represents the values of compassion, receptivity, surrender, trust, ease, beauty, stillness, abundance, and fertility. She is metaphorically represented in this book's image of the inverted triangle, which you will find on the cover and throughout the exercises at the end of each chapter. This inverted triangle represents the Divine Laws of Light (see below), while also symbolizing the force of Mother Earth or gravity, the energy of the Gatherer, who uses her magnetism for manifestation. The triangle represents her chalice, her yoni, and her womb. She represents the unseen, the keeper of the great mysteries, the Great Mother and the Goddess.

Divine Laws of Light: The combination of Information, Truth, and Love, physically expressed as an inverted triangle, representing the Light Work in action (see also *Information, Truth,* and *Love* definitions).

Gaia: The personification of Earth and the name that will be used when referring to our planet in this book.

Goddess: The original "God," also known as Prime Creator, and the essence of all that is, including you.

Family of Light: Members from other parts of the universe who have incarnated on this planet at this time to trigger their own cellular memory and that of others, to inspire the human race to remember who we are as sovereign free beings, altering the frequency of this planet back to its original state of Light, creating a new reality (see also *Renegade*).

Living Library: The infinite, cosmic intelligence that pulses through every living cell on Gaia, ever-connected to the infinite information stored in the entire universe.

light codes: Ancient wisdom and cosmic intelligence stored deep inside your physical DNA, waiting to be activated and brought into your consciousness through feeling, breath, human connection, sacred spaces, prayer, ceremony, ritual, movement, and expansive experiences.

Light Language: The language of your soul, holding your unique frequency and the essence of your higher self, allowing you to create a two-way communication with Source when you speak it. It is used as a healing method for activating your light codes, upgrading your DNA, clearing energetic density, transmuting trauma and receiving spiritual guidance. It comes *through you* by way of higher dimensions, channeled from other quantum and galactic realms.

Love: The master key. With Love, all the locks unlock and limitless possibilities become available.

immanence: The inward journey that allows us to experience the Divine in everything—most of all, in ourselves.

Information: The primary synonym for "Light"; a tool for personal transformation.

Matrix: A constructed representation of reality, maintained by patriarchal forces primarily led by the mass media, corporate capitalism, big government, Big Pharma, the food industry, and major social media networks, designed to keep us disempowered in a 3-D reality driven by fear.

New Earth: An evolving reality currently being birthed in real time by the awakening of a massive collective of human beings, also known as Lightworkers, who are healing past traumas, reclaiming their sovereignty, honoring Gaia and her resources, and leading their own awakened communities based upon the principles of Oneness, Love, and 5-D consciousness.

Pleiadians: A group of higher-dimensional beings from the constellation Pleiades, roughly 444 light-years away from Gaia inside the Milky Way, who have come from the past and the future to activate the Family of Light on Gaia; the original bringers of Light to humanity.

Renegade: A trailblazing leader of the New Earth; someone who is driven by a deep mission to wake up the world, motivated by Love, who has at times been outcast for her or his beliefs, opinions, and choices; also known as a member of the Family of Light.

Shadow: The pieces of you that are consciously and/or unconsciously hurting and need your love, attention, acceptance, and integration.

soul family: Your biological and/or nuclear family, whose souls chose you as their child and whom your soul chose as parents and siblings in return.

starseed: A soul that has incarnated on Gaia but is not originally from this planet and, as such, has often struggled with belonging and the acceptance of others since she or he was young. A soul who is here to "seed" a new consciousness of Light for humanity.

transcendence: The experience of connecting with Divine Source, God, or Goddess that exists beyond us.

transmission: A channeled message from a higher-dimensional being (i.e., an angel, spirit guide, ascended master, ancestor, or galactic being), which comes through a human being in written or spoken form.

Truth: Your own unique genetic blueprint based on your DNA, designed for your full unapologetic, authentic expression.

PART I

INNER LIGHT

You alone are the architect of your evolution.

—RICHARD RUDD, *THE GENE KEYS*

1

SOURCE

FINDING YOUR WAY BACK

Nothing can dim the light which shines from within.
—MAYA ANGELOU

When my grandmother passed away, I was a freshman in college. I was also in the middle of ending a relationship with the only boy I had ever loved, experiencing the sheer wreckage of heartbreak for the very first time. During the weeks and months after her passing, I didn't fully grieve. I wasn't sure I even knew how. Instead of thinking of her soft squeezes and the way she would repeat *"I love you, love you, love you"* in rapid succession, I distracted myself with my own despair over a dude.

When the school year ended, with my heart still ravaged over this boy, I convinced my parents to let me backpack through Europe by myself for a month with the money I'd saved from waitressing. (Looking back, I'm less shocked that they actually let me do this and more in awe of how brave the nineteen-year-old me was.)

The last week of my trip, I went to Ireland. I spent my first few days sightseeing in Dublin, eating soda bread, pub-hopping, and catching George Bernard Shaw's *Candida* in a local black box theater before heading down south to the tiny town of Kilkenny.

My first morning in Kilkenny, I sipped coffee, reveled in the street musicians' performances on the cobblestones, and let myself wander. Around midday, I descended upon St. Canice's Cathedral, also known as Kilkenny Cathedral, in the middle of the town square. Standing in front of its massive, ancient walls, I felt compelled to go inside, but I also felt a bit awkward.

Am I even allowed? I thought to myself.

At nineteen, I'd never stepped foot into any holy building other than a synagogue. I'd grown up in a predominantly Jewish Chicago suburb, and my religion was a core part of my identity. My life as a young Jewish woman was rooted in some of my favorite beautiful holy traditions, my Bat Mitzvah, countless sacred family memories, and a deep pride of my ancestral lineage.

Yet my relationship and connection with and to God was a little murky. Not because I didn't believe in a higher power, but because I'd never defined what that even *meant*. My faith was not a visceral experience, an inner knowing, or a soulful relationship to Source, but rather the adopted beliefs of my parents, Sunday school teachers, and rabbis.

I rationalized, given that the cathedral was built in the 1300s, that it was a historical site as much as a religious one, and I was simply a tourist enriching her travels, versus a Jewish person trespassing in a Christian space.

I stepped in, thinking I'd stay for a few minutes to check out the monuments, stained glass, and glowing wooden pews. I sat down in one and took a breath. As I breathed out, I felt a strong, palpable tingle around both my shoulders, as if someone or something was holding me.

I knew immediately, innately, and viscerally that it was my grandmother.

It didn't make any sense, but I knew in my body it was her. I began to sob. *God, did I miss her.* I deeply regretted not saying goodbye. I regretted not honoring her death when it happened, too wrapped up in my own selfish heartache over a guy.

I am so sorry, I said in my head.

As clear as a sweet angelic sound, I heard her respond: *There is nothing to be sorry for. I am here now. I have been watching over you this whole time you've been traveling alone, and I will be watching over you forever. If you ever need me, just call on me. I am always right here. I love you, love you, love you.*

I sat in the pew for over an hour, crying silently as my grandmother's spirit wrapped her arms even more tightly around my shoulders and didn't let go.

That moment in St. Canice's Cathedral was a pure discombobulation of everything I believed I *could* believe. It was also the beginning of my spiritual awakening.

After all, how could I have the most profound spiritual experience of my life up until that point, connecting directly to one of my angels, my own Jewish grandmother, in a *church*?!

That moment, sitting in that pew in Ireland, was at its core my first initiation *and* my invitation. An invitation to develop a relationship to Source that is not dictated by a rabbi, priest, religious book, my parents, a spiritual text, or any guru. It was the invitation to develop a relationship that was wholly and fully *mine*.

THE MANY INVITATIONS

Channeling the distinct voice of your dead grandmother in a random chapel in a foreign country sounds a bit, well, inconceivable. I totally get it. Yet it was that precise moment that changed everything. Sitting there in that pew I experienced the initial spark of what would become a deep journey to build a *real relationship* with God, Source, Oneness, The Universe (insert whatever moniker you choose) on *my* terms. This meant expanding my own understanding of as many faiths, modalities, and spiritual practices as humanly possible.

This wasn't about converting. It was about getting *curious*. It meant opening my mind (and my heart) to what felt true *to me*. It meant deepening my capacity to understand the multitude of religious and spiritual beliefs that exist beyond my own upbringing. More than anything, it meant developing a profound reverence for how other human beings connect with the Divine, based on their Indigenous, cultural, and geographical heritages. I am by no means an expert in them, but I do know that opening up my mind to understand more diversity of beliefs, with an expanded, inclusive, and humble spirit has made me a more expanded, inclusive, and humble person. Studying new faiths and ideologies has, above all, deepened my understanding of the Divine itself and my connection to it.

My connection to my grandmother's spirit was an initiation into the *angelic realm.* That moment in Ireland opened up an ability to commune with archangels such as Uriel, Gabriel, and, most significantly, Michael, who helps to "cut chords" of lower vibrations that no longer serve us. Archangel Michael has helped me countless times to dissolve unhealthy attachments to people, situations, and energies that are holding me back, as well as to "cut" projections and psychic attacks from others that don't belong to me. I feel infinitely lighter every time I work with him. This opening into the angelic realm at large has become so strong that, just like my grandmother suggested, if I ever need any of them, all I have to do is ask.

I grew up believing in one God. Hinduism is one of the faiths that called me in strongly, based on its beliefs in various deities who represent the many aspects of the god Brahma. When I discovered Ganesha (the elephant Hindu god of protection and new beginnings), Lakshmi (the goddess of abundance), and Saraswati (the goddess of learning and knowledge), it opened my understanding of what God could look like and feel like, and "who" I could pray to and meditate with.

As my spiritual intuition grew and my connection to Source became more embodied, I naturally gravitated toward *the wisdom of Mother Earth.* This opened up a whole new gateway into shamanism, plant medicine, nature, and Indigenous traditions. We cannot talk about connection to the Divine without recognizing the long lineage of the Indigenous people of this Earth, whose families were brutally raped and uprooted from their homes, their lands pillaged and colonized, and their cultures appropriated. We owe a great debt of restoration to their peoples, and to the sovereign, reverent lessons of their traditions. Part of any spiritual quest is to not only seek to transcend into higher dimensions but to ground into the beauty of this great planet called Gaia, and this is something that we can all learn from

Indigenous cultures who innately cultivated a planetary harmony through love and reciprocity for all living things.

Indigenous tribes across North and South America, Africa, Asia, and Europe honored the sentient world of the animal kingdom and interpreted their world of messengers, meaning, and their star wisdom. Whether it's a butterfly, a rabbit, a crow, or a deer, never let the presence of an animal pass by without reflection. According to many Indigenous faiths, these animals are called *spirit animals;* they enter your awareness in that precise moment, for a specific reason, with a specific message based on what you're currently experiencing in human form. As I began to better understand their teachings, a newfound conscious connection to animals deepened, and it opened a new understanding of God.

On my spiritual journey over the last decade and a half, I have been humbled and honored to participate in sweat lodges and drumming circles led by Native American descendants, and I have traveled to their homelands in the United States, specifically in Santa Fe and Sedona. It was on a recent trip to Santa Fe that I met with a shamanic practitioner named Michele Ama Wehali, or "Mother of the Waters." Prior to my visit, we took a short call to prep, and the only direction she gave me was to pay attention to any animals I saw in the days leading up to my session with her. The night before our appointment, I had what was without question the most vivid, lucid, and unforgettable dream of my life.

In the dream, I was at a big, fancy gala, surrounded by people I didn't know, when a big black horse started charging through the ballroom out of nowhere, headed straight toward me. The closer it got, the more terror I felt. As it bolted nearer, my body clenched, anticipating it running me over. I felt as though I were about to die. As it fast approached me, it abruptly stopped mere millimeters from my face and gazed straight into my eyes. I knew this horse. Pure, raw, deep, intense love flooded through me, and I could feel the horse's all-encompassing, mutual love for me. It was a love so deep, it ached. This horse was mine. We had finally found each other. I woke up.

The next day in my shamanic session, I shared my story with Ama Wehali, who reflected back that the horse is my *power animal,* the animal assigned specifically to my life's path at birth. The horse is a spirit who must run free, unbridled by constraints of others, who thrives in her independence, whose strength outweighs her beauty, and who can be a bit (okay, a lot) highstrung at times. She was me. The horse's spirit was my spirit. This profound understanding and intimate connection to the horse has helped me more fully accept myself and has healed a lot of self-judgments. There is a reason animals are referred to as "medicines" of the spirit world.

I am forever grateful to Ama Wehali, the Native American land of Santa Fe on which I was blessed to receive medicine, and all Indigenous people who, like the horse, have always deserved their own birthrights of freedom. Let us never take for granted what they unwillingly sacrificed for us to be able to share stories like the one I have just told.

My appetite for spiritual knowledge further deepened, and I was hungry for more. This led me straight into the mysticism of astrology, which helped me better understand my own unique blueprint. It blew my mind to learn that the time, place, and date I was born, combined with where the stars, planets, asteroids, and other bodies in the cosmos were in that exact same moment would determine my personality and the course of my life. **Astrology is less of a crystal ball and more of an anchor point to help you make sense of the ups and downs of your life.** The deeper I got into astrology, the more "believing in the stars" rang true. This wasn't "woo." It was a science, and an extremely complex one at that.

To demonstrate one facet of this, let's talk about the "big three": our sun sign, rising sign, and moon sign. The sun sign represents our ego and external motivations; it is the sign most people associate with their birthdate. Our rising and moon signs are determined when we look at the location and time of our birth. Our rising sign represents the energy or personality we put out in the world, while our moon governs our most internal, emotional nature. I'm a Leo sun, Virgo rising, and Cancer moon. Being a Leo sun, my fiery drive, passion, and extroverted confidence, along with my meticulous, type A, always-of-service Virgo rising always felt in conflict with my hyper-sensitive, solitude-craving, introverted watery moon in Cancer. For the years running my digital magazine in Chicago, I would host the biggest monthly social events all around town. While a part of me thrived in this world, I also hated it. The truth is, I was the girl who wanted to be the first to leave the party she threw, go home alone, take a salt bath, listen to emo music, and cry. I never understood it until I learned my astrological chart. The more I studied it, the more my whole life made sense, as did the course of my romantic relationships, cities I was drawn to, and career aspirations. The more I charted my chart, the more I began to understand that I wasn't just an earthly being but a cosmic one.

In addition to all these modalities, I found great support with plant medi-cines and the scientific study of the universe itself. My deepest journeys with medicines like ayahuasca, psilocybin, MDMA, and specifically bufo came with the culmination of my quest to understand "Source." The first time I ever "smoked the toad" (also known as *Bufo alvarius*) was in Jamaica in 2017. Bufo is a psychedelic medicine, which comes from the Sonoran Des-ert toad, that activates your pineal gland with the molecule 5-MeO-DMT, a naturally occurring compound in the brain capable of inducing a powerful psychedelic state.* Some describe the ceremony as a "death," after which you are born again.

For context, a couple weeks before this experience, I was at home with my husband watching *60 Minutes,* which just so happened to be featuring NASA's latest discoveries from the advancement of the Hubble Space Tele-scope. Based on the telescope's findings, it turns out the universe is *billions and billions* times *bigger* than they had originally believed. The TV seg-ment showed images that Hubble had captured of these galaxies. Our TV

---

* Sadly, there is an over-glorification and lack of responsibility in the collective right now when it comes to partaking in and administering plant medicines today, as well as appropriation of the Indigenous cultures they come from. My decision to work with them has been a deeply personal choice. Additionally, I have worked with healers and shamans who held the utmost integrity and reverence in my ceremonies. I highly encourage you to do your own research. I am not promoting anything here but rather authentically sharing what these journeys have taught me and how they've helped me heal.

projected pictures of countless sparkling, multicolored star clusters, layers upon layers deep within the ethers. These images burned into my brain, as did one NASA scientist's comments, when he casually remarked in the interview, "Human beings are literally made of stardust."

Flash forward to that moment in Jamaica on the cushioned floor, one-on-one with a beautiful, loving, integrity-filled, and empowering shaman. The medicine hit, and within moments, my whole body exploded and my mind dissolved into what can be described as an orgasmic *bliss* I did not know existed. Only, I didn't just explode or dissolve. I *became*. What I *became* were the same images I saw of the universe on TV a few weeks earlier, but vastly more vivid. The star clusters expanded into eternal, endless, infinite sacred geometry. All of the universe was within me; I was within it; there was no separation; and in this state of Oneness, a singular Truth downloaded into my body, my consciousness, my soul: *it's all Love.*

After the initial "explosion," I began to float down back into my body and started to see everyone who had ever hurt me the most come into my awareness. These were also the people I loved the most: my family, ex-boyfriends, and former friends. As I saw each of them, I could see Planet Earth as a tiny grain of sand in a truly infinite universe, and I saw that we choose to incarnate here for a microcosm of time so that our souls may *evolve*. Not just evolve but *remember* that visceral Truth: *it's all Love.*

An hour later, the journey was complete, and I became coherent enough to finally speak. "I understand it now" was the first and only thing I had to say.

A COSMIC HOMECOMING

These invitations and journeys affirmed my long-held quiet belief that human beings are not the only sentient species in the universe. However, it was not until one particular healing session in 2018 that this inner knowing was validated.

That summer, I connected to a healer named Arya. I was told her gifts were impossible to explain. Those who were lucky enough to get a session with her called her the "real deal" and encouraged me to not ask too many questions but *just go*. I eagerly made my appointment with her, and to my surprise, there was not much inquiry on her part about who I was or what my intentions were. By the same token, she gave me no instructions on how to prepare. All I was given was the location of her home and a polite request to be on time. When the day of my session finally came, I found myself in her sacred space, lying on her massage table, and with a single candle burning on an altar. She played no music, offered no plant medicines, didn't wave any crystals or recite any chants or prayers. All she did was put her hands on either side of my head and ask me to close my eyes; she closed her eyes as well, and we remained that way in still silence for an hour.

Lying there on her table, completely "sober" and coherent, I began to journey. Visions started to unfold. Where I "went" can only be described as another world, another planet. Landscapes of purple and blue crystalline structures, open archways as tall as buildings, and meadows filled with iridescent sparkling vegetation filled my view. Everything seemed ancient, timeless, new, and translucent all at once. The sky was not blue or black like ours but lavender, and I could see other planets in their full, detailed form in the sky right above me, among multicolored star clusters. A sensation of *home* flooded me. It all looked and felt so familiar. I could sense there were other beings around me, but I did not physically see them; I could only feel them. As I did, my heart flooded with a sense of safety I had *never* felt before. I began to cry tears of joy. Before I knew it, I was descending back into my body, back into Arya's room, when I saw the numbers "11111111111" flash in front of my face like a barcode.

When I opened my eyes and sat up, I recalled to Arya what I had just seen. She had seen the *exact same thing*. I could not believe it. Upon confirming our matching visions, she matter-of-factly stated, "You are Pleiadian, Jessica. They are your star family, and you just visited your original planet."

My initial reaction was: "*I'm sorry, whhhaaaat? The Pleiadian—who?*"
I didn't understand what she meant. My rational mind wanted to laugh in
her face and immediately deflect what I had just heard. It sounded fucking
ridiculous. Instead I got really quiet. I tuned in to my heart. What I had just
seen was as real as any vision I could ever recount. The feeling of "home"
(and the peace and safety it instantly brought me) was physically palpable. I
knew in my soul what Ayra had just shared with me was true. I didn't need
any other verification other than what I had just experienced. In Ayra's reflection, I felt more seen than any other healer, shaman, coach, teacher, or
medicine woman had ever made me feel.

That session sent me on a deep path to know, understand, and connect
with the Pleiadians on my terms and in my own way. The Pleiadians are a
group of extraterrestrial beings that come from the Pleiades constellation,
one of the brightest star clusters in the Milky Way galaxy, with over three
thousand stars, including the seven "suns," also referred to as the Seven
Sisters. Some say the Pleiadians are from "the future." It is believed that
they are returning to Earth after shaping the dawn of humanity hundreds of
thousands of years ago. In the Pleiadian reality, time is not linear, so it's safe
to say they have always been here. Their job is to help human beings activate
our remembrance of our Light, the power of our own thoughts, so that we
may create our own reality and ultimately lead ourselves back to Love. *This is
their mission.*

This personal expedition meant delving deep into their sacred texts,
particularly books by Barbara Marciniak, who channeled Pleiadian transmissions into her books *Bringers of the Dawn, Family of Light, Earth,* and
Path of Empowerment. It was through my studies of Marciniak's work, along
with dozens of other writers, resources, and teachers, that I learned of terms
and ideas such as "Family of Light," the "Living Library," "renegades,"
Light as Information, the "free-will zone," "cellular memory," and most of
all, *the power of thought.* We will be exploring each of these concepts in the
coming chapters, and their teachings will be core through lines of this book.

My most significant observations came from not what I was learning but how these learnings made me *feel*. With each word, it felt like I was coming home to myself—like a warm embrace from a family I had always known but somehow forgotten. An affirmation of everything I knew to be true in my cells but could never articulate. They explained to me, just as I have shared with you, the reason I resonated with their messages in the first place was because I, too, am a member of the Family of Light. Of all the faiths, religions, angels, deities, and plant medicines I have communed with, it is the Pleiadians and their transmissions of Light that have spiritually shaped me the most.

In my studies, I came to learn that there is an alignment of the placement of the Temple of Hathor in Dendera to constellations connecting to the star system of Pleiades.[1] The story of Seven Hathors, or Seven Goddesses, is connected to the Seven Sisters of Pleiades, and this has been reflected throughout various religions and cultures. The Pleiadians came to Earth to create a new human consciousness and were instrumental in creating various civilizations, cross-pollinating species, and enacting a new phase of humanity. They are known to activate through sound, and it has been said that Dendera holds their specific frequency. Years later, these teachings would explain my light-body activation in the Temple of Hathor in Dendera on my spiritual pilgrimage to Egypt and why I so clearly knew that the voices that were speaking through me were the Pleiadians. This is why their messages were so potent. It was Hathor's message that day that inspired me to finally come out of the spiritual closet to write this book and to own my voice as a leader of the feminine frequency, so you can own yours.

SOURCING YOURSELF

Maybe you've heard of the Pleiadians, maybe you haven't. It doesn't matter. I'm not here to convert you to believe in extraterrestrials if it doesn't resonate. I am simply here to teach you a newly empowered concept of Light through my own lens.

My intention in this book is nothing more than to help you awaken even more deeply to *your own* **authenticity, reclaim your feminine power, and ultimately remember:** *you are the Light.*

The Pleiadian teachings have been my personal accelerator in this understanding, as have been my uncovering of all faiths, religions, angels, deities, and dogmas that were beyond what I inherited from my religion of origin. **I'm not asking you to believe in anything that doesn't align to what feels true to you. Take what works for you here, and leave the rest.**

That's exactly what I've done. The entire point here is to open your mind, humble your heart, and get you curious about *your* connection to Source over adopting beliefs handed down to you by others.

This curiosity can become a path to *curation* of what makes sense to your soul. As co-creators of our own lives, we get to be the curators of our own Light. Because the common thread among all these faiths, religions, and dogmas, as I have translated them, is Love. Learning how to develop our own personalized, intimate, and curated relationships with Source can be a renewed beginning of our own unique spiritual journeys.

There is so much talk about the "spiritual journey" these days that it's easy to displace where we started and where we are going. It's easy for the average woman to unconsciously surrender sovereignty of her own core beliefs based on what her parents told her, what her friends might be doing, what the latest podcast she just listened to said about the moon, or what the Instagram meme she just scrolled through glorified about ayahuasca.

This isn't about anyone else. This is about *you.*

This is my invitation to you as you read through this book: start to examine and unlock the truth of what *you* believe. Open your mind and your heart to the endless spiritual stories, beliefs, practices, and sacred sciences that exist in the world and in the history of time. Align with what *feels* true to you.

This is how you find your way back.

Back to what, you might ask?

To you.

Because you are the ultimate Source.

ACTIVATING OUR CELLULAR MEMORY

The greatest connection you will ever experience to Divine Source lives within you, because it *is* you.

You may have heard this philosophy before, but let's take it one step further. Through the lens of cosmology—which is the astronomical scientific study of how the universe formed the stars, the structure of galaxies, space-time relationship, and the nature of all living things—everything possesses a "cosmic intelligence." This is the Information, or "Light," that I will be speaking of in this book. This Light is stored inside your physical body as much as it is stored in the stars, because according to the study of cosmology, we are all the universe.

Our assignment as human beings who have incarnated at this time is to awaken our own immanent design. Many religions speak to the concept of *transcendence*, which is elevating up and out of ourselves to reach the Divine without. *Immanence* is the journey within, to unlock the divinity, the Light that already lives inside *you*.

When we look at cosmology from a Pleiadian perspective, your cosmology is your physical cellular memory, or "codes," that comprises the memory of all that has ever occurred in the universe, which is encoded right inside the cells of our DNA. This gives the concept of being a Lightworker a whole new meaning. We are literally made of light.

Some scientists believe that over 90 percent of our DNA is "junk," useless and dormant.[2]

What's another word for "dormant"? "Asleep." This decline of our fully activated light codes has been more than an evolutionary progression of our biology; it has been *by design*. This inoperative slumber of our DNA, otherwise known as our cellular memory, has been predicated on paradigms of patriarchal control that have arisen on this planet over the last couple of thousands of years, designed to keep us unconscious of our own power. These patriarchal systems, also known as the Matrix, are now in the form of world religion, corporate capitalism, Big Pharma, big food companies, mass media networks, and major social platforms. They prefer that we stay asleep. You were most likely called to this book because you are *awakening*. As you wake up, you *remember*. You are a part of the Family of Light, here to bring Light (Information, or cosmic intelligence) to the dark (lack of information, or ignorance), to help shift the vibration of our planet, Gaia, back to her original state of harmony and love. We do this through our awakenings, activations of our light codes, and the remembering of who we really are.

To activate these dysfunctional and dormant programs inside our bodies is more than personal empowerment; it is our evolutionary imperative. According to Richard Rudd in his book *The Gene Keys*:

> Research into DNA has demonstrated that one of its more unusual electromagnetic properties is its ability to attract photons (elementary light particles). . . . It is this ability of DNA to weave light around itself that reveals its true hidden role within your body—to act as a superconductor whose sole purpose is to exponentially increase the frequency passing in and out of your body. This in turn leads to a complete transmutation of the fabric of your being. . . . It signifies the extraordinary birth of a completely new kind of human being—*homo sanctus*—the sacred human.[3]

In this book, and particularly in the first section, "Inner Light," we are going to learn how to activate our cellular memory, recall the light codes stored in our DNA, and return to our sacredness.

We will do this by learning how to clear the *emotional* body to unlock the full spectrum of our human experience. This means allowing ourselves to *feel* the complete range of all our light and dark feelings with a deeper awareness. By simply feeling our raw, fully expressed emotionality (especially the unpretty emotions), we move energetic density out and bring in more light feelings. This is an alchemical process that creates true transformation in our lives.

We will learn how to move out density in our *physical bodies* that is blocking our cells from generating pure Light. This will include reframing the bullshit programs we have been conditioned to believe about our bodies, put upon us by impossible beauty standards, the health-care system, and the suppression of the feminine, designed to keep us stuck in a loop of self-loathing and self-sabotage. We will be incorporating somatic practices as we reclaim our physical vessels as the beautiful self-healing technological machines that they are.

Finally, we are going to reclaim our power through our cosmic birthright, which is *joy,* and once and for all step out of our collective slumber of victim mentality and claim radical responsibility for the wondrous, magnificent, and inconceivably rare gift it is to be a human being at this exact moment in the history of time.

Reading this book will be an activation of your cellular memory. Like a cosmic alarm clock, it is here to wake you up to the Light that lives within you.

By doing so, we wake up the world.

THE DIVINE LAWS OF LIGHT

Activating our own cellular memory and quite literally *re-membering* that we are the Source is not just a personal evolution: it is a planetary revolution. (In this "re-membering," we are recalling, recollecting, and restoring the *members,* or aspects, of our higher consciousness that have been displaced and disempowered in this 3-D reality, so that we can become fully whole.)

We are moving out of the Piscean Age, an era associated with the introduction of world religion, the patriarchy, and individualism, and into the Age of Aquarius, a time purported to center on the collective "we." There has been much debate as to when the Age of Aquarius technically began, or if it has begun yet at all. There is no debating that in the last few decades, there has been a clear shift of humanity's deeper desire to understand itself. We have seen this with the explosion of ancient practices, such as yoga, meditation, and plant medicines, into the mainstream. There is a massive demand for New Age healing modalities like astrology, numerology, the Enneagram, Human Design system, past-life regression, and mediumship. We are simultaneously witnessing and participating in the return of ancient healing practices like Reiki, acupuncture, breathwork, and shamanism. Conscious communities are popping up everywhere; books like *The Law of Attraction* by Esther and Jerry Hicks have become international bestsellers, while "spirituality" and its subsequent coaching sector has become a multibillion-dollar industry worldwide.

You can point to the turning of a new astrological cycle, chalk it up to the advent of the Information Age, or credit (or blame?) social media's ability to disseminate all this new conscious content. No matter how you slice the sugar-free, gluten-free, dairy-free, vegan cake, there is no doubt that a progressive expansion of our collective consciousness is afoot.

In order for this new paradigm of Light to be set into motion—one that is evolving us beyond a three-dimensional, patriarchal construct of duality, disempowerment, control, and fear that such aforementioned forces would like to keep us sleeping within—we cannot look upon this as any sort of trend. **The future of our humanity depends on our authenticity and embodiment into this awakening.** When we do our own Light Work, by integrating our shadows and *remembering* we are the Source, we activate an entirely new reality. This reality is rooted in *Information, Truth,* and *Love,* which I transmitted from Hathor and the Pleiadians in Dendera in Egypt as the Divine Laws of Light. These Laws are what comprise *5-D consciousness,* a new dimension that is available to all of us by way of our hearts, versus the 3-D construct that keeps us stuck in our minds. This 5-D realm holds unconditional love, unity consciousness, and unbridled creativity. Hathor and the Pleiadians called this the *feminine frequency.* When we collectively activate our 5-D consciousness by embodying these laws, we create a New Earth.

As we journey through this book together and do the Light Work, which involves examining some of our most extreme and painful shadows about ourselves and the world around us, I am going to encourage you to call upon these Divine Laws of Light—Information, Truth, and Love—and commit to embodying them in your own unique expression. Each of these three "laws" are codes within themselves. Each Law contains a rich wisdom that is intended to support your own awakening and healing. When you work with these laws, you activate the cellular memory system of your body as much as it does the complex memory system of this New Earth.

Let's look at them with deeper context and examine what each of these Divine Laws encompass.

Information: The cosmic intelligence of Light pulsing through all living things in the universe, including you. Information unlocks personal power, a connection to the universe, and our place within it. As such, this inspires a sense of Oneness within humanity, and thereby a reverence and reciprocity for all life on Gaia.

Truth: Your own unique genetic blueprint, based upon your fully activated DNA, designed to be fully expressed in your lifetime. This unlocks authenticity, freedom, courage, and self-sovereignty.

LOVE
harmony, abundance,
compassion, 5-D consciousness, peace

INFORMATION
personal power,
connection,
reverence, reciprocity,
and Oneness

TRUTH
authenticity, freedom,
courage,
self-sovereignty

Love: The building block of the entire universe. Love is intended to be felt, known, and shared by all who exist on Gaia. Love activates harmony, abundance, compassion, peace, and, ultimately, 5-D consciousness. When Love exists, all possibilities exist. It is the ultimate key that unlocks all the locks.

This trifecta of Information, Truth, and Love crafts the symbol of the Light Work: an inverted triangle. You will see this triangle reflected at the end of each chapter, within the Light Work exercises, meditations, and tools, called "the Invitation + the Key." The Divine Laws of Light are stored within each exercise to activate your codes. For example, when you are struggling with accepting your body, access your *compassion.* When you find yourself judging other women, tap into *Oneness.* When you're afraid to raise your prices and charge more for your time, recall your *courage.* The Divine Laws are here to support you, but it will be your job to do the work.

For when you do, this new *Information* stored in your cells will set free your *Truth* so you can be an example of *Love* in this new 5-D reality. This is what is available to you in this book. Before we begin, let's do a little unlocking.

UNLOCK TO ACTIVATE

Maybe, like me, unlocking takes an extraordinary experience, like the visitation of your grandmother's angelic spirit to hold you while you cry into her ethereal arms in the most unexpected of places. It could start with a simple questioning of what you were taught to believe by your parents, pastors, rabbis, or communities. You could send yourself on a deep dive into dogmas, faiths, modalities, Indigenous traditions, and beliefs beyond your own current understanding and come to know new deities, angels, spirit animals, and extraterrestrial star families. I encourage you to expand your own limitations of beliefs, for when it comes to Source, it is metaphysically boundless.

The Light starts and ends with you. Sure, transcendence allows us to touch the Divine, but immanence allows us to touch the Divine within ourselves, and we do not have to look far. Each and every one of us is not only filled with Light, we are *encoded* with it. It is pulsing through your cells at this very moment. It's time to flip on the proverbial light switch inside your cosmic body and see something new.

Before we journey through the rest of this book, we must take the first step of remembering our own Light within. To do a little brave questioning, get curious, and begin to curate our own unique relationship with Source and, therefore, ultimately with ourselves with a new multidimensional understanding.

A critical caveat: if you have current religious beliefs, spiritual practices, and ideologies that guide your life already, that's *amazing*. Start there. I will forever be incredibly proud and connected to my Jewish heritage and identity. If you have been questioning what you believe, or if you believe anything at all, *fantastic*. Begin right where you are. No matter where you are on your journey, it's already perfect. The only part of your belief system I'm asking you to "stretch" is to consider that *you* are an equally divine part of whatever you believe in, if you don't believe in this already.

This is the entry point into your Inner Light—unlocking your cellular truth and remembering *you* are the ultimate source. It might take a minute to fidget with the lock and open what may be a very sticky door. This should be a gentle process, as you begin to dig a little deeper into what you believe, why you believe it, where that belief came from, and to view your personal role in the Divine with more responsibility and, above all, excitement! How incredible is it to know you are a member of the Family of Light, here to recall your DNA and live the path of a Lightworker rooted in Information, Truth, and Love in this brand-new paradigm of humanity. Okayyyyy, co-creator of the New Earth, I see you!

It's now time to see yourself. For it is in this unlocking that you activate the ultimate source of Light: *you*.

The Invitation: Create a Connection to Source on Your Terms

- Taking a look at the Light Work inverted triangle, which aspects of *Information, Truth,* and *Love* do you feel the most connected to? Why?
- What beliefs, practices, qualities, or aspects of your religious or spiritual upbringing do you align with the most?
- What beliefs, practices, qualities, or aspects of your religious or spiritual upbringing do you align with the least?
- When, where, and with whom do you feel most connected to Source?
- What does it mean to you to be a co-creator of the New Earth?
- What *Information* do you believe you possess inside your cells that has yet to be expressed?

The Key: Stargazing Ritual

You are made of stardust. That's not woo, my friend, that's science. Even NASA says so. The next time you catch a clear night's sky where there are stars present, practice this stargazing ritual to help you get in touch with your cosmic nature and your cellular memory. Find a comfortable place to lie down on the earth, and with your eyes open, begin to scan the sky. Perhaps grab a friend or gather your Radiance Realm, and do this exercise together. When you feel called, land your eyes on a single star. Notice how it shifts when you bring it into your awareness. Most of all, notice what comes up inside you. Hold your gaze for up to twenty minutes (and of course blink if you need to!) and witness the sensations you feel in your body, what emotions arise in your heart, and see if you can "hear" any messages. When you are done with the ritual, write down what you experienced in your Light Work journal.

Please visit jessicazweig.com/unlock to access all the Invitations and Keys.

2

EMOTIONS

THE KEEPER OF KEYS

They say you are emotional. I say you are all the
way alive. Life is an emotion. Feel it.
—JAIYA JOHN

Years ago, I went to the woods of Wisconsin on a women's personal development retreat that was entirely designed to get us in touch with our emotions. As a passionate Leo sun, hypervigilant Virgo rising, hypersensitive Cancer moon empathic starseed, I couldn't contain my eagerness as the weekend kicked off. I was ready to *feeeeeeeel* my sadness, *cry out* my pain, *break open* my heart with connection, and dance with my sisters like a fool.

I certainly wasn't expecting to feel . . . anger.

After days of group coaching, processing, journaling, crying, and dreaming out loud, about forty of us descended upon an open field covered in gym mats, like it was straight out of PE class. One of the facilitators of the retreat was standing in the center. She welcomed us officially to the "Anger Gym." She was holding a bat. At first we thought this was a joke.

We gathered around in a semicircle as the facilitator demonstrated the Anger Gym exercise. She raised the bat directly above her head, took a deep breath in, and as she swung toward the mat with full force, let out the most ferocious roar I'd ever heard come out of an adult woman. It came from deep inside her body. The roar immediately morphed into dozens of howling, vicious screams as she began beating the mat with all her fury.

All of us stood around shell-shocked. Rage isn't an emotion that is often witnessed by strangers. We're supposed to keep our rage contained to the privacy of our own homes, right? Well, not that day.

We were each handed a bat of our own as we dispersed around the field, blinking at each other out of the corners of our eyes with shades of awkwardness and resistance. With bats in hand, we took a collective breath as we grounded our feet and lifted the bats above our heads. The facilitators told us to begin.

Imagine forty grown-ass women beating the shit out of a mat-covered open field, screaming our faces off, roaring from deep inside our bodies, tears spilling down our red-hot faces as we wailed sounds we didn't even know we possessed. The facilitators of the retreat walked around us, shouting at us to not stop but go deeper.

It sounds absolutely wild in hindsight, and that's exactly what it was: *wild*.

We women are not taught to own our wildness. In fact, we are taught to be the opposite: contained, composed, pretty, polite, and kind. And when we do act out on our rage, we get grounded, rejected, fired, broken up with, or called psycho. Ironic how rage always incites more rage, right?

Rage is not only sacred, but it's sacredly *feminine*. The "Divine Feminine" often gets categorized as tender, soft, compassionate, and loving. While that characterization isn't necessarily inaccurate, it doesn't convey the full magnitude of what makes the feminine *Divine*. Our wombs, where we literally create the universe, are the ultimate black void. Here lives the space before life, the portal of birth, and the beginning of all there is. When we are birthing anything, whether that be babies or the next versions of ourselves, that feeling is orgasmically excruciating. We contain multitudes: from the frequency of Hathor's pure pleasure to the don't-fuck-with-me Mama Bear ferocity. Get in touch with *all* of it and you will discover not only your

Divine Feminine, but your Dark Feminine. Be cautious of women in their rage. They are indestructible.

That afternoon, with my bat in hand, I channeled that rage. I had been holding so much of it inside me for *years*. Primitive screams of sheer wrath purged out of my body as I pounded the ground beneath me, envisioning the faces of all those who had repressed me, judged me, betrayed me, rejected me, and scarred me. (This even included parts of myself I hadn't yet forgiven.) Through the continual screaming eventually came tears of ferocious indignation, until I couldn't raise my bat any further. After about thirty minutes, my breathing slowed and I fell to my knees. Something in me fully, wholly surrendered.

I could feel something within my body shift. In all this releasing came a clearing, a cleansing, and an alchemizing. I felt light as a feather.

Never in my life had I gotten *that* in touch with *that* much anger all at once. I had been subconsciously hiding behind a silent stigma that screaming like a wild woman (let alone holding a bat in front of dozens of other people) would be nothing less than downright terrifying to me and everyone around me.

It wasn't terrifying at all.

It was beautiful, purifying, and *instantly* healing.

That afternoon I understood the transmutable and transformative power of my own darkness. I began to feel safe within my own rage. I stopped shaming myself for not only my rage but the shame itself. I discovered that this heaviness inside me wasn't something to avoid, but something to explore and ultimately embrace. I began to understand that these dark aspects of ourselves are alchemic doorways into deeper parts of our true essence, which is Light. This is where our true power is found.

Our traumas, whether severe or mild, can stay stuck so deep within our energetic and physical bodies, we don't even notice how much they're steering the car called our "lives." When we work to clear them through somatic practices such as screaming, crying, dancing, moving, and shaking, we upgrade. That doesn't mean we will never be triggered. However, in this upgraded state, we no longer need to make these emotions our identity, but rather our tools.

As I have shared, this is a book about Light, but in order to ascend into it, we must come to know our dark. If we live our lives without ever accessing our darkest of the dark, it keeps us unconsciously controlled by it. When we face it, it loses its power over us.

Do you know what's more radical, revolutionary, and alchemizing than a woman in her sacred rage with a bat in her hand, beating the shit out of the ground?

A woman in her *joy*.

JOY, THE POWER KEY

After my mountain's summit, the depths of my burnout, and upon returning from Egypt, I reflected a lot on the last few years up until that moment. Going from a one-woman consultancy (with zero strategy and zero dollars) to an internationally recognized agency, with a twenty-five-person team, two offices, a number-one bestselling book, and a top-ranked podcast, having served more than thousands of clients across the globe made me proud and grateful. It also made me a bit regretful.

I realized how little I enjoyed it. Not just my career but my life.

I decided from that moment forward I would only measure my success (both professional and personal) by how much fun I was having. I decided my "job" was not to answer one hundred emails per day, sit on dozens of Zoom calls, launch products, and hit quotas. I decided to recall the unconscious debt I felt I owed to the Matrix, the hamster wheel, and the hustle, and to take back my chips. From now on, joy was my job.

That's not to say I threw my fiduciary responsibilities out the window. I simply was not going to be ruled by them anymore, nor continue the victim mentality keeping me in a perpetual state of resentment and heaviness toward my business. As a practice, I began to cultivate joy everywhere in my life, my body, my heart, and my mind. No act of joy was too big or too small.

I started blocking out time on my calendar for "fun" which was as legitimate a time block as my "executive meetings." I started my days with walks outside, where I blasted my favorite music in my earbuds and danced like a fool without a care in the world for who saw me. I dared to close my computer at 3 P.M. on a regular basis and to take the afternoon off to go meet a friend for coffee. I made a point of catching live music, a comedy show, a new restaurant, or an ecstatic dance party every weekend. I went to Michael's and bought myself a fresh batch of colored pencils and a sketchbook and made art in my free time.

At first, in making my joy my job, I felt . . . guilty. There is a deeply etched program that we cannot experience joy for joy's sake. That our positivity can be too annoying, our laughter too loud, our dancing too bold, our smiles too plastered, our pleasure too selfish, our success too prideful, our gratitude too cheesy, our fun too indulgent. Um, *says who*? Yes, we incarnated in these human bodies to heal and transmute our trauma (and that of our ancestors), but we are not meant to live there forever. As we move through the dark, we move it *out.* When we do, we create more space. In that space, we reach a deeper capacity to feel the *joy* as much as our pain. If that's not the aim, I don't know what is.

Positivity is a vibration that emits magnetism. When we are in our joy, we are an open channel for life to flow through us. Joy is the lubricant of abundance. Abundance creates our expansion. Our expansion impacts our success. The higher we vibrate, the more we effortlessly co-create our desires with the universe. These high vibrational emotions operate like a symbiotic continuum. The more *joyous* we are, the more pleasure we experience, the more bliss we allow, and the more play we create, the more abundance, success, and expansion we attract. **Joy gets us into alignment.** The more I made joy a conscious practice, the more capacity I had to receive more of what I wanted. Since this *unlock,* I have made more money, have had better sex, magnetized more opportunities, found deeper connections to friends, and, ultimately, have experienced more peace than ever before in my life.

How we *feel* is the way to unlock it all, and joy is the power key.

Some might say that this key is not given but earned. I believe this is a key we discover when we simply commit to the quest of activating our Light and fully believing we deserve to hold it.

The deeper we go inside our own dark feelings (sorrow, shame, rage, embarrassment, hopelessness, loneliness, desperation, betrayal, pain, and heartbreak) the more deeply we can feel our light feelings (personal power, connection, trust, freedom, harmony, abundance, trust, peace, self-sovereignty, courage, reciprocity, reverence, authenticity, compassion, and Oneness), the aspects that make up the Divine Laws of Light.

To experience it *all* is the crux of the human experience.

When we allow ourselves to fully *feel* everything in our lives, the exquisite pain *and* the exquisite beauty that come with being here in this life, this key becomes not only our holiest gift but the ultimate tool. As we work with this tool of our dynamic emotionality, take responsibility for our thoughts, beliefs, and behaviors, and ultimately integrate all that pain and beauty into one, we *unlock*.

Our emotions are our most sacred key to the Light.

Each emotion is a key unto itself, a cosmic device to access the full magnitude and magnificence of our human experience. The willingness (and the power that comes with it) to feel your full range of feelings is what makes you a Lightworker.

Let yourself soak that in.

What if each of these keys could unlock more safety, more connection, more joy, more healing? Are you trying to avoid dark feelings? Is it your rage, your shame, your neediness, your loneliness, your sadness, or your pain you're running from? Or is it your unapologetic joy that you are evading? Remember that you are the lock itself. Allow yourself to go *all the way in* to unlock. Each and every one of your sacred, valid, and holy emotions is your key. You possess multitudes. You contain the universe. You, as a woman, *create the universe.* You store coded infinite Information inside your very own DNA. When you don't let yourself feel it all, you are robbing yourself from the most wildly beautiful existence that is needed for you to express on this planet. Not just for your own healing but for Gaia's.

So feel it all.

Take all your keys, as the Keeper of Keys, and unlock.

There is nothing to be afraid of.

THE GREATEST ADVENTURE YOU'LL EVER TAKE

We know now that the universe possesses a cosmic intelligence that pulses through everything on Earth: humans, animals, insects, plants, rocks, and even grains of sand. Each and every vibrating being on the planet contains *Information*. This is why it is technically, uniquely *intelligent*. This is otherwise referred to by the Pleiadians as the *Living Library*.

We human beings are the "library cards," or the keys to unlock this Living Library and the multitudes of cosmic intelligence it possesses. The Living Library is the vast knowledge and cosmic intelligence of all timelines, dimensions, and realities stored in all life-forms on our planet, Gaia. This knowledge and Information has been kept hidden and suppressed by the Matrix, a constructed representation of our three-dimensional reality, which has been created and maintained by toxic patriarchial forces designed to keep us disempowered within the lowest vibrational state of them all: *fear*. Fear lacks information, and therefore, intelligence. It's what leads us into the dark. This is why Light is Information.

Lightworkers are so deeply needed at this time, as we can access something that no other species on the planet can *consciously* access with the same deliberateness and capacity we can: the full spectrum of emotions. This breaking free of the Matrix, and therefore the dawning of a New Earth, starts with our *feelings*.

With all due respect to their beautiful sentient existence, elephants, ants,

and eagles cannot "awaken." Not, at least, to the full spectrum of consciousness that we can. Our awakenings occur because we experience the full,
multidimensional depth of all emotions available to the *human* experience.
We came here to have this experience, and a critical component of this assignment is to allow all our emotions to be felt. This is the key to transmuting the emotional density that is holding us back from turning on our Light
to full blast. This is the key to opening up the Living Library and bringing
back our personal and collective sovereignty.

Transformation (the journey of metamorphosis) leads to transmutation
(the complete changing of form, substance, or appearance into something
new). This is what comprises evolution itself. This human experience isn't
meant to be a cakewalk, my friend. We are not only members of the Family
of Light and Lightworkers, we are Light *Warriors,* destined to evolve. This
requires going through the painful polarity of this human experience so we
can expand our capacity to know ourselves wholly, which in turn activates
our *Truth,* our own authentic blueprint here to be fully expressed. When we
embody this state, we awaken new DNA and our light codes turn on, literally providing deeper Information to the world we touch. When we unlock,
awaken, and *remember,* we help to shift the planet back to its original state:
Love.

The more you feel your emotions, the higher states of consciousness you
can access. The higher states of consciousness you can access, the more
you can tap into your true multidimensional power. The more you tap into
your true multidimensional power, the freer you become. The freer you become, the more empowered you are. The more empowered you are, the less
able you are to be controlled.

You are a fucking renegade. I keep telling you just how important and
needed you are, and I hope you're beginning to understand why. You know
your assignment.

This starts with a commitment.

It is the commitment to take the deep, profound, never-ending, adventurous, and sometimes treacherous journey *within.* To get in touch with

your emotions, especially the dark ones (like rage) and the light ones (like radical joy).

The Light Work isn't for the faint of heart. It's not meant to be pain-free, guilt-free, or comfortable. We must push past our comfort zones, and sometimes even our limits, to expand and evolve our Light. We must strive to reach unknown territories so that *we can become new* and true to who we really are. We become the Light.

It's going to bring up *a lot.* The Light Work is designed to bring a new consciousness and radical personal responsibility to every area of our lives, and this can be (and will be) *emotional.* It is intended to crack you wide open. The more open you are, the deeper *within* you can go into your unconscious, disempowered states, *and* the high vibration states of bliss, wonder, gratitude, and joy. This is your portal.

Once we can fully claim the full spectrum of our feelings, an unshakable authenticity emerges. This is the Divine Law of Light called *Truth,* one of the three components to the Light Work. When we allow ourselves to feel everything, the embodiment of who we uniquely are crystallizes. We finally, fully trust ourselves. The need to find the answers, the validation, and direction outside of ourselves dissipates. We stop outsourcing. We become our own inspirations. We become empowered. We become magnetic.

What do magnets do? They attract. Like attracts like. This is related to quantum science as much as it is spiritual. If you're in a frequency of light, of joy, of love, of abundance, of radiance, you are going to call in more of that same vibration. Like I have said, we cannot shortcut our way there. We cannot bypass the dark to get to the light. We have to feel our way there.

Starting now, and into each and every chapter moving forward, you are going to be asked to adventure into your emotions in ways you haven't before. We are going to explore our relationships to our physical bodies, our personal power, our family systems, our romantic relationships, our friendships, our relationship to money, and more. I am going to ask you to take off your armor, your defenses, and the protection gear you've been carrying with you for most of your life, which has been keeping you safe, stuck, and dimmed. The more open, exposed, and raw you are on this journey, the better it will be for your evolution and healing. The better it will be for the planet's evolution and healing. This is the revolution you came here for, renegade.

Adventures aren't "adventures" because they are a breeze. What makes an adventure is its new territory of pushing past your comfort zone, finding your edges, reaching treacherous ground, and discovering just how capable, strong, and resilient you are. It is there that you reach new capacities for true, authentic joy. This makes you *fully awake to your own life.*

The vastest landscape lives right inside your soul. This is your adventure. Adventure is the portal into the Light. Your emotions are your map.

The greatest adventures are led by the most daring of warriors.

THE LIGHT WARRIOR'S PATH

In the days following my light activation at the Dendera Temple in Egypt, after the cellular upgrade to my DNA had occurred through the channeling of Light Language, *everything hurt.*

While the apex of intensity had worn off after that initial explosion of light, my physical body was still in an extremely tender place. It took so much energy to talk, walk, and eat. I had no appetite or energy for anything. I just needed to rest.

Nonethless, there I was on an international spiritual pilgrimage, with a super-jam-packed itinerary, trekking across an African country by foot, on buses, and on planes; sleeping in new hotel beds every night, with 3 A.M. wake-up calls; and surrounded by seventeen other people going through their own personal stuff. It was, to say the least, a fucking lot. I had no choice but to power my way through the physical pain, body aches, weakness, mental fatigue, and emotional exhaustion and to keep going.

On one particularly rough afternoon, sitting in Luxor International Airport, waiting for our plane to arrive, trembling in a lounge chair, dehydrated and too exhausted to get myself up and walk across the small terminal for a bottle of water, I remember having a conscious thought: *Only a warrior could do this.*

Perhaps, you could say I was just trying to make myself feel better, but I knew in my heart exactly what was happening to me: I was being initiated. That singular knowing changed my entire perspective on my pain. When I left Egypt, I had never felt so light, so in my heart, so *alive.* I had faced so much of my pain, shame, and darkness, and in doing so, I alchemized it and came out on the other side . . . new. I had walked the path of the warrior.

I want you to remember that every time you face the dark, whether that be a failure, a hurt, a disappointment, a trauma, a loss, a heartbreak, or even a physical sickness, you are being initiated. Go in, don't go around. Let it hurt. Move into it . . . and then move it out, clear it out, cry it out, journal it out, breathe it out, dance it out, or pick up a bat and beat the shit out of the ground outside. Every time you have an opportunity to laugh, dance, sing, draw, connect, or delight in the simplest or most intense of pleasures, dive in. Don't just dip your toe in fun. Who cares who's watching or what people think? Call back the false programming that your joy might take away from someone else's. You came here to feel it all, express it all, and have it all. When you feel every single multidimensional emotion humanly possible, your DNA upgrades. Your light codes activate. You evolve your soul into more of its authentic expression. It is always going to be challenging in the moment, and that's just perfect. Let yourself feel it. You are capable, resilient, and strong enough. You are a warrior, after all.

It is a huge task to carry Light on this planet. This task is meant for your highest evolution. When you evolve, you help the world evolve. The events that manifest in your life—the magical *and* the painful—are divinely designed for you to live your Light. Living your Light is the most courageous thing you can do, warrior.

Are you ready?

Of course you are.

It's time to get out your sacred keys—your emotions—and dive deep. Use the following questions and journaling prompts to connect with yourself now. This is the warm-up to the work. As I've said before, there are no short-cuts to the Light. The adventure is long, endless even. The darker you go, the greater capacity you will have to hold the Light, activate the Light, and be the Light.

In committing to this work, this path, you become a way-shower.

Set the path ablaze, starting now. Starting with you.

The Invitation: Unlock Your Full Range of Feelings

- What has been your deepest heartbreak, biggest failure, or biggest disap-pointment? Write that story and let yourself feel it.
- What has been your purest, most unadulterated, over-the-moon joyous experience? Write that story and let yourself feel it.
- Looking at these two circumstances, what were the primary emotions you felt?
- What did feeling these emotions teach you?
- How did they change you?
- What new Information do you now have because of these circumstances, and how can you use it to serve others?

The Key: Emotional Alchemy Practices

Now that you have spent some time accessing your darkest and lightest emotions, pick one of the two circumstances you wrote out, and read it out loud to yourself or to your fellow Radiance Realm members reading this book with you. As you do, become conscious of where in your body it lives.

Is it in your chest, your stomach, your throat, your back, your hands? Do you feel compelled to cry, scream, laugh, or sing? How does this emotion move through you? Record it. Now it's time to move it, clear it, shake it, and create more space for your cellular memory to open and to awaken. *This is the alchemy.*

Set an intention for where you want that emotion to go and how you want to feel when you're done with the alchemy practice. For example, you might want to clear your anger so you can feel free, or expand your joy so you can feel powerful. Create a sacred time and place to simply be with yourself. Choose one of the following modalities: breathwork, journaling, soaking in nature, screaming, dancing, chanting, or yoga. As you practice it, gently notice what's happening in your body. (You can use "Your Light-worker Resources" in the back of the book to support these practices.) Once complete, journal how you feel. End this practice by writing down in your Light Work journal, or reciting aloud the Pleiadian mantra: *"My emotions are my key to unlocking my multidimensional self."*

Please visit jessicazweig.com/unlock to access all the Invitations and Keys.

3

BODY

YOUR SACRED VESSEL

be careful
i am fertile
do you know i thought i was barren?
someone told me that story
it took so many accidental gardens
for me to realize
i had sun in my fingers
—ADRIENNE MAREE BROWN

I received a bachelor's of fine arts in acting from the University of Illinois. I shined in college, getting cast in leading roles like Desdemona in *Othello,* mastering dialects like Cockney and the Queen's English, earning my sword-fighting certification, all while *barely* passing my electives like astronomy, geology, and all things math. (I like to make the joke that when I graduated college, I knew how to do only two things really well: wait tables and be dramatic.)

I also gained the freshman fifteen.

(Actually, it was closer to thirty.)

Nonetheless, with my formal degree and classical training in my hand, I hit the audition circuit hard. With the help of a brand-new agent, I scored a coveted meeting with one of the biggest commercial directors in the city of Chicago just a few months after graduation. I remember walking into his office at twenty-three years young, wide-eyed, hungry to start my career, and practically salivating with the hope that my talent could open this exceptionally serendipitous door that I'd gotten lucky enough to knock on.

I waited patiently in Mr. Director's fancy lobby, examining the massive photos of his work with Michael Jordan and Cindy Crawford. As I sat there, lost in a mix of my own anxiety and awe, his perky assistant finally entered, escorting me quickly into the director's office. He was sitting at a massive desk, clean and chic, as he waved me toward the armchair placed across from him. I sunk down as I felt him size me up. Before I could even formally introduce myself and tell him my name, he abruptly asked me to stand right back up.

"How much do you weigh?" he asked.

"Uh," I murmured. "I don't know. . . ."

"Well, do you know what size you are?" he pressed.

"I . . . I'm a size eight. Um, maybe a six . . . ?" I wobbled.

"Okay, well. If you want to be an actress, you're going to need to lose about twenty-five pounds at least. That, or get yourself to a size two. If you want to be on camera, preferably a size zero. You can sit down now."

I did.

"So tell me your name," he finally asked.

That moment in that director's chair wasn't just the beginning of my acting career. It was the beginning of my life as a young adult woman in the world.

I was already insecure enough, having grown up in the 1990s and early 2000s, where Kate-Moss-heroin-skinny was the ideal, while I was born into a body that was short, curvy, and adored sugary carbs. (Starbucks's cinnamon scones were a personal favorite.) From the time I was young, loving my body for exactly how it was shaped, what it craved, and how it moved through the world was something that never came naturally to me.

That singular conversation became one of the biggest catalysts of an obsessive insecurity that plagued me for over a decade, from that moment forward. It was that one conversation that sent me into years of disordered eating, restriction, compulsive working out, and body dysmorphia. If there was a fad diet that existed in a book, I read it and I tried it: Atkins, Paleo, Mediterranean, Raw Vegan, Master Cleanse, Weight Watchers, Whole Body Reset, Keto, Whole30, Skinny Bitch diet, the Mayo Clinic diet. Books about these diets all used to sit on my bookshelf, and whichever particular trend I was on, it would consume my every waking thought.

When it came to working out, I chased just as many shiny pennies down even more rabbit holes: SoulCycle, Barry's Bootcamp, CorePower Yoga, weight lifting, and marathon running, all in an attempt to burn calories, lose weight, and, well, get skinny.

Skinny I got. In fact, I became so thin that I didn't get my period for two years in the midst of my twenties. I deprived myself so much of food that I would go through bursts of binging my entire kitchen. I had days when I didn't leave my house because I felt so "fat." I turned down plans with precious friends, important business meetings, and even opportunities to connect with loving and safe sexual partners because I didn't want to get naked in front of anyone. I cried constantly about how my pants fit, and I walked through life with the constant loop of hyper-self-consciousness about my body running through my head 24–7, like a mental radio station that I could never turn off.

Maybe you can relate?

I want to acknowledge that I graduated college back in the early 2000s, and we have come a long way since then when it comes to body confidence and body positivity. Just a few years before this book was published, I was at the office with a handful of my younger employees, who were mainly women in their early twenties. We were gathering around to take a group photo on my iPhone, and as soon as the shot was snapped, I grabbed the phone and jokingly said, "Do I look skinny?" My twenty-three-year-old staff member blinked at me with a smile and said, "Jessica . . . skinny is no longer in. *Confidence* is in." Slightly embarrassed, but even more in awe of looking at the face of a young woman the same age as I was in that director's chair, I could barely believe my ears. I had to hold back tears.

There are still severely dangerous subliminal campaigns targeting women with the advent of social media and what it is doing to shape our culture today. Women young and old are now driving toward the ideals of Kardashian-shaped bodies, perfectly filtered skin, celebrity-endorsed bone-broth diets, and cosmetically altered faces.

When we look past the content and into the con*text,* we can see that this isn't about our bodies at all. It's been about control: control over our bodies, yes, but also control over our thoughts, feelings, beliefs, and behaviors. These are all of the aspects that make up our Light.

Women have been programmed to believe that, in order to be worthy of love, to be worthy of being seen, to be worthy of shining our bright fucking Light into the world, *we have to look a certain way.*

This is all programming and very calculated conditioning. It's like we have been societally roofied by the patriarchal desire to keep women figuratively, literally, energetically, metaphysically, and physically *small.*

For literally hundreds of thousands of years *before* the start of patriarchy, civilizations worshipped the feminine. The very first feminine deity discovered somewhere between 230,000 and 800,000 years ago was called the Acheulian goddess, or the "One Who Birthed the Universe." She was a voluptuous figure, revered for her representation of fertility. Similar statues have been uncovered throughout the Near East, Australia, China, Africa, Sumeria, Turkey, and Egypt, denoting that our ancestors believed God was a female.[1] (Um, actually, she was. We'll talk more about that later.) As Hathor and the Pleiadians told me in Egypt, *we are all pieces of the Goddess.* Part of activating our Light requires us to remember this not just in our minds and hearts but in our bodies.

None of us can look at ourselves as victims here, because we're not. We are not victims to the Matrix programming, our societal conditioning, or even social media. We are far more powerful than any of that.

We have been put under a spell.

It's time to wake the fuck up.

THE SPELL OF SICKNESS

After my body dysmorphia in my twenties came my autoimmune disorder in my thirties.

For an entire decade, I battled chronic sinusitis, brain fog, fatigue, migraines, and inflammation. These bouts would come every other month, capsizing me for weeks at a time, keeping me in a constant rotation of dozens of antibiotics, steroids, doctor's visits, and, ultimately, the inability to get out of bed without relief for years straight. When the Western medicine protocols stopped working, I eventually had sinus surgery, and the recovery was brutal. The results of the surgery weren't perfect, taking my infections down from ten times a year to five, and I depressingly told myself at least it was progress. Every time I came down with an infection, I wanted to die, and that is not an exaggeration. The mental darkness, helplessness, and hopelessness was worse than the physical pain.

However, nothing compared to the psychological programming I claimed as a "sick person." I would tell anyone who would listen to me just how immunocompromised I was. My cabinets became a full-on apothecary of every supplement, herb, tincture, or oil I could learn about on Google. I would travel with at least three gallon-size ziplock bags filled with the stuff. My hunting down of the herbs, tinctures, and oils was my own initial attempted antidote to healing, but I was doing it in blind desperation, and therefore nothing worked. I kept my ENT (ear, nose, and throat) doctor on speed dial in my constant state of panic and found myself back in his office on the regular, pleading for prescription drugs. "Being sick" became more than my habit or lifestyle. It became my identity.

What was perhaps the most concerning was that I had completely surrendered my self-sovereignty to Western medicine, which not only epically failed my body but convinced me that it had all the answers. This is one of the most dangerous spells of them all.

I felt truly powerless.

I had not yet come to realize that my body, as the Pleiadians say, is a magnificent self-healing, self-repairing system and an organic wonder that I had yet to truly appreciate.[2]

By my late thirties, I got sick and tired of being sick and tired, and began to take my power back when it came to my health. I started doing my own research, ditched Western medicine as my foundation, and turned to holistic practitioners whom I trusted. Their first and primary message for me to accept was and still is, *I am my own healer.* My diet became less restrictive and controlling and more nourishing and nutrient-dense. I upped my mineral intake, while adopting the incredible, life-changing benefits of parasite cleansing and coffee enemas. I learned how to track my menstrual cycle, sync it to the moon, and honor my body's mood, hunger, and energy based on the four different "seasons" of my body's infradian rhythm, which is diffrent from the circadian rhythm. Our circadian rhythms vacillate within the twenty-four-hour cycle of the day, based upon the rise and fall of the masculine father Sun. As women, we get a bonus rhythm—the infradian—connected to the thirty-day cycle of the feminine Moon, which impacts our entire female being. The seasons of a woman's twenty-eight-to-thirty-day cycle are the follicular phase (spring), the ovulation phase (summer), the luteal phase (autumn), and the menstrual phase (winter). I stopped popping literally twenty-five daily supplements and now take zero to a few, depending on the day. Eastern modalities such as acupuncture, meditation, cupping, yoga, and the incredible power of breathwork has kept my "chi" (life-force energy) strong, allowing me to experience true vitality.

Above all, I began to understand that my body is a physical repository of everything that I have *emotionally* experienced, as well as what my ancestral bloodline has experienced. All the joy, pain, and trauma has been stored in my DNA. The negative projections and psychic attacks from people who did not have my best interests at heart were also living in my body, as I had not yet learned how to protect myself. All of it was literally clogging my energetic system, and as a result, impacting my physical body in subtle and overt ways. Learning how to create better energetic boundaries, finding my sovereignty, and transmuting ancestral trauma through sacred ritual, somatic practices, psychotherapy, and plant medicines have helped me to clear my sacred vessel.

At the time of writing this book, I have not had a sinus infection in five years and haven't stepped into a doctor's office since. In fact, I rarely get sick at all. My body is younger, lighter, clearer, and more optimized than it has ever been in my entire life. I self-selected to reprogram *myself* by understanding that I am indeed a self-generating healing machine, took my health into my own hands, reclaimed my power, and *dissolved the spell of sickness.* This took years of research and seeking out trusted, fully sovereign, fully empowering healers and practitioners, as much as it took my own awakening to the power of my own body. We are all this powerful.

Sadly, I am the exception, not the rule. Many, if not most, people are sick-identified.

In my opinion, "the rules" have convinced us that it's normal to feel like shit all the time. That it's normal to view your doctor as someone who knows your body better than you do. That it's normal to pop prescription medications like Tic Tacs. Our bodies have been programmed, controlled, and colonized by the major corporate systems of the food, pharmaceutical, and media industries, which, according to many reports, profit trillions of dollars per year off our sickness and, most of all, our ignorance.

We do not have to look far to understand the impact of this collective spell. In the last thirty years alone, disorders like ADHD have increased by 819 percent, bipolar disease in youth by 10,833 percent, chronic fatigue syndrome by 11,027 percent, fibromyalgia by 7,272 percent, and hypothyroidism by 702 percent, to name a few.[3] These numbers are fucking *staggering.* Do you think it's a coincidence?

On a daily basis, in our modern Western lifestyles, we are unknowingly inundated with the negative impacts of seed oils, blue light, sedentary lifestyles, processed foods void of nutrients, depleted soils from conventional farming practices, poisonous tap water, electric and magnetic fields (EMFs), pharmaceutical drugs, vaccines, a disconnection from Gaia, and the toxic media. This is not an accident. *This is by design.*

As members of the Family of Light who have incarnated at this time, we must *reclaim our bodies.* We must see through the programming. We need to heal our bodies so that the "exception" of empowered, optimized, self-generated, sovereign personal health is the rule. This is really how we create a New Earth. For if we are not vibrantly, vitally *healthy,* how are we going to have the strength to shift consciousness and reactivate Light on this planet in the first place?

What can you do right now to enact this shift? Start by stopping the self-criticism, self-loathing, self-depriving, and, most of all, stop surrendering your self-sovereignty to someone who spends five minutes with you a year, just because that person wears a lab coat. When we are hateful toward our bodies, sick, and hooked on meds, we are vulnerable. When we are vulnerable, we can be controlled.

◆ ◆ ◆

Wake up to your own power and become your own healer. Start talking to your body with love, appreciation, and empowerment. Turn off the mainstream media and start to do your own research. Before changing any medical program you are currently on, find established, licensed health practitioners who genuinely want you not only to heal but thrive, and create a new plan with them. Reprogram the false programs and dissolve your own spell. It can only start with you.

Most of all, learn to listen to your body as much as you learn to love it.

I'm actually not here to talk about calories, Big Pharma, or Kim Kardashian. You can find a million other women talking about the traps of diet culture, the danger of social media, the diseases caused by corporate farming, the power of holistic health, and/or the latest workout fads. I could certainly write a whole diatribe about my daily diet, the supplements I actually do take, and all the steps I took to change my workouts to a more gentle and self-loving approach. I will say, quite transparently, that I still struggle with my body on certain days and get a post-traumatic tinge of anxiety if my throat is mildly scratchy, although not at all to the severity of what it once was. I now see food as a gift of nourishment and pleasure versus the enemy. I use working out as a tool for longevity versus a punishment. I relate to my doctors as my partners, not my gurus.

This is part of the problem. We fixate on the micro (the right habits, the perfect supplements, the best foods, the worst workouts) *and* condemn the macro (the Matrix that keeps us hooked on all of it), and by doing both, we have so deeply missed the point.

ASCENDING FROM THE MICRO, THE MACRO, AND INTO THE MULTIDIMENSIONAL

I'd like to invite you to ascend beyond the micro, the macro, and into the multidimensional truth of what your body *really* is.

It's not a weight or a size or a shape. It's not gluten-free or allergic to pollen. Your body isn't skin and hair and muscle and skeleton and fluids.

Your body is a sacred technology.

It contains light-encoded filaments carrying a vast amount of data and information that provides you access to multidimensionalities (expanded states of quantum consciousness and access into higher dimensions), all completely unique to your own soul's blueprint. It is a deeply powerful, important, and holy vessel carrying your soul through this human form on Gaia. Your body, which is made of flesh and blood and bone, is encoded with DNA-storing light. That light contains a cosmic set of Information that only you contain, that only *you* can fully express through *your* unique body in *your* own unique way, with *your* own unique understanding, your *Truth*.

We *think* we are here to heal from eating disorders, obsessive working out, body dysmorphia, comparison, and chronic illness. However, I believe what we are *really* here to heal from is ancestral trauma living inside our DNA, cultural and societal disempowerment, and the incessant patriarchal oppression of the Divine Feminine power that lives, and has always lived, within all of us. This oppression, which has been passed on from the generations of women before us, has led to the eventual, perpetual dormancy of our DNA, or our light codes. We're not just here to *heal it.* We are here to *activate* it. This activation begins with the words we say about our bodies, the thoughts we think about our bodies, and the consciousness we bring when we move our bodies. Our DNA responds to our own attitude more than anything. The ability to reprogram our bodies with our own thoughts is truly astounding.

It's time we honor our beautiful, luscious, self-generating, deeply intelligent, light-encoded cosmic physical vessels.

If we can truly come home to the pure gift that it is to be in this human body in the first place, remember that we are literal Goddesses, and realize that we possess miraculous powers to heal ourselves fully from the inside out, then can I ask you this question: Who gives a fuck how your jeans fit?

With our physical, technological human vessels, we are billionaires. Infinite, endless potentiality lives inside our cells, allowing us to cleanse, to clear, to heal, to expand, and, most of all, to *feel joyous to be in our bodies* in the first place. If we are going to be Lightworkers in the world, we have to have the capacity to hold Light within our own bodies first. Not just in our hearts, minds, and souls but in our bodies. It must start here.

EMBODYING THE VESSEL

Embodiment starts with the physical experience of feeling fully alive and safe within our own bodies, loving how they feel and trusting they know how to heal itself. The aim of embodying our vessels, above all else, is joy. That is the true upgrade. When we feel this sense of pure joy in our own bodies, we create alignment everywhere else in our lives. We become more invincible to the powers that want to keep us suppressed when we are in our joy.

The Matrix, instead, has taught us to despise being in our bodies instead of loving them, and this programming runs deep within us.

So what is the first step to embodying the vessel called your body in order to carry Light?

You must begin to cultivate a true relationship with it.

We are so used to telling our bodies what to do: *Get up at this time, even though you're exhausted. Work out for this long, even though you're depleted. Eat only so much off your plate, even though you're still hungry. Power through five meetings in a row on your period. Take this pill because your doctor said so, even though you don't fully understand exactly why or what it does.* If our bodies signal to us a complaint, such as tiredness, hunger, moodiness, or pain, we often ignore it. These signals are divine yearnings calling for our attention, but instead we view them as a nuisance. How can you create a loving relationship with *anything* if you neglect it?

Your body is speaking to you at all times. It wants to be in right relationship with you, and by "right relationship" I mean equanimity. It wants you to trust it, but it needs to trust you, too. It wants to give to you, but it needs you to give back to it, too. Think about all the things your body does for you without you ever asking it to. It pumps your heart; detoxifies your organs; digests your food; oxygenates your cells; neurologically permits you to walk, talk, stretch, and express; purifies your system as you sleep; and produces billions of other physical functions every second of every day. In return, we often criticize it at best and abuse it at worst. How is that equitable? How is that even *just?*

It's not a right relationship.

So how do we get into the "right relationship" with our bodies? It's not as simple as eating cleaner, sleeping more hours, and adding in physical movement. All those lifestyle changes can be supportive tools, of course, but honoring our bodies as sacred technology and aligning them to joy requires us to start tending to them on a cosmic and cellular level so that *all the spells dissolve.* We cannot just remove ourselves from the spell in our minds.

We must use our bodies to do so, too.

I want to remind you what Hathor and the Pleiadians shared with me in Egypt that afternoon in November 2022: *We want you to understand how lucky you are to be in a human body . . . and not just a human body but a woman's body. You could have incarnated as a man, but you didn't. You chose to be a woman, and you are therefore one with us, the Goddess.*

We want you to remember just how lucky you are to have this human experience right now. It is meant for your enjoyment, for your pleasure, and for your bliss.

This is the core purpose of our bodies: to enjoy them and to cherish them as sacred technology. I was reminded of this truth at the Temple of Hathor, but it was two other goddesses in Egypt who told me what to do with this new Information. It was these goddesses who helped me dismantle my own spells and tend to my body in a completely different way.

INSTRUCTIONS FROM THE GODDESS

Speed, hustle, and grit are all part of the programming, or the spell. Women are hooked into the belief that if we want to grow, achieve, be seen, and make a difference, we have to go, go, go. So we set goals; work out harder; overschedule our calendars; climb the ladder; always scan for the next opportunity; stay on alert for what we're not doing; pop the pills; slam the caffeine; plan for the next job, home, vacation, or baby; say yes when we mean no; people-please; and rush our way through life. This isn't entirely our fault. This is how the world works, one that was designed by men for men. Like fish swimming in water, we are unable to see the system we live in because it's so all-encompassing.

The first thing you need to learn how to do to embody and align your vessel is to *slow down.*

On the morning we visited Philae, the Temple of Isis, we had to get up at 4 A.M. in order to have private access to the grounds before the doors opened at 7 A.M. It was there in the predawn that I stepped into her Holy of Holies, the most powerful chamber on the entire grounds, a place where only the high priests and priestesses were once allowed to go. I got down on my knees, curled over them, and put my forehead on the floor. Within moments, I could feel my heart fill with an almighty *motherly love.* This feeling coated my cells like mother's milk, as powerful waves of this energy started to move through my body. I picked up my head from the floor, with my knees still on the ground, and sat up. In an instant, I exploded into what can only be compared to a psychedelic trip similar to on Bufo, although I was on zero medicine. As I dissolved into this beautiful Oneness, I was able to hear Isis's words come through me. She could see the years of me pushing my body mentally, emotionally, and physically into the ground. She could feel my burnout, and she knew precisely just *how tired I was.* She gave me permission to rest. She told me that I had to treat my body as I would treat the most precious, tender thing in my life. She commanded me to love my body with as much devotion as I love her, the Divine Mother, as I was a piece of her. She instructed me to *"slow down enough to be able to watch the seasons change, witness the flowers bloom, and hear the wings of fairies flutter."* These were her words to me. That is how slow she told me to move. I knew then that this wasn't just an instruction for me but for all women.

Since that communion, I have tried my best to slow down to the speed of the rotation of Gaia herself. I actively seek out boredom and gentleness, making rest a sacred practice. I put time on my calendar to literally "do nothing." I go outside every day, rain or shine, warm or cold, and walk for at least ten minutes. Do I experience these luxuries of spaciousness every week, let alone every day? Not always. Life persists. It can definitely be challenging to slow down if you run a business, raise a family, work a big job, and want to make a difference in the world.

This isn't about changing your entire life. *It's about tweaking the pace with which you engage it.*

Creating actual, palpable quiet in my life as a practice *has* indeed allowed me to watch the seasons change. Slowing down has permitted me to witness not just the flowers bloom but my own thoughts, too. As a result of this level of deep rest, gentleness, and slowness, my body has not only softened, it has opened. These regular practices have *activated* the following sacred technological gifts:

- *Lightness of being,* by unhooking from a busy schedule, creating freedom in the mind and therefore the body
- *Rooting to Gaia* on nature walks, creating safety in the body, and healing of the nervous system
- *Enhanced intuition,* with consistent silence and solitude, creating sheer presence, and trust in my intuitive, psychic gifts

The second instruction I received in Egypt was from Sekhmet, the lioness goddess of war and healing. Leading up to this trip, I was completely physically depleted due to my burnout. Add severe jet lag on top and my first twenty-four hours in Egypt were fucking rough, to say the least. As soon as we landed, I felt as though I was on the verge of getting seriously sick, and, as I've shared, *I rarely get sick.* I told our group leader I needed to tap out of the first day's activities and instead try to sleep. That night, I crashed for fifteen straight hours, and in my dream, I had an unmistakable, undeniable visitation from Sekhmet. When she appeared, I was hit like a Mack truck with the flu. My throat was on fire, I couldn't stop choking, and I sweat through my sheets. This went on for hours, and I could feel Sekhmet chewing me up in her lioness teeth as I violently tossed and turned. Finally, the aches, fever, and inflammation just *stopped.* I continued to sleep like a baby, and when I awoke hours later, I was 100 percent fine. I did not feel sick at all. Before Egypt, I had only heard of Sekhmet in my peripheral awareness, but in truth, I knew nothing about her. That night stands as one of the most powerful visitations by a higher being I have ever had. As the goddess of war and healing, I knew Sekhmet had intentionally accelerated my sickness (which felt like a war within myself) so that I could clear it out and wake up the next morning fully recovered and *healed*. Sekhmet doesn't just "war" for the sake of warring. She wars to heal. Her entire mission is ensuring that *all* things are in right relationship on the planet. For me, this started with my body. Sekhmet has become one of my favorite goddesses of all time.

Naturally, I could not wait until the day on our itinerary when we visited her private chamber, the Temple of Ptah, at Karnak. Immediately upon entering her tiny chamber and beholding the massive statue of her, I could not believe the message she gave to me. It was instantaneous and crystal clear. I felt my vagina and my womb literally tingle. I looked into the eyes of her statue, and in that moment, I *heard* her speak to me. "*You think you're powerful now, Jessica? It's time to connect with these parts of your body. Turn this on. Find your roar and your sexual fire. You will become more powerful than you know.*"

This instruction sent me deep into an exploration of activating untapped technology within my body, using the power of my feminine anatomy and physical power. This has turned up my fire, turned on my Light, and gotten me deeply in touch with my physical feminine power. The most transformative tools I use today are the following:

- **Primal growling**, a somatic practice that connects you to sacred rage and transmutes stuck emotions into a sense of freedom within the body, while activating new neural pathways of strength, confidence, and power.
- **Diaphragmatic breathwork**, which oxygenates cells, releases stagnant unconscious emotions, opens up your pineal gland (or third eye) to see into other dimensions, and upgrades your DNA.
- **Ecstatic dancing**, which gets you out of the mind and into the body with physical liberation and joy, moves negative energy, and detoxifies cells on a physical level through sweat.
- **Yoni steaming**, an ancient, Indigenous, and *beautiful* practice, cleanses the womb space, regulates your menstrual cycle, and

eases cramps, stagnation, and bloating while connecting you with the holiest of holy systems in a female physical body (this also supports better sex and deeper orgasms).

Slowness, dancing, breathing, screaming, nature walks, and yoni steaming—these practices have transformed my right relationship with my body while *unlocking* its sacred technological gifts of Light, leading me deeper into my intuition, freedom, power, lightness, safety, confidence, femininity, and cosmic connection.

There is no workout in the world that can provide these types of benefits. None of these practices can be found in a diet book or from social media.

They come from the Goddess herself. They come from *within you*. Your body is more than just a body. It is a piece of the Goddess.

She is divine. She is a vessel of Light.

She is asking you to love her.

She is asking you, Lightworker, to use her, channel her, and honor her in a way you never have before.

As you embody the Goddess and honor her codes, you can activate your body's *frequency*.

ACTIVATING YOUR LIGHT CODES THROUGH FREQUENCY

We are here to create a New Earth that is going to be free, and by now, you realize you must free your own body, which is a piece of our Great Mother Gaia herself.

You have learned that in order to build your right relationship, you must dissolve the spells that have programmed you to despise your body, abuse her, ignore her, and allow her to be suppressed by the mass systems designed to keep her sick and in the dark.

You have discovered new practices of **gentleness** (the magical healing powers of *boredom* are real), **rest** (naps are a spiritual practice), **play** (hit up your local art store, pick up materials that turn you on, and make things with your hands), **growling** (summon *your* inner Sekhmet, find your roar, and let her rip), **dancing** (check out "The Lightworker's Playlist" in "Your Light-worker Resources" section in the back of the book and get movin'), **yoni steaming** (I've also listed my favorite yoni steaming brand in the resources section), and simply **walking outside** as ways to embody the technological vessel called your body.

With this new information in hand, the final step is to activate our bod-ies' frequencies, so that these new frequencies can become available to everyone we meet and, over time, the whole planet.

We do this with our chakra system, which helps us to fire up the codes of our true essence, our Light. When more Light is brought into your body, it activates light-encoded filaments and helps rebundle DNA, establishing a frequency change. Your frequency is more than your vibration: it is your unique genetic blueprint, otherwise known as your identity. Your frequency is your Truth.

Some might be familiar with the "chakra system," which reflects seven major energy centers in the physical body that correspond to specific nerve bundles and internal organs. These seven major chakras run from the base of our spines to the tops of our heads. If these energy centers get blocked, we can experience physical and emotional symptoms related to a particu-lar chakra. Clearing, balancing, and activating these physical centers in our bodies helps us to heal physical and emotional blocks, shifts our energy, and impacts how we show up in every area of our lives.

Since the maxim "as above, so below" is usually true, what is perhaps happening in your life emotionally most likely will manifest itself physically or vice versa. Our chakras can provide a powerful road map. Thus, I have provided a deeper look at what each of the chakras represent, how to activate the unique frequency of each one, and how to know which chakra needs your attention most, based on what's transpiring in your body and in your life.

Our **first chakra,** the **Root Chakra,** the color red, sits at the base of the

spine, connected to our sex organs and perineum, and represents our connection to the earth, the physical world, and our primal sense of safety. To
clear and activate the Root Chakra, practices like coffee enemas, yoni steaming, grounding into the earth, and using essential oils like amber and ginger
on our feet are powerful tools and practices. If you have been stuck in survival
mode; suffer from anxiety or panic attacks; deal with constipation; struggle
making commitments to people, places, or opportunities; or feel like you're
not fully present in your life, healing your Root Chakra will serve you greatly.

Our **second chakra,** the **Sacral Chakra,** the color orange, sits at the
womb center for women or the lower abdomen for men, and represents our
creativity, sexual power, and our ability to literally birth things into the world,
whether that be our children, projects, ideas, or dreams. To activate our
Sacral Chakra, sex and self-pleasure are powerful practices, as is anything
that gets us into a juicy creativity flow, like drawing, dancing, and making
"fun" a sacred ritual. If you are addicted to work; live in hustle mode; lack
joy and inspiration in your work; lack sexual pleasure; feel resentful toward
people, partners, and life in general; or struggle with fibroids, cysts, endo-
metriosis, or severe period cramps, this can all be a deeper indication that
your Sacral Chakra could use some tending. Firing up your Sacral Chakra
can aid in lighting your juicy, passionate fire and transmute these physical
ailments. (For the record, I was disconnected from these first two chakras
most of my life and was a textbook case for almost all of these symptoms.)

Our **third chakra,** the **Solar Plexus Chakra,** the color yellow, sits at the na-
vel and represents our connection to our own personal power, confidence, and
ability to manifest. To bring our Solar Plexus Chakra online, self-affirmations,
self-reflection, and yogic poses like upward dog, bridge pose, and camel pose
are powerful activators. If you are the type of person who needs other people's
approval or permission; if manifesting money does not come easily; if you lack
clarity on what to do with your life professionally; or if you struggle with stomach problems, IBS, or any gastrointestinal issues, then clearing, healing, and
activating your Solar Plexus Chakra will support you immensely.

Our **fourth chakra,** the **Heart Chakra,** the color green, sits at the center of our chest and represents how we give and receive Love, the foundation of the Light Work triangle. This chakra is vital to our overall emotional well-being and ability to be in balanced relationships with the self and others. Practicing anything that gets you inside your heart, whether that's journaling, spending time with people you love, playing with children, practicing gratitude, and/or working with the frequency of rose in crystal or essential-oil form are all great activators. If you are prone to pushing people away; take a while to open up; often judge others; keep to yourself as a form of protection; or struggle with acid reflux, chest pains, asthma, or shortness of breath, you may want to look at clearing, opening, and healing your Heart Chakra.

Our **fifth chakra,** the **Throat Chakra,** the color blue, sits at the center of the neck and represents our ability to speak our Truth, let our voices be heard, and express our authenticity. To activate our Throat Chakra, practicing primal growling, Light Language, chanting, and singing, as well as finding ourselves on podcasts, stages and platforms where we literally use our voices, or simply asking to be heard in our everyday conversations, are all incredibly supportive practices. If you buckle every time you are asked to publicly speak; feel silenced at work or in a relationship; lack direction with what to do with your career; speak softer than most; or struggle with thyroid issues, swollen glands, sore throats, or throat cancer, your Throat Chakra could benefit from your attention.

Our **sixth chakra,** the **Third Eye Chakra,** the color indigo, sits in between the eyebrows and represents our connection to our intuition, our psychic gifts, and the use of our imagination, and empowers us to "see" beyond the veil of illusions. Our Third Eye Chakra strengthens when we practice meditation, work with Blue Lotus oil, and practice Holotropic Breathwork, which induces altered states of consciousness by breathing in and out through your mouth, releasing blocked emotions, memories, and energy. If you often deal with betrayal; feel like "you should have seen that coming"; question your instincts; struggle with migraines or headaches, sinus infections, brain fog, or fatigue, your Third Eye Chakra might be blocked and is calling out for its clearing.

Finally, our **seventh chakra,** or **Crown Chakra,** the color light purple, sits at the very top of the head, serving as our direct line to the Divine. The more we open this chakra, the more cosmic Information and communion with higher dimensions we are able to access. Our Crown Chakra activates anytime we learn something new and inspiring, whether by reading, watching, or listening, as well as when we clear our energetic bodies by burning sacred plants, like sage and palo santo. If you often feel stuck in your life, feel that you can't access higher wisdom, lack inspiration, or even feel like you're being attacked by energy and entities that do not belong to you, or if you struggle with lightheadedness, fainting, or vertigo, your Crown Chakra could use your tender loving care.

According to the Pleiadians (and many other spiritual teachings), we actually possess not seven but twelve chakra centers. The twelve-chakra system supports not only our connection to our own bodies but to our bodies' place within the entirety of the universe. Working with these twelve chakras allows us to access new energy outside our human forms to get in touch with higher dimensions, ultimately supporting our expansion, activation, and healing. These additional five chakras ascend from our crown and are linked to our own auric fields.

The **eighth chakra** is the **Soul Star Chakra,** the color silver, which supports your connection with your "higher self." Whenever you are seeking wisdom from within, drop into a meditation and focus your mind's eye on the area a few inches above your head. You might even feel a tingling sensation when you do. Don't force this; just listen. You have greater access to this piece of you than you may realize.

The **ninth chakra** is the **Spirit Star Chakra,** clear in color, which supports our unique Divine path. This chakra connects us to the angelic realm, which I first personally discovered in that tiny chapel in Ireland when I felt my grandmother's spirit come to me for the first time. Similar to the eighth chakra, simply call attention to the area located a few feet above your head and get still. These supportive realms communicate more directly with us when we directly ask, just as my grandmother told me to do.

The **tenth chakra** is the **Universal Chakra,** which is gold, and merges our human experience with Universal source energy. When we activate this through visualization, meditation with scalar waves, breathwork, and essential oils (I recommend frankincense), we can experience powerful sensations of balance and healing as we tap into pure Source consciousness.

The **eleventh chakra** is the **Galactic Chakra,** which is iridescent, and allows our ability to astral travel into the multitude of quantum realms, which we can reach with the support of deep meditation, crystals, high-frequency music, and healers and guides. The first time I activated this chakra was with Ayra, my healer mentioned in chapter 1. With her assistance in a deep meditation, I was able to access my connection to the Pleiadians for the first time. I recommend working with Moldavite or Libyan Desert Glass crystals in meditation to support accessing this chakra. (More about these crystals can be found in "The Lightworker's Toolkit" toward the end of this book.)

And the **twelfth chakra** is the **Divine Gateway Chakra,** where we experience a pure, complete, and encompassing connection to Divine Source. The twelfth chakra color is diamond white light, which was distinctly the "color" I saw in Dendera in my light-body activation. My advice to access the twelfth chakra is what I've been saying this entire chapter: practice clearing your vessel, get into nature, activate your light codes, and remove the density in mind, body, and spirit. You don't need to fly to Egypt to access this. You are embodying sacred technology with infinite abilities right now.

There are a multitude of ways for us to clear, activate, and engage our frequencies, and these are just a few examples with which you can experiment. Try one chakra, one practice at a time, and see how you feel inside your body and your spirit. The chakras are energy centers, designed to align to your most authentic energy, your highest frequency. When we tap into this frequency, we come back to who we are meant to be: fully expressed, sovereign, healed, and balanced Lightworkers.

When we activate our light codes through this frequency shift, we become more than conscious creators; we become *conscious re-memberers of who we really are.*

Remember, it all starts with breaking free from the spell and building your right relationship.

BUILDING *YOUR* RIGHT RELATIONSHIP

Imagine waking up tomorrow and being completely free from the spell. Imagine walking through life fully awake to the self-generating healing power, the gift, and the joy it is to be in your physical body. Imagine feeling fully safe to move your body, express your body, and be in your body however you want to. Imagine your body as your best friend and that there is no one that either of you listen to, trust, honor, cherish, worship, respect, and love more than each other. Imagine using your body to emanate and inspire more love, acceptance, and freedom to all the other bodies around you, simply by being in your frequency.

This is the body of a Lightworker.

It's all possible. It's time to love your body, listen to your body, and activate your body more than you knew possible and to ultimately feel more joy being in your own skin than you've ever felt before. *This is how you activate all the Light within you.* It is waiting for your remembrance. It has been waiting to be in right relationship with you your whole life.

The time is now. She is so excited, grateful, and ready.

Can you feel it?

As you do the following meditation and write your answers to the following questions, I want you to feel your answers in your body. Sense *where* in your body your responses feel true, uncomfortable, scary, or safe. Your body doesn't lie, so *listen to her.* That's all she has ever wanted from you. She holds sacred, untold Information. She stores infinite codes. She contains technology that can heal you and the world.

It is up to you, my friend, to tell her story. To remember her power. To honor her needs. To activate her gifts. To live her Light.

The Invitation: The "Right Relationship" Body Meditation

Find a quiet space and comfortable seated position, close your eyes, and take three slow, cleansing breaths in and out. Scan your body with your mind, simply becoming aware of your entire physical vessel, from the top of your head, to your neck, shoulders, chest, torso, hips, lower spine, thighs, shins, and toes. When you feel this awareness of your whole body, ask your body the following questions. You can speak them out loud or simply say them in your head. Wait for the answers. Don't rush or force this. There is no wrong way to do this. Be patient and allow your body to talk to you. Practice what "listening to your body" feels like to you.

"What do you want me to know?"
"What do you need from me?"
"What would feel good to you?"
"What spell do you want me to release you from?"
"What chakra needs the most attention?"

In your Light Work journal, write down what you heard. As you review the answers, dissolve any judgments toward your body or yourself. Your body might tell you it's hungry or tired. It might tell you it feels anxious or energized. Did it define a "spell" you have not yet named? What new Information did your body share with you? There are no wrong answers here. Just observe and tune in to what it feels like when your body "talks." Her frequency is alive and real.

The Key: Embodiment Practices and Chakra Clearing

It's time to give back to your body. She's done so much for you, and she is so grateful for your attention, for your love and your tenderness. Choose any of the practices you learned about in this chapter, such as walking in nature, breathwork, ecstatic dancing, primal growling, or yoni steaming. If you feel a particular chakra is needing to be cleared, activated, or tended to, refer to the twelve chakras and call on the tools, such as yoga poses, essential oils, or meditations for each. Refer to "The Lightworker's Toolkit" in the resource guide toward the end of this book for guidance on specific meditations, music, oils, crystals, as well as my favorite spiritual wellness brands to amplify these practices. Remember to follow Isis's instructions: move slowly and be gentle on this journey. Your body is your temple. She is sacred. Honor her as such.

Please visit jessicazweig.com/unlock to access all the Invitations and Keys.

4

POWER

CLAIMING RADICAL RESPONSIBILITY

Within our core self is an indelible blueprint of unrivaled individuality—the singular being that each of us exists to express.
—MICHAEL BERNARD BECKWITH

Before I fell in love with entrepreneurship, the theater was my original crush. My entrée into that world started in high school, surrounded by my fellow thespian outcasts, intoxicated by the magic dark before the curtain drew, the shortness of an anxious breath before the lights flashed onto the stage in front of a live audience, and the metamorphic capacity one could find inside to become someone else. In the theater, I had found my people and my passion.

There was just one problem: I wasn't very good at acting.

At least, that was what was being reflected back to me over and over again by consistently, exclusively getting cast in the ensemble.

One afternoon, I found myself crying in the office of my acting teacher between classes. "I just don't get it, Mr. Conway," I said with tears dripping down my cheeks, and holding in the snot from my nose. "I rehearse like crazy; I take copious notes in your lectures; I study the top actors in class. My heart is in this; I love nothing more than the theater . . . and I'm not even getting the smallest of parts." I felt so defeated by it all, I was considering quitting the department altogether.

It was there in his small office that Mr. Conway kindly but firmly said something to me that would change the course of my life: "You're not getting cast *not* because you're not talented, Jessica. The reason you're not getting cast is because you don't believe in yourself. No one is going to believe in you until *you* believe in yourself."

He was correct. I didn't believe in myself *at all.* I had been riddled with inescapable insecurities for as long as I could remember. Growing up to be a gawky, awkward, and chubby teenager while trying to cope with a dysfunctional home in a predominantly affluent community, where everyone seemed to have a "perfect" family, a "perfect" body, and a "perfect" life, will do that to you. My disbelief in myself was so deep and so unconscious, of course I could not see it. In Mr. Conway's reflection, I could never unsee it from that moment forward. I decided right there and then that I was going to fake it until I made it. For as long as I needed to, I would pretend to believe in myself until others started to as well.

That following year, I got cast as the lead character in the main stage play, *The Miracle Worker.* I played Annie Sullivan, the teacher who taught the blind and deaf Helen Keller how to read, write, and speak. I was so committed to the role, I dyed my hair from blond to red and perfected my Irish dialect. We got standing ovations each show. I finally felt worthy.

This newfound worthiness inspired me to go to college for acting, and upon graduation, I got into one of the most competitive acting departments in the United States. The year I got in, they had only accepted twelve students in the country. I finally felt special.

This specialness sparked my drive, and upon entering the "real world" after college, I dove right into the acting industry in Chicago and immediately landed an agent, garnering my SAG and AFTRA cards (Screen Actor's Guild and American Federation of Television and Radio Artists, respectively) from equity plays, commercial gigs, and voice-over jobs. I finally felt successful.

While pursuing my "successful" acting career, I met a sexy older guy in the music industry, who became my boyfriend. He wrote songs about me and helped me with my headshots, as photography just so happened to be his favorite hobby. He loved taking pictures of me, and I loved being his subject. I finally felt beautiful.

When acting ran its course five years later and I got sick of the body-dysmorphic pressures and perpetual narcissism that came with that industry, I got a spark to start my own business: a food and fashion blog for women. So I quit acting altogether. I also quit the boyfriend. This made me feel free.

When that online magazine became the biggest platform for women in the city, I grew hundreds of thousands of followers on social media, hosted the hippest parties in town, got invited to social events nearly every night of the week, and was coined a "lifestyle expert" on local TV segments. This made me feel influential.

I also started being able to skip every velvet rope at every nightclub in town and walk straight in. This made me feel *super fucking cool.*

When I left the magazine to go start my second business, the SimplyBe. Agency, I got more clients than I knew what to do with, hired a big team, and started making more money than I ever had in my life. This made me feel powerful.

When the business started to gain national recognition, I won awards, achieved major press hits, and got a six-figure book deal. This made me feel important.

When it all started to feel overwhelming and the burnout began to rise, I started hiring almost every business coach, therapist, healer, astrologer, medium, acupuncturist, and shaman to give me the answers. This made me feel validated.

Along the way of chasing the spiral of worth, I never stopped and went back to hold that sixteen-year-old girl, crying in her acting teacher's office. When he gently remarked, "You don't believe in yourself," I never slowed down enough to ask her, *Why not, sweet girl?* Instead, I chose the outward path of proving my power and *earning* my worth. The catch is that it worked. I faked it so well that I did indeed make it. The crescendo of my life's success, outside validation, and professional accomplishments grew to be so loud, I could never hear the Truth of my higher self shouting at me the whole time:

Hey, Jess . . . aren't I enough? You know, just me, being me?

It would take me years to tend to that little girl crying in Mr. Conway's office and to get to the root of her unworthiness. It would take me decades to *remember* who she really was.

And when I finally unearthed this new Information, I found my true power.

TRUE POWER

What makes you feel *truly* empowered?

Perhaps it's quitting a job you hate so you can feel *free*. Or leaving a shitty relationship so you can be *loved* more purely. Maybe it's starting a business so your gifts become *needed*. Say it's publishing a book so your voice can become *important* in the world. It could be transforming your physical health so you can feel *confident* in your own skin. Or maybe it's advocating for a bigger salary so you can experience greater *worth*.

What if all those things went away tomorrow?

Take away quitting the job, the breakup of a bad relationship, a successful career, a bestselling book, an "ideal" physique, all the money in the world, and any other outside affirmation or accomplishment. Imagine *none* of those things ever happened and never will.

Would you still be empowered? Would you still be innately, inherently *powerful?*

The truth is yes.

We are born free, loved, needed, important, and worthy.

We come out of the womb empowered. However, because this human experience is one big amnesia trip, our environments, parents, schooling, teachers, friend circles, and systemic cultural and societal factors cause us to forget this truth. So we spend the majority of our lives seeking empowerment in as many places as we can and feeling oh-so-empowered when we find it, versus *embodying the power we already possess.*

There is a difference.

Picture a child and how embodied, authentic, unapologetic, imaginative, and empowered her or she innately, instinctually is. **That freedom, that magic, that *power* still lives inside you. It's not lost. You've just forgotten.** Believing your power can be found, given, anointed, affirmed, or validated is a lie. To believe your power is found anywhere outside your own being is ironically disempowerment in action. It's part of the programming.

So we grow up. We become functioning, well-meaning adults in the world and start to unconsciously, frenetically look for our power like a lost set of keys that has been in our pocket the whole damn time.

The outsourcing begins.

The fire torches and lamps come out, and we start searching. And we search for it *all, everywhere.*

We look to the right college degrees and careers to validate us. We look to therapists and coaches for guidance. We look to our bank accounts for safety. We look to our mentors for wisdom. We look to our doctors for the answers. We look to books by authors we respect and podcasts hosted by experts for direction. We look to fashion, beauty products, and our workout routines for more confidence. We look to plant medicine ceremonies, crystals, Reiki, moon circles, and the like for healing. We look to our friends for advice, our partners for connection, and our parents to fulfill our lifelong unrequited needs that most likely catalyzed the void in the first place.

We outsource our power over and over and over again.

Along the way of this rather aggressive search party, we forget the most sacred Truth of them all:

We are the power source.

We are the spark within the flame of that torch. The light in the lamp itself. The treasure trove of answers. The key to unlock the lock.

When we fully wake up to this realization, the need to look to the next right job, the perfect relationship, the spiritual guru on Instagram, the author on the bestseller lists, the meditation teacher on the internet, the corporate assessment that affirms our personalities, or the next bigwig expert feeding you "inspiration" simply dissolves . . . and we *remember*:

We are the source of power itself.

There is nowhere else to look to be needed, guided, loved, worthy, or *allowed* other than inside yourself.

When you *really* look . . .

You will see that you are, and always have been, your own inspiration.

CLAIMING RADICAL RESPONSIBILITY

A few years ago, before the happy marriage, the successful career, the bestselling book, a loving sisterhood, and a body I now treat like sacred technology, and before I got the memo that I inherently possess infinite worth, I was a victim to my whole entire life.

Whether it was my husband's scarcity that was preventing me from quitting a cushy corporate job to go off on my own, or blaming the weather for always fucking up my flights out of O'Hare when I needed to be somewhere important, or the economy that wouldn't let me get ahead as an entrepreneur, or my parents for not modeling a functional relationship, or Instagram's constantly changing algorithm that would mess up my launches—life was always happening *to me*.

Everything that wasn't working the way I needed it to was everyone else's fault. Never mine.

It was around this exact same time in my life that I came across the teachings of the Pleiadians. The words from the Pleiadians are light codes within themselves and therefore have a density and a richness in each and every statement. These words are intended not to be simply read but absorbed thoughtfully as new programming into our psyches and souls. As I got deeper and deeper into their material, something activated within me. I felt the power of their words and therefore felt self-empowered.

The more I read, the more I began to remember the truth of who I really am, which is pure power and potential. It was in this remembrance that I had to dismantle the victim version of Jessica. The one who had been unwittingly sitting in the passenger seat in the car called *her life,* allowing the opinions, circumstances, judgments, fears, agendas, other people, even the weather, to be in the driver's seat. For years I had been so consumed by my own anger, resentment, fear, and insecurity that I completely forgot the car was actually mine, the keys were in my hands, and the map that was taking me from where I was to where I wanted to be already exists within my very own heart.

There was nothing to outsource.

Realizing this was the exact pivot point to begin to build a life that was not only fully empowered but fully authentic and, most of all, impactful to the world around me. There was no shortcut to get here. There's no user manual in the glove box. Sure, I've worked hard at things like growing a business and amassing wealth, but I haven't been especially lucky, either. Yes, I've grown a large platform by "simply being myself," but I still put a ton of time into it and strategy behind it. Yes, I pour a lot of energy and resources into working on my marriage, my friendships, my travels, and my spiritual practices, but I make a lot of mistakes and don't have all the answers. It's not like I've found some grand "secret" to living my Light.

I've simply found the one singular personal choice that can change the game: *claiming radical self-responsibility.*

The Light Work is a practice, a daily commitment, and a constant choosing of our own personal responsibility in the co-creation of our own lives. The core teachings of the Pleiadians are for us to remember that we are not just empowered but that we are *self-empowered.* How we awaken to that self-empowerment is by taking *radical responsibility* for every aspect of our lives.

I'm talking about who we really are, how we show up, what we choose to believe, how we behave, what we allow, who we associate with, what we accept, what we hold on to, what we release, and what we dedicate ourselves to. It's all up to you.

It's about claiming every single magnificent part of us: our beauty, our brilliance, our kindness, our empathy, our talents, our creativity, our courage, our resilience, our radiance, our willingness to forgive, to accept, to grow, to give, to give a shit, to put in the work, to be vulnerable, to believe in ourselves, to simply be ourselves.

It's also about claiming all the parts of ourselves that just aren't that cute: our mistakes, failures, meltdowns, selfishness, laziness, diva moments, princess tendencies, judgments, obsessions, blaming, shaming, persecuting, martyrdom, and above all, the victimhood.

All. Of. It. Is. Your. Responsibility.

Yep, that's terrifying.

It's also liberating.

This guidance I received from the Pleiadians set me on a path to lay down any remnants of victimhood and take back my true power.

That's when everything really changed.

If you are ready to claim radical responsibility, your whole life might just change, too.

Part of claiming radical responsibility for our lives starts with taking responsibility for how we *think* about our lives.

THOUGHT IS. THOUGHT CREATES.

Thought *is*.

Thought exists, just like this book you're holding or the coffee you might be drinking or the friend you're going to meet for coffee once you're done reading this book. It exists in the world as a form of matter that is as real, tangible, and accessible as anything you can touch, see, or feel.

Thought *is,* and therefore thought *creates.* Realizing this singular concept can change your entire life. It's the real flex in becoming a radically responsible, conscious co-creator of your reality. It's one of the most powerful and, dare I say, exciting principles of this reality and is a core message of the Pleiadians. "Thought-forms are vibrational blueprints that hold instructions for manifesting reality," as Barbara Marciniak channeled in her book, *Path of Empowerment.*[1]

As I have walked my own path of empowerment, I have witnessed transformation after transformation in every aspect of my life, due to not only claiming my worthiness and quitting the "outsourcing" but, above all, harnessing the power of my own thoughts.

Here's an example: At thirty-three I went broke, which was nothing short of a truly traumatic experience. I told myself constantly that I was bad with money. It was that mental story that sent me straight into financial scarcity, after all. When I finally got enough courage to rub my two remaining pennies together and start my next company, the SimplyBe. Agency, I had done about $300,000 in sales in my first year in business and needed a bookkeeper. In my first meeting with him, I blurted out, "I just need you to know that I am *really, really* bad with money. . . . I am *really, really* going to need your help here." He blinked at me and responded, "There's no way you would have made $300,000 in your first year in business if you were 'bad at money.' That's clearly not true, so don't tell yourself that anymore." It was such an honest reflection, I couldn't help but take his advice to heart.

From that moment on, I stopped telling myself that story. In fact, I started telling myself the opposite story. "*I am good at money*" became my mantra. A year later, I made a million dollars. Seven years later, I've made multimillions. It didn't happen because I somehow got better at spreadsheets. It happened because I reversed my story and changed my thoughts.

Before I met my incredible husband, Brian, I was the girl who was always unlucky in love. This again *was my story.* The guys I wanted never wanted me back; the guys who wanted me I could care less about. All the good men were gone. All the bad boys only wanted sex. No one was emotionally available.

Story after story flooded my mind in my entire twenties and early thirties. After the final narcissistic douchebag broke my heart, I remember having the conscious thought that I was "done" with any man who wasn't fully emotionally available and wanting to pursue *me*. A week after making that mental decision, and *changing my thoughts,* I got set up with my husband. This is a *true story.*

As I mentioned, for years I self-identified as a sick person and clung deeply to my autoimmune disorder in my every waking thought. A huge part of getting healthy was, of course, finding empowering holistic practitioners, new modalities for clearing my physical body, and learning that I was indeed my own healer. But I also stopped telling myself and everyone around me that I was the type of person who got sick all the time. I stopped thinking it to be true and stopped speaking it into existence. With the exception of writing about it in this book, I rarely discuss my history with sickness, as it is no longer my story. I honestly don't think about it. When I stopped mentally fixating on it, I started getting healthy, and *that* was the real game changer.

In one of my very first months of business with my agency, I scored a coveted meeting with a bigwig tech founder who had just raised $50 million and was looking for a personal branding firm. After nervously greeting him in his office, we sat down at his glistening conference room table, and he immediately launched into his prolific background as an expert in computer sciences, artificial intelligence, big data, and innovative transportation technology. The more he talked, the more my heart sank in my chest and beads of sweat began to ooze down my forehead. *What the actual fuck am I doing here?* I thought to myself; *I do not belong in this room.* When he was done with his introduction, it was time for mine. I had no other choice but to tell him my story. I cleared my throat and meekly launched into how I had a background building campaigns for some of the biggest Fortune 500 brands in the world, growing large organic social followings through the power of compelling content, and building credibility in the market as an expert in PR. The more I talked, the more he leaned in and his eyes widened. This man was impressed not by an imposter, but by . . . *me.* From that moment forward, I stopped telling myself "I don't belong" anywhere.

Sure, I might not have the same smarts, experience, and background you have. No one's got what I've got. *That singular thought* changed the trajectory of my entire business. Today, that tech CEO is my largest and longest client, at six years.

When you access the truly unlimited and *very real* magnitude of your own thoughts, you do more than reclaim your personal power; you reignite your codes of consciousness. You recall the purpose of the Living Library, which is to activate unlimited Information, or *Light,* including and especially the Light that lives within you. You *remember* who you really are.

Are you remembering how powerful you really are by now?

If not, I encourage you to think it so . . . and so it shall be. There can be no other way.

THE NAME OF THE GAME

Flashback to Egypt. I'm at the end of my trip, after days of weakness and rawness after my light-body activation.

We were taken by our guides to a man named Gamal, a ninth-generation Reiki master, chakra master, and essential-oil shaman. (Yep, that's a thing.) Each one of us dropped one hundred dollars to spend fifteen minutes with this powerful stranger so that he could read our energy and tell us what he saw.

I stepped into his small room in his beautiful essential-oil store in Cairo and sat down across from him on a bench. He took one look at my face, and he said, "You must learn to love your pleasure more than you love your suffering."

You see, even after years and years of acting on my own self-empowerment, I had gotten lost in the sea of outsourcing myself. The majority of my thirties entailed a lot of hustling for my worth, spending tons of cash on courses and coaches to give me the answers, and chasing accolades for validation (I am *human,* not a Pleiadian, after all). This is what led to my crash and burn*out*.

It was all my own unconscious disempowerment. My unconscious addiction to the drama of the human experience. Sometimes we have to go through the same lessons over and over again until we fully learn them.

Since that auspicious meeting, I have repeated Gamal's words to myself every single day: *"You must learn to love your pleasure more than you love your suffering."*

That statement is a mantra as much as it is a directive. In that one statement, I am reminded of the power of my own mind. That my experience simply comes down to where I put my *focus.* That I have a wonderful, beautiful, and frankly unbelievable superpower . . . to harness my own thoughts.

Thought is.

Thought creates.

Therefore, you are the result of your thoughts.

This is the name of the game.

It is indeed a game. It is important to remember that you are a soul inside of a body called by your name for a microcosm of time against the infinite, spinning on a rock around a star among trillions of other rocks and stars inside trillions of other galaxies across the universe.

One of the dopest "rules" in this reality is that our thoughts create experiences. I came back from my trip to Egypt new, and I made the commitment to focus on my joy, my play, my fun, and my rest. Pleasure was the medicine I needed. As a result of consciously shifting my focus, I have become lighter. I have remembered my power. I have healed. Today, it's not that I suffer less. I am no longer capsized by my suffering *because* I am more conscious of my own thoughts.

You don't have to go sit down with a shaman to create your own reality. If you're wondering where to start when it comes to empowering yourself, look no further than your own mind. Much of our pain, fear, and disempowerment comes from our unconscious thought patterns.

The Light Work is here to hold a big shiny mirror up to our common unconscious behaviors, patterns, and beliefs that *so many of us* share as women. When we name them, claim them, and reframe them, we can ulti-mately integrate a new way of being.

Because when you can claim all parts of yourself (your dark and your light, your shame and your power, your shit *and* your shine), you become . . . unstoppable.

The greatest flex of power there is? Joy.

JOY, THE GREATEST FLEX OF POWER THERE IS

One of the most self-empowered women I have ever known is my mother's best friend, Terri.

Like me, my mom treasures her girlfriends and spends a lot of quality time with them. For me, growing up, that meant I had constant exposure to Terri at coffee dates, mall visits, and home hangs, and her presence in my life left a huge impression on me. At eighty years old, Terri is as much of a spitfire as she always was. She's fabulously dressed, bounding with endless energy, genuinely interested in everyone around her, and is, hands down, one of the most positive people I've ever known.

Twenty years ago, Terri unexpectedly lost her only son to liver cancer, which spread quickly. After his death, I remember her saying, "You've got to live for today." That became *her* mantra.

I've never seen a person so palpably choose *not* to be a victim to her cir-cumstances. That is not to say she didn't grieve her son's death. Of course she did. I watched her cry for years on my mom's shoulder. Losing a child is by far one of the most devastating, heartbreaking, and horrific things that can happen in this human life. Instead of letting the grief define the rest of her life, though, Terri used the pain to empower how she would live it. She claimed radical responsibility for how she responded. She honored his untimely death by fully living her life. She is one of my greatest inspirations.

Like Terri, I have worked hard on overcoming my own victim mentality. Once I claimed radical responsibility for myself, I moved into an empowered state of creating my own reality, which was driven by my ego's (healthy) desire to feel better. From this more empowered state, I was able to manifest a lot of incredible things in my life and career. Yet with all these external validations pointing to my success and fulfillment, parts of me still felt incomplete at best and burned out at worst. With my victimhood dissolved and my empowered consciousness unleashed, I was nonetheless still operating in a masculine vibration of creation, versus the feminine vibration of *co-creation*.

To *co-create* your life with the magic of the universe actually only requires one conscious choice.

Get into your joy.

Joy is different than happiness. Happiness is a fleeting emotion, whereas joy is *a conscious choice.* When we choose it, it becomes the lubricant to abundance. It is the speed-rail train to alignment. It's the portal into magnetism. It's the most potent pathway to healing available.

Cultivate joy as a practice, and you will come to find a whole new sense of empowerment that lives within your heart, your mind, your body, and your soul.

I know that I'm not alone in traditionally focusing on suffering. How could we not with the vicious news cycle, broadcasting one tragedy after the next, the inequities across the human race, not to mention the daily grind many people feel they need to run just to survive?

We are not here to ignore, deny, or bypass anything. The deeper we can dive into our darkness, let ourselves feel ours *and* the collective pain, the bigger of a container we can have for the joy it is to transcend and choose how our lives can be. What we forget is just how much self-sovereignty we have over our choices. Our thoughts. Our power.

THE LIGHT WORK (REALLY) BEGINS

You now understand that you are free to create your own relationship with Source, on your own terms, which reminds you that . . .

. . . you are the ultimate source of Light.

You now realize that you possess a sacred key to live a fully activated life using the power of all your emotions. It is safe to feel it all, and the more you do . . .

. . . the more multidimensional you become.

You now understand that your body is a sacred technology, longing to build a right relationship with you as you walk within its vessel from this moment forward, knowing . . .

. . . you store infinite codes of light, of cosmic intelligence, of healing within your cells.

As we journey together throughout the rest of these pages in Outer Light and Future Light, it's now time to bring all this light you've cultivated within to the world around you: your family, your lovers, your friendships, your career, and the world at large.

Life is not happening to you.

It is happening *for you.* This is the point of empowerment.

When we connect to Source, life starts to flow within you and all around you.

When you tap into your codes, honor your body's sacred technology, activate your joy, reclaim your thoughts, and harness your *true* power, you co-create your life, this life, and reality itself.

You remember who you really are.

You become the Lightworker.

An Invitation: Claiming Radical Responsibility

- What outside sources give you a sense of validation? Name as many as you can. Examples could be: money, my job, status, my romantic relationship, awards, my social following, my astrologer, my parents, my social circle, my beauty, my body.
- How does this outsourcing validate you exactly? Can you explain it?
- Name a situation in your life that you felt happened *to* you.
- How can you reframe this story as something that happened *for* you?
- What did it teach you?
- How did it stretch you?
- What new *Information* do you now possess because of it?

The Key: Pleiadian Power Affirmations

When you feel a bit of victim mentality creeping in, when you notice yourself outsourcing validation, when you start ignoring the little girl in you who just wants to know she's enough, when you start doubting your abilities, call on the following Pleiadian power affirmations. Say them silently to yourself in your mind, recite them out loud, chant them in meditations, write them down in your journal, set them on your desktop or phone screen, frame one on your desk, put them on sticky notes all throughout your house. There is no wrong or right way here. You are empowered to make them your own.

- *I am the source of my power.*
- *I am the light within the lamp.*
- *I am the spark within the flame.*
- *Thought is. Thought creates.*
- *State of mind is the name of the game.*
- *Joy is my job.*
- *I commit to loving my pleasure more than I love my suffering.*
- *I claim radical responsibility for my one precious life in this human form.*

Please visit jessicazweig.com/unlock to access all the Invitations and Keys.

PART II

OUTER LIGHT

When you step into the thing you are, the world does not
burn, but glows more brightly with the light you bring.

—BRIAN ANDREAS

5

SOUL FAMILY

HEALING YOURSELF HEALS THE WORLD

Pain is not part of life;
it can become life itself.
—FRIDA KAHLO

F lashback to Jamaica, 2017, in the presence of my shaman, dissolving into Infinite Oneness as the medicine Bufo pulsed through my body. It was at that moment I understood more than just the truth of the universe. I understood the truth of my human experience.

I chose it.

Or rather, my soul did. I believe my soul chose this timeline, this body, this gender, this personality, the people I love, the people who hurt me, the lessons I came here to learn, and the journey my life has taken. It had all been a soul-choice.

This also means that I chose my biological family.

After the initial explosion into the infinite universe, I slowly began to dissolve back into my body and embody this understanding in real time.

My mother's soul, my father's soul, and my brother's soul were the first to come into my conscious awareness. I could see all four of us floating through the starry black skies, connected to each other through what looked like a cosmic spiderweb. All pain, hurt, resentment, and triggers dissolved, and in their place was a love so pure, divine, and palpable. I knew then that we had all journeyed through *eons* of lifetimes together and in different forms of relationship. In what past specific dynamics I couldn't name or see, but my soul knew, without a shadow of a doubt, that we had all chosen each other to be a nuclear family in *this* lifetime.

Perhaps you've heard the term "soul family," or maybe you haven't. I have heard people correlate this concept to "a chosen family," or a circle of close friendships and partnerships. The terms "soul tribe," "soul fam," and even "soul mates" can all be credited with the experience of finding and then *choosing* your people as you grow and get older. Finding this core group no doubt feels like fate and soul alignment. It can feel like a *homecoming*. Surrounding yourself with people you align with, feel safe with, and vibe with can be very healing. Because you *consciously chose them*.

I believe your *true* "soul family" is the family *you* didn't choose at all. Your soul—not your human form—chose your biological family, and their souls chose you, too. You might struggle with this idea a bit, or you might struggle with this idea a lot. After all, if you're like most people on this planet, your childhood upbringing was far from perfect. If you're like me, home wasn't always the safest place, which is what propelled you to go out and search for that feeling of "home" in others, like friendships, communities, and romantic partners. You might ask yourself why you would *choose* something so painful, so traumatic, so uncomfortable, or so unidealistic to be the home you were born into?

The answer is simple:

For your soul's highest evolution.

When you accept your chosen soul family as your biggest initiation toward your deepest path to healing yourself, you heal the world.

You might just heal your family in the process, too.

SHINE BRIGHT LIKE A DIAMOND

In this human experience, as the Goddess Hathor shared, you came here to experience bliss, joy, pleasure, empowerment, and embodiment.

Yet, you didn't come here to coast.

You came here to get your heart broken, to burn, to fall apart, to ache, to grieve, to lose, to fail, to bottom out, to cry, to crack, and, yes, even to suffer. This is how you find the depths of your bliss, your joy, your pleasure, your empowerment, and your embodiment. You came into this body, into this life, at this time to experience it *all*, my friend.

There is no other place in our lives that this paradox plays itself out more than within our biological soul families. Without a doubt, our parents, siblings, children, grandparents, aunts, and uncles present us with the most formative relationships we have. These are the people we come out of the womb loving the most, and as a result, they are the ones who hurt us the most. This contradiction literally *forms us*.

Say you are a heterosexual, or sexually fluid, biological woman. Your relationship with your father most likely will influence who you date and fall in love with. Perhaps your mother-daughter dynamic has had the most impact on you, as this relationship commonly produces a "love-hate" experience based on the desire for both mother and child to have their emotional and psychological needs met. The "mother wound" can form us in profound ways, as it's one of our most complex relationships in the human experience.

Regardless of sexuality or gender identity, our parents' relationship can and most likely will shape our perspective on how we approach romantic partnership at large. Sibling dynamics shape our personalities, work styles, and who we choose as friends and why—all of which can vary based on what order in the family you were born in or if you have sisters, brothers, both, or none at all. On the flip side, when we become parents, our chosen children give birth to *us*, literally *re-forming* who we are as soon as we bring them into the world.

This "formation" is not unlike the making of a diamond. Like a diamond, your soul is precious and rare. Diamonds are either formed naturally in the earth or human-made in a lab. You too were made of this earth *and* by humans. A natural diamond, when exposed to extreme pressure and extreme heat, can take up to 3.3 billion years to form. (Side note: *your soul might just be that old.*) Lab-made diamonds, in comparison, start with a carbon seed (a beautiful metaphor for your soul) and are exposed to temperatures of 2,000 degrees Fahrenheit and pressurized to approximately 1.5 million pounds per square inch. Either way, all that pressure and heat that it takes for a diamond to form sounds rather excruciating, doesn't it?

◆ ◆ ◆

I bet living with your nuclear family was, at times, excruciating, too. Whether you were raised by your biological parents, adopted parents, or by extended family members or other guardians, your soul family is the ultimate refinement. You came into this life and chose the family that would put you through *your* specific proverbial (but no less painful) heat and pressure. From the pain comes the beauty. Just like diamonds themselves, you are one of a kind. No other diamond went through the extremes of *your* exact parents, childhood wounds, memories, and traumas. That's what makes you magnificent and literally priceless. When you look at who you have become based on the pressurized formation based on your family, can you see what an absolutely rare gem of a human being you are?

You were born into your family for a very special reason:

You were born to form your Light.

You were born to shine your Light.

You were born to shine as bright as a diamond.

THE GREATEST DARKNESS AND
THE GREATEST LIGHT

To say my family system was complicated would be an understatement. From the outside, we looked like the quintessential middle-class American family. My mom was a school teacher who sat on the PTA; my father was an accountant; my younger brother excelled at sports; and I, the first and only daughter, was the creative one who shined in the theater department. We took family vacations, spent weekends with our grandparents, played Capture the Flag, and caught fireflies with our neighbors on our tiny square block where the house we grew up in was. While there was a *ton of love* in my childhood, there was also a lot of dysfunction.

I don't think there is a family system in the world that doesn't have dysfunction. Of course dysfunction is on a spectrum, which inevitably leads to all sorts of micro and macro traumas in our lives. This doesn't mean our parents were all universally bad or ill-intended. It simply means that, like you and me, they were human. They came into this world with just as much shadow and light as everyone else, raised by their own parents, who came with theirs. I am not a parent, but I do know that being a parent is by far and away the most challenging initiation into the Light due to the programming and unconscious conditioning it exposes. Or, as one of my mom friends recently said, "If you want to bring your ego to your knees and see just how truly flawed you are, have a child."

One of the most significant, painful, and beautiful relationships is the one that I have with my father. He came from a first-generation American mother and an immigrant father who faced several years of challenges due to financial instability. His parents struggled to raise him and be fully present, not because of their lack of love but because of their lack of resources. Flash forward to my dad's adult years, and out I came as his first and only spitfire of a daughter. I know that I was the most precious thing in his life, being his first and only little girl. It was when I hit puberty that things got intense, to say the least. He had a temper, and I had an attitude. My displaced rebellious hormones combined with his own unhealed childhood trauma led to, well . . . what created mine. He didn't have the tools to respond to who I was becoming and how to raise me with the consciousness I needed. Not because he didn't love me or want to. I have always known my father's love for me is fierce and unconditional. During my adolescent and teenage years, however, he struggled to show it. Throughout that time, I felt like he had to learn "on the job" how to parent. So I guess you could say I became his greatest teacher, and he became mine.

Today in my forties, I hold no resentment toward him for any of it. This peace didn't come overnight. I have spent years unpacking my anger, sadness, and trauma in therapy and through somatic healing, journaling, breathwork, and psychedelic modalities. I have even unpacked it with my father directly, in some of the most difficult, honest, healing, beautiful, and transformative conversations of my life. It was in my relationship with him that I found my source of strength, resilience, and self-belief. These attributes serve me in immeasurable ways today, as an entrepreneur, as a wife, as a friend, and even as a daughter. It was also in watching my dad transform his life from one of financial struggle to that of a self-made man that I learned some of my strongest and best qualities: tenacity, grit, morals, and self-actualization. These qualities have defined and, most of all, *refined* me as a woman in the world, and I couldn't be more grateful to the Universe that he is my dad. Due to all of this and more, my relationship with my father has been my soul's greatest initiation.

My mom is the sweetest soul there ever was. She is a quirky, hilarious, and genuine little light that flutters through the world, and everyone loves to be around her. She is as good to her core as goodness itself. I like to believe most of my kindness and my compassion came from her. But, as in many married couples that came together in the patriarchal boomer generation, my father was the breadwinner and my mom was a schoolteacher, and it created an imbalance in our household. My mom was the best "mommy" there was. She packed little notes in our lunches, sang us lullabies, and kissed our boo-boos. However, she seemed to be somewhat disempowered in her relationship with my father due to their financial dynamics. She always encouraged me to be an "independent woman," and yet I had a tough time reconciling with this advice, because my perception was that she was financially dependent on my father.

I didn't have a model of a strong, empowered woman to look up to, and I believe that's why I became one. The specific shadow and the unique light in my relationship with my mother defined my loving heart *and* shaped my drive. It also fueled a lot of resentment that I have spent years unpacking. For the past few decades, not only have I come to fully accept who she is, I have found so much gratitude in her choosing me as her daughter and in my soul choosing her as my mom. Do we still trigger each other in our human form? Fuck yes. That's the mother-daughter dynamic. I wouldn't trade it in for anything.

My younger brother and I have been on quite the journey, too. He and I are less than two years apart, and even though he's the younger one, he is far wiser. I believe he has an ancient soul. I tell him all the time that he is way more mystical than I am, but he never really takes it in. (Maybe one day he will.) The truth is, we couldn't be more different. As kids, I was the introverted, artistic, emotional, thespian outcast. He was the "popular" one, who played varsity sports, had a dozen best guy friends, and had a steady girlfriend. When shit hit the fan at home with our parents, I would step in and rebelliously fight, while he retreated quietly inside himself and avoided everything as best he could. For years, we were in the same house but lived in completely different worlds.

It wasn't until my mid-twenties that I had an epiphany about my brother. His soul chose to come into this family as much as mine did, and therefore our souls uniquely faced the same trauma and pain from our parents, as well as all the incredible love they gave us. That exact darkness and that exact light from our childhood upbringing, only he and I will ever truly know. That fact alone has made my relationship with my brother the most cherished, revered, and sacred soul connection of my life.

We have taken very different paths in our adult lives. He's a dad of three kids; lives in a house with basketball nets, swing sets, and barbecues decorating his suburban yard; and works at a steady career in finance. When I tell him about my belief in aliens, he looks at me like an alien, and we laugh. I tell him all the time that if I hadn't chosen him to be my brother, I would have chosen him to be my friend. I don't think he completely understands what I mean when I say that, cosmically speaking. That's okay; I don't need him to. He's become my dearest friend anyway.

There is no perfect family, but it is in our initiations that we can accept that we are indeed perfect for each other.

Even in our most challenging experiences with our families, whether that be abuse, neglect, abandonment, or simply poor modeling, there is always a dichotomy of what the experience is really offering us. Yes, traumatic experiences in our families deliver pain, anger, hurt, and sorrow that might never go away. The harsh criticism I received from my father, the disappointment I felt from my mother, and the emotional abandonment I experienced from my brother still hurts when I really reflect on it. I get to *choose* what I do with these hurts. So do you. Unlike your soul's choice to come into your family (one that you in your human form and egoic identity had no control over), **you *do* have control over what you make of your soul family relationships, the stories you tell yourself about them, and how you walk through the world because of them.**

I want to acknowledge that there are people in the world who have suffered severe trauma within their family systems. While I believe our souls choose our earthly situations, I do not believe our human selves choose trauma or abuse. I am in no way excusing horrific behavior or letting anyone off the hook for the consequences of their actions. We often need to receive professional support for these traumatic experiences on a human level, and I profoundly encourage that. Our responsibility is for our own healing, never for the abusive actions of others.

All of us have either experienced some degree of physical, psychological, or sexual abuse or know people who have. As I have stated, the greatest unlock to living your Light (and by that I mean your *happiest, fullest, safest, most impactful life*), is to lay down the victimhood. This doesn't mean that the pain of these experiences ever goes away. We might just spend our whole lives unpacking what happened in our soul family, and that's more than okay. It's important to remember that it didn't happen *to us*. It happened *for us*.

In one of my most memorable, painful, and frankly life-defining arguments with my dad, he told me he was going to call me "Jessica Zero" because I was going to amount to nothing. I was fourteen. While my father doesn't even remember this moment, I nonetheless spent my whole life from that moment onward trying to prove my father wrong. Even though it was only said to me once, those two words, "Jessica Zero," propelled my entire entrepreneurial career. It also instigated my unconscious addiction to work, obsession with achievement, downward spiral of proving my worthiness, and eventual burnout. All I ever really wanted to do was make my dad proud of me, and I've created a lot of beautiful, abundant things in the world because of it. The greatest gift has been where all that fire, ambition, and "proving" eventually led me to: peace, joy, and my *true power*. It is only from that paradox that I have come to understand that my worth comes from not what I do but who I am.

When a parent says or does something vicious to their child, that child *is* the victim. Like you, I don't believe that anyone, especially children, should be harmed in any way, ever. You are no longer that child. You are now the conscious, integrated, empowered adult who can choose to begin to heal and choose different options. It is your birthright to live fully in our joy. It is your birthright, therefore, to heal.

You can let the pain of your past define you, or you can let it *refine you*.

CALLING ALL STARSEEDS AND
CIRCUIT BREAKERS

By this point, I don't have to tell you that you're a Lightworker. You know that you are. You have renewed the source of your Light; you're freer than ever to express your emotions; you're tapped into the sacred technology, beauty, and safety of your body; and you've come home to your true power.

Imagine being an example of what is possible to your family. Imagine being the one who gets to wake members of your family up to *their* power, their beauty, and their own unique source of Light.

Not by *telling* them what to do, how to think, where to live, what books to read, and/or what podcasts to listen to, but by you *being the Light in action*. We are often so triggered and hooked into our family story that we lose sight of just how powerful we can be. These triggers and hooks are our soul assignments. We are of a generation that is living in a new paradigm of an evolving collective consciousness. We are living in a time when we have a different level of self-awareness and the tools to support this exploration, in a capacity that our parents, their parents, and their parents' parents did not.

What a privilege, an honor, and responsibility this is! This is the responsibility of all members of the Family of Light.

The soul family that birthed you, and your ancestors that birthed *them* . . . they need you. They need you to be a circuit breaker. Yes, their DNA informs your DNA, but you do not have to repeat their unhealthy habits, their pain, their unconscious behavior, their trauma, or their programming. You, Lightworker, get to choose a different path and set the stage for your future generations to come. Allow yourself, and allow your children, to go forth and lead a new world of coexistence, acceptance, generational harmony, health, and wealth. May the unique lessons of your soul family be the gift that brings more abundance, breaks barriers, and heals traumas for the New Earth rising.

This is why healing yourself *heals the world*.

THE FIGHT FOR LIGHT

A few years ago, on a particularly heavy night in the middle of the pandemic, I had what can only be described as an angelic visitation from the spirit of my great-grandfather. I had been quarantining for months, alone in my room, crying after a particularly stressful day running my business, fighting with my husband, and fearing for my health, my sanity, and the world. It was there in that moment that I felt a very clear presence "enter" the space. I have no explanation that it was my great-grandfather other than just an utter and total knowing.

He had died years before I was born, and even though I had never met him, I had always felt close to him. During the 1920 German occupation of Soviet Ukraine, as the German army was taking over Eastern Europe and antisemitism was rising, I had heard the story of how my great-grandfather killed a German soldier who had put a gun to his stomach in the streets, attempting to steal his coat. For six weeks, my great-grandfather hid for his life in the Carpathian Mountains.

The programming of *survival* is deeply etched into my own DNA. I am acutely aware of how the trauma of literally running for your life, scraping for security, and living in a state of fear has impacted the "circuits" of my own soul family. It was these unconscious beliefs that shaped my own parents, specifically my dad, and therefore the lens through which I grew to see the world. By choosing to be the Light within my own family system, I don't negate what it is they experienced in their own lifetimes, but I take the best of who they are and what they taught me—the *refinements*—and apply them to how I move through the world as an adult.

As soon as I felt my great-grandfather in my room that night, he gave me a very clear instruction: get out a pen and write. I channeled the following poem:

I am my great-grandfather's great-granddaughter.
I am a warrior princess

built for the fight of Light.

I easily tire, but I am never worn.

My soul knows . . . it's always time.

My DNA is encoded with

magic

miracles

gifts, unmatched.

A channel of fire burns through my heart.

I am born again every day.

I was born to burn bright.

I am my great-grandfather's great-granddaughter.

His blood runs through my veins

filled with fire and heart and flames

of white lava truth.

It's time to unravel

to know it's all okay.

It's school, this place called Earth.

I am a student

an ambassador of Light.

I am here to see the Light

and be the Light

and know the Light

and show the Light

and burn people blind with the Light

so they become their own source of Light.

I am my great-grandfather's great-granddaughter.

He gave me his spirit of flame and fight

of Love, furious with might

of strength to stand up and claim what's right.

It's time to unravel

into the truth of it all

down down down
into the knowing
into the unpolished essence of my cells
that make up this vessel
called
his great-granddaughter.
I am here to live his legacy by
living free
empowered to
truly
simply
be.
I hope you are proud of me.

I hope you are proud of you, too. Family is heavy.

Maybe this chapter brought up some tears, as it did for me. By accepting, trusting, and honoring that your soul-family experience was chosen for your soul's refinement (despite how hard it might have been), you can activate your Light in new and profound ways. You are not a victim to any of it. The pain was and is your gift. The blood of your ancestors runs through your veins. This is also a gift, should you choose to transmute it into your new way of being. You get to choose what you do with it. This is true power. This is Outer Light. You have taken one of the biggest steps you can take to live it.

While this might seem like some sort of conclusion, this is only the beginning. I've offered the following questions for you to go even deeper within. To feel the pressure and heat of the diamond that you are. Find that bright-diamond Light within, so that you can shine without.

When you do, let it burn. Let it burn so brightly that the world can feel you heal. So that the world can heal, too.

The Invitation: Honoring Your Soul-Family Experience

- How can you reframe your most painful childhood memories as your "re-finements"? Who did you become *because* of them, not *in spite of them*?
- If it's true that you all "choose" each other, write down why you think you chose your family and why they chose you, too.
- How have they taught you to know yourself, love yourself, and take a stand for yourself?
- What perils, pain, and trauma did your ancestors face?
- What about their past are you circuit-breaking?
- What family traditions, rituals, and aspects of your ancestral lineage are you carrying forward?
- What new *Information* are you here to offer the New Earth because you chose your soul family and they chose you?

The Key: The Diamond Visualization + Mantras

Before doing this visualization, I recommend that you be in a state of calm, relaxed presence. Do your best to clear environmental distractions, like phone notifications, background noise, or other people's energy. Also, do your best to clear yourself from emotional or mental distractions. This visualization is best done in a state of neutrality. When you're ready, find yourself in a comfortable seated position, close your eyes, and take three deep, slow cleansing breaths in and out.

Bring to mind a past family hurt, and witness where that feeling sits in the body. As you tune in to this sensation, picture red-hot heat burning into this space; it is the hottest fire you have seen or felt. As you feel the heat rising, imagine a brilliant, sparkling, bright diamond emerging from the flame. Stay focused on this diamond, tuning in to its beauty, its radiance, its perfection. Stay with the diamond as long as possible, until the family memory begins to disintegrate into the fire. The diamond is you. Open your eyes and record in your Light Work journal what you experienced.

You can use the following opening mantras to start to channel key messages that Spirit, your ancestors, or your own soul has for you:

- *I am my father's daughter / I am my mother's daughter / I am grandmother's granddaughter, here to live . . .*
- *Their blood runs through my veins, pumping with . . .*
- *My DNA is encoded with . . .*
- *I am here to heal, transform, and transmute my lineage by . . .*
- *I am here to live their legacy by . . .*

Please visit jessicazweig.com/unlock to access all the Invitations and Keys.

6

ROMANTIC RELATIONSHIPS

LOVE'S A WITCH

Enter now into love without conditions, roses and orchids,
wren and crane, seemingly cracked or perfect,
it's all the same. It's all equal in love.

—ARIEL SPILSBURY

A few years ago, in a particularly contentious couple's coaching session, after a particularly contentious fight, my husband, Brian, and I were at an impasse. I was deep inside my burnout and feeling resentful toward everything and everyone in my life. I needed my husband to take care of me. I needed him to help me make it better. I just *needed* him. The more I tried to communicate how badly I needed him (in a rather passive-aggressive way), the more he pulled away. The more he pulled away, the more upset I got.

After more than a decade of doing deep work on our relationship through therapy and coaching, we didn't fall into this dance too often. So when we did, a part of me chalked it up to #marriage. *Couples fight,* I would always tell myself. *There's just no way around it.* Something needed to shift that day, and I was convinced it was Brian. I had popped off in a tirade

about how disappointed (okay, *fucking pissed*) I was at Brian for not showing up and taking care of me in this incredibly dark time, in the *exact* way
I needed him to.

Our coach, Annie, interjected, "Jessica, it's not Brian's job to meet your
needs. It's yours."

I'm sorry, what? A part of me wanted to punch her, and the other part of
me wanted to walk out of the session.

"Should Brian meet your needs," Annie continued, "it's a gift. It's not
an obligation. His only obligation is to himself, and your only obligation is
to you."

Like a baby deer in headlights, I stared blankly back at Annie, digesting
what she had just thrown at me.

The truth.

A truth I had once discovered but had recently forgotten. Her words
weren't just a necessary dismantling of my entire dynamic with my husband,
but a remembrance of who the most important person in my life *really*
was: me.

I had learned that same lesson Annie had just dropped like a bomb,
many years before, during the hardest and most transformative years of my
life: being single. Here I was in a relationship with my forever person, playing out those same shadows of neediness. This was a darkness I thought I
had transmuted, but when we are on the path toward our Light, it's never a
straight line.

Most of us have to learn the same, painful lessons over and over again
until we finally remember the Truth. We have a lot of *unlearning* to do as
well—a lot of romantic narratives and fantasies from which to break free.

Because we are more than just our number-one priority. **We are our own
greatest loves.**

THE FANTASY BEGINS

Anybody else remember reading Shakespeare's *Romeo and Juliet* for the first time and thinking to themselves, *Yep. That's* exactly *what I want?* (Maybe without the death part.) Or you might have watched *The Notebook* and set the Ryan Gosling and Rachel McAdams type of chemistry as your desired standard.

(Was it just me, guys . . . ?)

We have all been fed similar subliminal messages that "love is forever." That when you find your "person," that love should be so great, so intense, so deep, you'd be willing to die for each other. That is extreme, but nonetheless, most women I know dream of an all-encompassing kind of love. That intoxicating, sweep-you-off-your-feet romantic connection that only happens to a lucky few. We intuitively know falling in love is a risk. We don't have to look far to see how love can wreck your heart and leave you in shambles. Just look at the movies, love songs, romance novels, and even our own families of origin. This can make the idea, the chase, the search, the *longing* that much more exhilarating. At least that's how I looked at it. I always *wanted* the fantasy, so I didn't care how the story ended. To touch and to taste that kind of profound love with another human being, even just for a moment, always seemed worth the gamble.

It wasn't until I was twenty-three that I indeed found a Romeo. He was *fourteen* years older than me, mysterious, artistic, passionate, made his entire world about me, and required I do the same for him. For the five years we were together, we were in our own vortex bubble of codependent love addiction. We were hooked so hard on each other, I didn't realize just how much of the rest of my life I let dissolve during that time. Namely, my close friendships, my career, and, yes, even my relationship with my family. My boyfriend and I got matching tattoos of the infinity symbol (mine on the small of my back), because it really did feel like we were going to be together forever. When the bubble popped and it all dramatically ended (as it always does in addictive, codependent relationships), my heart shattered into a trillion pieces.

For months on end, picking up those pieces looked like curling up in a fetal position in my junior one-bedroom apartment in Chicago, lights off, room pitch-black, clutching my third roll of toilet paper (because a single Kleenex box just wasn't enough) as I wailed most of the day. Once that relationship ended, it wasn't just that a piece of me was missing. My entire self-identity disappeared, too.

It would take me a lot of time and tons of therapy to not only heal the heartbreak but to get to the bottom of where my yearning for such an all-consuming desire to love and be loved came from in the first place. It was there inside the depths of my first real traumatic breakup that I realized the problem wasn't that I was choosing the wrong partner, idealizing love, or romanticizing drama to a fault. (Although those were certainly concerning behaviors.)

The *real* problem was that I felt totally, inherently incomplete with myself.

If I really wanted to heal, I had to look not at the ex-boyfriend, not at the relationship, but at myself for the first time in my life.

I had to look *deep*. As deep into the void of my heart, my body, my soul as I could go. I had to learn how to fill that void myself.

1 + 1 = 11

Filling the incompleteness inside ourselves is never a straight line. Some of us spend our whole lives trying to figure out how to feel complete and never get there. In those few post-traumatic breakup years, I kept repeating the patterns of chasing emotionally unavailable men. When that didn't work, I dated a woman, who made me feel more loved, safe, and honored than I'd ever felt, but none of it was ever enough. I still kept playing games, pushing people away, becoming needy when I felt lonely, chasing the "high" of the dramatic reunion after a big fight . . . rinse and repeat.

The greatest transformation came when I quit dating. For almost two years, I made the conscious choice to stop searching for The One and instead cultivate an intense, loving, deep, and raw relationship with myself. This act itself was a leap of faith into my biggest fear: being alone, which, at the time, was the same thing as being lonely.

Loneliness is a dark void. It is in that darkness where you meet your Light.

Day by day, bit by bit, I began to trust this unknown void. While the void certainly was painful, it provided a newfound spaciousness and a newfound freedom. I began to fill it by deepening my friendships, which expanded and enriched me. I poured myself into my entrepreneurial career, which started to flourish. I traveled to new and adventurous places. I discovered yoga and found a new community at my favorite studio. I journaled religiously and got more in touch with my inner voice. I kept up with therapy, even when I started feeling better. This consistency kept me accountable to my own independence and self-healing.

During this precise time, swimming in my oceanic feelings of persisting loneliness, I was out to dinner with some girlfriends when I saw a woman sitting a few tables over, all by herself, reading a book, drinking a martini, and clearly lavishing in her own company. Something about witnessing her activated me. It was a subtle permission slip to start walking through my life as a single woman with not only more courage but more pride. One evening, I tried it. I took myself out on a date. It was all at once exhilarating and terrifying. This "rush" became my favorite practice: sitting at a wine bar alone, or going to a Mexican restaurant, telling the hostess "a table for one, please," and ordering tacos and tea.

I started to build the muscle for aloneness, which was different from being lonely. Aloneness, I came to learn, was far from an empty experience but so *full of aliveness.* I began to fall in love with this feeling, and therefore my life, but most of all, myself. This apex of self-discovery was so significant, I wanted to commemorate it. So one evening, I went to a tattoo parlor and inked "1 + 1 = 11" on my right rib cage.

Nope, it's not a math equation, but a metaphor. It means: be a whole person. The number 1 in many faiths is the symbol of unity. In many monotheistic faiths, the number 1 represents God, or The Universe itself. The expression of 1 + 1 = 11 is the idea that whole people attract whole people. When they create a union, they do not bend, shift, and reshape to the number 2, which is a number that holds no physical similarity to its original expression. The two 1s remain intact, true to their original form, standing side by side as the number 11. Not only is the number 11 mathematically greater than 2, it is the angelic number of spiritual awakening.

Whole people attract whole people. These types of relationships are not founded upon the infamous *Jerry Maguire* quote, "You complete me." Rather, you become complete within yourselves by doing your own work. From this embodied state, you are then able to explore love with another from a new kind of emotional set point: one that is safe, expanded, authentic, vulnerable, and infinitely more fulfilling.

Another way to look at it is this: **people can only meet you as deeply as they have met themselves.**

During those years I was single, I finally met myself. I gave myself the space to experience a new full spectrum of being in this human existence: from excruciating loneliness to exhilarating aloneness and everything in between.

It was there, inside that spectrum, that I found my own wholeness.

It was there that I decided I wanted a partner who had found his, too.

It was there that I did.

REWRITING THE FAIRY TALE

I met Brian when I turned thirty. He was an emotionally available man who had done his work (and still does) and was looking for love. I remember knowing on our blind first date that I was going to marry him. Together, we have built a beautiful life, are partners in business, are raising two furry babies, and are sheathed by our passionate connection, unending physical attraction, never-ending laughter, mutual respect for each other's autonomy, and a genuine friendship. I got to ride off into the sunset with my very own 11. Twelve years and going strong, baby. How lucky am I, right?

If only it was that simple.

Yes, whole people attract whole people. Just because you're a whole person doesn't mean that you're a perfect person, let alone a fully healed person. Whole people still find themselves in couple's therapy. We are human beings, after all, not fully evolved Pleiadians.

If our family systems activate our deepest shadows and our highest Light and set the foundation for what we came here to heal, I believe our romantic partnerships are the containers that allow us to actually do the healing. Not because of the particular person we get into partnership with, but *who we become* in response to them.

Relationships are the ultimate container for growth because they hold up a gargantuan mirror to all your shadows. If I'm being brutally honest, I *still* have a propensity for drama, fears of being alone, a bit of codependency, and a passive-aggressive communication style. Being with my husband didn't quell those patterns but rather brought them to the surface. Throughout all the work that I had done, and as my coach, Annie, had pointed out, I *still* unconsciously believed it was my partner's job to take care of me emotionally, to please me, to serve me, to hold me, and to heal me.

I still *outsourced.*

Inside my own container, I have learned that it's not your partner's job to *resource* you. It's yours. Should your partner choose to take care of you, hold you, serve you, and please you, consider it a bonus.

This can be an incredibly hard pill to swallow. It was for me, and I've spent the majority of my marriage digesting, dismantling, and remembering this fact. The feelings of incompleteness are etched deep inside our human DNA, regardless of whether we are in a relationship at all. What's actually critical to understand here is that we don't need to be in a relationship to unearth, integrate, and ultimately learn to *love* these parts of ourselves. Whether we're single, dating, married, heterosexual, queer, trans, monogamous, polyamorous, or open, we can all forget that we are always the source of our own Light. The more we search for that sense of completeness in another, the more painful it becomes, even in the "healthiest" of relationships.

Your closely cultivated relationship with self is the only place in which you can *remember* your wholeness. That's because, as you now know, *you are the Source*.

Sure, a relationship can be an accelerant of growth. However, a relationship is not, nor will it ever be, a fairy tale. It's time to rewrite the fairy tales we've been programmed to believe and ditch the desire for a happy ending.

The happy ending is always going to start with you.

You are always The One.

I'm not here to tell you how to find a partner or be a better partner once you do. I'm here to invite you to remember that the ultimate love affair will *always* be the one you have with yourself. Just like all great love affairs, it might just be messy, painful, uncomfortable, and sad at times. If you commit to becoming your own source of love, it will become the most empowering, beautiful, freeing, nourishing, exhilarating, pleasureful, fulfilling part of this human experience.

It is, in fact, the reason for your human experience: to know your own power and to become the source of your own Light.

I don't know about you, but that sure sounds like a fucking fairy tale to me.

The best part? *You* are always the leading character.

LOVE'S A WITCH

Some say love's a bitch. It's painful, often doesn't end well, and if it does last, it takes a ton of work. Love's also a witch, playing tricks on us, and there's no more potent trick than the craving we have for love itself.

When our cravings for love are not met, we turn to whatever is going to satiate our appetite to be validated, seen, important, needed, desired, and wanted. If we can't get it in a relationship, we'll quench our thirst on social media, get our hits from shopping, swipe left, swipe right, throw ourselves into our work addiction, keep ourselves distracted with reality TV, numb ourselves with food and alcohol, and consume, consume, consume to fill the void.

Our appetites to love and be loved are insatiable. The trick of the witch is that the "fix" has been right under our noses the whole time. It is in fact our very own whole faces, whole bodies, and whole *beings* that are here to love us more deeply, more completely than any other human on Planet Earth ever could.

Yes, relationships are containers, and our partners are our mirrors, but there is no one more beautiful, intriguing, stimulating, and challenging than the person staring back at you in your own mirror. Your relationship with self is the *ultimate* mirror, and falling in love with what you see is the very spell that Love has been trying to cast on you for your entire life.

I'm not just talking about what you see physically but *who you are.* Have you ever tried to soul-gaze with yourself in the mirror? To simply soften into your own eyes until the image of yourself intoxicates you, dissolves you, and becomes one with you? It's not dissimilar from what most of us search for in a partner, right? *This wholeness.* Realizing that this Love is always available to us *inside us* is the ultimate unlock into our Light.

Most of us don't have the time or inclination to sit in front of the mirror all day spouting affirmations at our souls. So how do we venture out into our lives to fully live this expression of wholeness? How do we get used to being with ourselves so intimately? How do we call upon the witch who will fix our fears of loneliness? How do we sit in the discomfort of not reaching for anything else to *consume* but our own presence? What if you took all that energy pining for someone else to fill all your needs, and you started to fill your own?

It requires us to be courageously unafraid of *being* with ourselves. That's where we meet ourselves and realize the witch is on our side. She wants us to remember how powerful we are, with or without a relationship.

Even in the most beautiful serious relationships, your needs will never be fully met. You will still long to feel completely held, seen, and desired. Being in a relationship can still feel incredibly lonely.

However, in our relationships with ourselves, we are never alone.

When you embody this empowered state of independence, you then have the roots to grow a happy, healthy *interdependent* relationship with someone else.

INTERDEPENDENCE: THE GODDESS MOVE

Being an independent person is a beautiful thing, but it certainly has a shadow side of its own. We can get too comfortable, too particular, too at ease being alone that we make no space for a partner. Codependency, on the other hand, might seem like a natural evolution of a close relationship, and I'll admit, it's nice to be needed and to need someone. Codependency, though, is the crux of most relationship breakdowns.

When I first started dating my husband, all I ever knew was codependency. In previous partnerships, we were never apart. Trips, events, weekdays, and weekends turned into black holes of togetherness, never coming up for air. For the longest time, "having a boyfriend" meant Friday nights at concerts, Saturday daytime errands, Saturday date night, Sunday morning sex, followed by Sunday brunch, and ending with Sunday laundry, home-cooked dinners, and Netflix. It was all I wanted, because it was all I knew. This level of obsession never ends well, as one partner or the other eventually needs space, changes, or desires something beyond the invisible four walls of the twosome, which can be incredibly threatening to the entity called your relationship. The neediness and resentment then starts a feedback loop, and left in its wake is one big toxic soup of codependency.

When Brian and I first started dating, one of the first things he told me about himself was his passion for golf. What he *didn't* tell me was that for half the year, I would be on my own for the weekends. You see, my husband isn't just passionate about golf: he's *obsessed* with it. That obsession takes him out of our bed every Saturday and Sunday morning at 6 A.M. and doesn't return him home until 4 P.M. For the first few years of our relationship, golf became my nemesis. I resented the sport as much as I resented Brian for abandoning me every weekend and leaving me "all alone." We would fight constantly about it, as I would guilt him with statements like "I might as well not even *have* a boyfriend, because the one I do have is *never here.*" (As I mentioned, I've never lost my flair for drama.)

I didn't realize it at the time, but Brian's insistence on maintaining his own autonomy through his passion was a gift. It held me accountable to maintain mine. Being madly in love with a person and being madly in love with yourself do not cancel each other out. On the contrary, they deepen the strength, health, and connection of the relationship.

Today, in my partnership with Brian, we have found a beautiful equilibrium of interdependence. It is an acceptance that we do in fact *need* each other, rely on each other, and are impacted by each other's choices, energy, and actions. The pendulum has not swung so far that I feel I *cannot* live without him (which I can't), and we aren't so far apart that I feel like I *can* live without him (which I can, but I never want to). Interdependence, as I define it, means we are interwoven but not enmeshed. Separate when necessary, but always intimate regardless of distance or time. In love with each other and in love with our own lives.

Golf is no longer my enemy—or as I used to bitterly call her—"his mistress." She's my ally, as she helped me to sustain my relationship to myself that I worked so hard to cultivate when I was single. The dynamics of my partnership further inspired me to intently seek out even more opportunities to be with myself.

One of the most powerful practices I have cultivated to maintain interdependence in my marriage is an annual solo trip, which I've coined "alonemoon." In the last few years, I've spent weeks and months in Costa Rica; Santa Fe, New Mexico; and Ojai, California, by myself and with myself. When I first started taking these trips, I got the strangest feedback, mainly from women in my community: *What do you do with yourself all day? I would be so scared! Your husband lets you do that? Is your marriage okay? I think I would go crazy if I took a trip myself. Maybe one day I'll be brave enough to do that. . . .*

I never take these projections to heart. I know that everyone is on his or her own journey, and, more than anything, I know I am setting an example of what it looks like to embrace your fears, because I feel them, too, in being alone. These trips have given me the space to remember that I am always and forever my own "1"—where I can let the wisdom of my couple's coach, Annie, ring true. It's no one's job to fill me, complete me, or take care of me. Only I can do that. That, my friend, is the most liberating and potent form of empowerment that exists.

Being alone is no doubt uncomfortable. When you give yourself the space to sit with yourself, *you meet yourself* in a new way. It can be lonely, boring, and sad. The witch tests you all the time. The upgrade is to move through it anyway. In it you find your strength and self-reliance. When I come home from these trips, I am renewed not only in my personal power but in my connection to myself. I am more embodied in my own Light. I am also a more grateful, loving, and present wife to my husband.

You don't have to gallivant off to an exotic location to cultivate this light and love within yourself. A simple quiet walk in nature, journaling, processing with a therapist or a close friend are all beautiful practices to meet yourself. I encourage you to get in touch with your thoughts, prick your own wounds of loneliness, and shine light on the darkness in your own forms of aloneness. It is there that you build your own unique relationship with the witch of love, where she reminds you that she's not something you ever have to chase. You're actually right next to her, flying high on the broomstick, co-creating the joyride of your life as teammates.

Through the power of solitude, self-reflection, solo travel, and therapy, whether you are in a relationship or not, you find embodiment through self-love. That embodiment of confidence, self-assurance, and independence is sexy as hell. This turns up your magnetism.

You attract not only more of the right aligned partners from this vibration of wholeness but more of a fully aligned life.

There is nothing to ever chase. It's always been right there, within you.

TRUE ORGASMIC BLISS

On our stop at Philae, at the Temple of Isis, our group had gotten there before dawn to have a private tour of her incredible grounds before the doors opened at 7 A.M. to the public. (Those 3 A.M. Egyptian wake-up calls were no freakin' joke, but walking through these sacred sites in the dark before day came was *always* worth it.) As the sun rose over the low reservoir of the Aswan Low Dam, we could finally see the beautifully engraved walls of Philae in full effect.

Our Egyptologist summoned a small group over to a particularly rare and, according to him, "scandalous" hieroglyph in an inconspicuous corner of Philae. It was of Isis, the goddess of Divine Love, and her husband, Osiris, the god of fertility and the underworld, intertwined with one another. The love story between these two mythical figures has shaped not only much of Egyptian mythology but beliefs around how religion and, therefore, humanity at large, were formed.

In this image, Isis is holding the ankh, also known as the key to all eternal life, and she is placing it inside Osiris's mouth. At the same time, something more unusual is going on. King Osiris has his fingers inside Isis's vagina, and she is coming. The depiction of her ejaculation is an image of dozens of ankhs shooting out of her. It is a very special scene, and it is not seen anywhere else across Egypt.

It was standing there at the crack of dawn, listening to this story and taking in this image, that I had a sheer remembrance of a universal truth. The creation of humanity, and all eternal life, *began with bliss.* All birth begins with tantric orgasm. The key to living an eternally joyful life is to return to how it all started: pleasure. While this is factually obvious, I could feel the generations of misappropriated beliefs around sexual pleasure as "something to be ashamed of" begin to not only dissolve but *rewrite.* Standing there in Philae, I recalled codes of the Pleiadians in my cellular memory: *sexuality connects you with the frequency of ecstasy, which connects you back to Divine Source and to Information.*[1] Sex is the most spiritual, healing, and activating of experiences. Screw plant medicines (pun intended). Sex is the ultimate bridge to take you into higher states of consciousness.

It was only a few days later that I would meet Hathor, the goddess of pleasure herself. In her Dendera Temple in Egypt, she gave me the message that it was *my job* to experience pleasure, to prioritize bliss, and to make play a priority, not anyone else's. How on earth could I possibly outsource that, let alone even want to?

Yet that's all most of us do when it comes to seeking someone to fuck. Sexual pleasure is one of the primary (and most primal) desires, yearnings, and expectations we seek from a partner. There is nothing in the world like the sexual, orgasmic intimacy we have with our lovers. Sex, from a Pleiadian point of view, is a doorway to multidimensional ascension through our orgasm. There's a reason they call the best of them "mind-blowing," as your cognitive mind dissolves, as does your physicality, and you transcend to a place beyond this reality. (If you know, you know.)

The Pleiadians also caution us to be far more selective and less casual about who we sleep with. Sex is more than fucking with your bodies. It's a merging of your electromagnetic frequencies. This explains why you might want nothing to do with someone you've recently slept with, and yet you can't "get them out of your system." While I am all for sexual liberation, exploration, and freedom of all people everywhere (and having all the hot sex they want to), I can't help but agree with the Pleiadians. There is more to sex than simply getting off. Your body, as we have learned, is a sacred vessel, a doorway into other dimensions. You should not let just anyone enter it. I am not encouraging you to be a prude but rather to *remember* how precious, rare, and powerful you and your body are. After all, what's more precious, rare, and powerful than an orgasm that can blast you into the highest dimensions of multidimensional realities and instant quantum healing? Having that orgasm with someone you love.

By that same token, as you vibrate in the love of self, honor the self, and understand that the journey here is about self-discovery in relationship to others, you will come to see this is not about "monogamous versus promiscuous," "partner to partner," or "husbands and wives." It's about honoring your physical body and allowing for the gift of sexual pleasure to be a tool for your own highest evolution.

Next-level ascension into our orgasmic Light is not necessarily connected to a partner and their sex organs. Once we've discovered our wholeness—which by now I hope you've come to realize is the most magical love of them all—we can see just how pleasurable all of life can feel within ourselves.

When we are living lives that are full, whole, adventurous, brave, and in love with life itself, we literally turn on our Light. Partner or no partner, isn't walking through life *that* "turned on" what we're all seeking in the first place? To feel the rush, the high, the bliss, the orgasmic pleasure to be in this human body? Life began with an orgasm. Why does it need to stop? *Life can be an orgasm.* The Egyptian gods and goddesses know this and have never forgotten. Only we have. We have forgotten the orgasmic explosion we came from, only to search for it everywhere else outside ourselves, and especially to outsource it to romantic love, when the truth is that level of bliss lives within our cells at all times.

When we *remember* we are Love itself, our romantic partnerships then don't have to be obliged to ensure we are always pleased. Only *we* can do that.

We are the gift we've been seeking. We get to be that gift to our partners. We get to be the Light.

That is our gift to the world.

The Invitation: Find Your Wholeness

- What is your biggest fantasy about romantic relationships?
- Does any aspect of this fantasy hold you back from loving yourself fully?
- What are your fears about being in a partnership?
- What are your fears about being alone?
- Can you gently acknowledge where in your relationships, or in past relationships, you are codependent?
- If you could give the witch of love a name, what would it be?
- How can she become your best friend?
- How does receiving pleasure make you feel?
- How could you honor your desires more fully?
- What new *Information* do you possess about the power of true love and orgasmic bliss?

The Key: Take Yourself Out on a Date for One

Regardless if you're single, dating multiple partners, in a committed relationship, divorced, or otherwise, this key applies to *everyone.* Make a reservation for one at a restaurant you have never been to in a new neighborhood. (The aim here is to go somewhere new where you won't know anyone and can't lean on your favorite bartender for conversation.) Before heading out for the night, give yourself enough time to soul-gaze in the mirror. Let your eyes stare at yourself for just long enough that you feel yourself dissolve, creating a deep sense of wholeness within. Once you feel ready (as this experience can bring up a lot of beautiful emotions), put on your favorite music (suggested songs from "The Lightworker's Playlist" can be found in "Your Lightworker Resources" section near the end of the book), as you style yourself to feel the most beautiful, getting yourself into a vibration of joy, beauty, and confidence.

Before you leave for your date, grab a book or your Light Work journal. When you arrive at the restaurant, don't obsessively check your phone.

Give yourself the opportunity to truly be in your own company by sitting in the awkwardness. Keep yourself company by reading your book or journaling versus scrolling through Instagram posts and focusing on everyone else's lives. Pay attention to who is entering your awareness and stay open to what conversations may organically begin. If you don't say a single word to anyone but your server tonight, that's perfect, too. To make the night extra exhilarating, take yourself home, put on your sexiest lingerie, and pleasure yourself. Repeat this key as often as you like.

Please visit jessicazweig.com/unlock to access all the Invitations and Keys.

7

FEMALE FRIENDSHIPS

THE GREATEST MEDICINE OF THEM ALL

Women who love themselves, love other women.
—MARYAM HASNAA

On a Tuesday afternoon, in the middle of the work week, I blocked two hours out of my schedule to go to therapy. I was in a crisis, and my heart was bleeding. There seemed to be nothing more important than tending to this pain.

Sitting on the sofa next to me, facing my therapist, was my best friend of thirteen years, Megan. We had just had the most major falling-out of our friendship and hadn't spoken to each other for almost a month.

Despite my anger and hurt that led to this blowup, I felt an even greater sadness. The level of intimacy that we are able to achieve with our best friends is among the deepest we go in our entire lives, and not speaking to Megan for the previous few weeks felt like cutting off my oxygen.

I was gutted.

At forty, both of us had done enough Light Work to know that this falling-out was an opportunity for us to heal some of our greatest wounds when it came to being in healthy relationships with other women. It took a shit ton of consciousness, dedication, and guts to walk ourselves into therapy as two forty-year-old women . . . together.

Throughout our decade and a half of friendship, we had both grown together and apart. We expanded at the same time, at different times, in similar and different directions. We'd traveled the world together and laughed and cried across every proverbial and literal terrain. We had become each other's *biggest* cheerleaders, triggers, activators, and healers. We'd brought the darkest of the dark out in each other, and the brightest of the Light.

Nothing had ever taken us down like this.

Just a few weeks before our session, a simple misunderstanding about a girls' weekend led to an enormous disagreement, and all our unspoken truths, old stories, quiet resentments, negative assumptions, and imbalances boiled over to expose a dynamic that was no longer working.

Had we been in more of our own Light consciousness, this misunderstanding would have been a blip. Instead it was a breakdown. When the fire of our own furies calmed down and the ashes cleared, we came to see that we were both codependent on one another—and *that* is what we really needed to heal on that sofa.

The good news is that when you're really doing the Light Work, you're going to manifest friendships with other empowered women who are, too. The Pleiadians, as channeled by Barbara Marciniak, understand this well: *"you will find that when you live your light, you will draw to yourself others who are very interested in living their lives in the same manner, and your numbers will grow and grow."*[1] The not-so-good news is that we're also going to manifest friendships (and all close relationships, for that matter) that are the ideal match for us to heal our deepest and most profound wounds. When it comes to the closest relationships of our lives, I believe we choose them. Our souls come here to work out karma from our past lives in order to evolve into more Love. Based on either our childhood or ancestral traumas, we then get into relationships that are the ideal match for us so we can begin to heal.

For me, Megan had been "mothering" me in a consistent and dependable way that I never got from my own mom, which provided me safety within my fears of abandonment. For Megan, she took care of me in a way her own mom unconsciously required of her, which provided her safety within her fears of chaos. Like two jigsaw puzzle pieces, we were a perfect match for our unhealed shit.

It's this combination of befriending empowered women who bring out the best in us, while they activate some of our most unconscious, unresolved darkness, that becomes the perfect recipe for what I believe to be the *greatest medicine of all*: balanced, authentic, and responsible female friendships.

WALKING THE WALK

There's a special kind of activation that comes from female friendships. When things are clear and conscious, these friendships can provide the most nourishing fun we have in our entire lives. I can honestly say that my greatest memories have been made when I'm with my girlfriends. That's not to say I don't cherish the time I have with my husband, family, or work colleagues, but there's a heart-to-heart depth to friendships that cannot be replicated. If you have even just a few friends you consider your Sisters with a capital S, you're blessed. Sisterhood provides you a sense of unshakable peace, joy, strength, and love. We get to live the highest vibrations of the Divine Laws of Light when we are in integrated and loving friendships.

When things do get out of balance, we can experience some of our most profound pain and therefore our greatest opportunities to heal some of our deepest wounds and ultimately step into more of our embodied Light.

Maybe, like it was for me, friendship is an opportunity for you to heal your pattern of codependency, too. Perhaps you have a tendency toward jealousy, you default to competitiveness, you feel profound loneliness, you carry palpable insecurities, you are addicted to drama, you fear rejection, or you are prone to judgment and gossip. These are among some of the offenders in the dynamics of female friendships, and many of us either avoid facing them or are entirely unconscious altogether.

I have learned that when we stop hiding from these hard, often embarrassing, and shameful feelings and "come clean" with ourselves, we step into a massive portal of expansion and growth. This is the *work*. You can certainly walk yourself into a therapist's office with your friend, like I did (which I highly recommend you try at some point), but for the purposes of this chapter, let's take some baby steps.

Who are the women in your life that "trigger" you the most? Maybe these are some of your closest friends, women you *used* to be friends with, or perhaps they are women you follow on social media. There are no wrong answers here. Write their names down in your Light Work journal.

When you look at these women's names, what comes up for you? What is the exact feeling? Do your best to *name* it, and do not judge yourself. This is between you and you (and you and me), and I love you, Sister. We're in this together.

Regarding that named feeling, what's the story behind it? *Claim* that story as your own, not hers, not society's, not the circumstances surrounding it—but yours. This is not only incredibly empowering but incredibly freeing. It's okay if some tears come up here. Letting go of the stories we project onto other women and reflecting within is a radically vulnerable act. Claiming *responsibility* for our own part, our own pain, our own thoughts, and our own behaviors is downright terrifying. This is the darkness that leads us to the Light.

Now I want you to consider a more loving, conscious, and clear story about this woman or relationship. This is the *reframe*. Even if you don't fully believe this story yourself yet, that's okay. Simply write it down. Read it out loud to yourself a few times. Feel it in your body. Imagine yourself walking through the world with this belief. That's all you have to do at this step.

When you're ready, choose from an aspect of the Divine Laws of Light: connection, personal power, Oneness, reverence, reciprocity, authenticity, freedom, courage, self-sovereignty, compassion, trust, peace, and harmony.

Ask yourself: What would a practice, a ritual, a behavior, or an action look like if you were to *integrate* one of these laws into a new way of being in relationship with yourself—and with your friend?

For the longest time, I felt that in order for my friendship with Megan to work, she had to take care of me emotionally.

Simply *naming* out loud that I was codependent, with radical self-awareness, was sheer fucking liberation!

Claiming that belief (and behavior) as my own, with *radical humility* and *radical responsibility* was the catalyst toward not only a more balanced friendship with her but a more authentic relationship with myself.

Reframing that belief, with an *unshakable willingness to shift* into a more conscious story rooted in the Information that our friendship was a gift, not an obligation, the Truth that I am whole with or without Megan, and allowing Love to be the salve to heal our resentments, was the Light Work made manifest.

From that place, I was able to *integrate* a new way of being in relationship with her using the Divine Laws of *compassion* for past hurts, *reverence* for who Megan fully is, *peace* in who I fully am, and *trust* that our friendship possesses enough *freedom* for both of us to expand in our own unique directions.

Is our friendship today perfect? No. It *is* infinitely more balanced, conscious, and loving. The best part has not been upgrading our friendship, but upgrading ourselves as grown women.

That's the *real* flex of doing this work.

Because again, our wounds go deep—way, way back to what is our shared, inherited trauma and societal conditioning as women—and our friendships are here to help us heal them.

LET'S GO BACK TO THE BEGINNING

I was twelve years old, standing in line with my mom at the mall's food court, waiting for our order from McDonald's. I caught a glimpse of a woman out of the corner of my eye. Her hair was dyed electric blue, coiffed into a spiky buzz cut, and she wore thick eyeliner and bold lipstick of the same exact color. She was wearing a tie-dyed spandex dress, fishnet stockings, and platform Mary Janes. I tugged on my mom's arm out of reflex.

"Mom . . . ," I said quietly.

She did not hear me.

"*Mom,*" I emphatically whispered. She blinked at me.

"Did you see that lady standing over by Sbarro? She looks *so* crazy. Mom . . . doesn't she look *soooo* crazy?"

My mom's head slowly turned away from me in the direction of the stranger I was alluding to. She blinked again and then looked back toward me.

"Jessica," she said patiently, "when that woman got dressed this morning, looked at herself in the mirror before she left her house, *she* thought she looked amazing. That's all that matters."

That woman I saw across the food court when I was twelve years old is the same woman who was sitting next to me on the sofa at my therapist's office when I was forty years old, and is the same woman who is reading this book right now.

We are all each other's mirrors.

Every one of us wants to feel beautiful, needed, respected, admired, loved, and honored. Remember this. When we cast negative opinions, judgments, and projections toward other women, we aren't just doing them a huge disservice: we are cutting ourselves off from our own Light as well.

My mom did her best to raise me with compassion and empathy. That moment at the mall, judging a perfectly beautiful stranger, was one of dozens of moments I was guided to open my heart to a new perspective by her.

Despite my mom's best intentions, I grew up in the same world as you did. A world that taught me that I wasn't thin enough, smart enough, pretty enough, good enough, or cool enough. As a direct result, I have unconsciously scrutinized and criticized many other women throughout my life. As that unconsciousness morphed into a conscious *responsibility* through my own Light

Work, I realized that this scrutiny actually had nothing to do with what I saw in other women, but rather everything that I could not yet see in myself.

For a long time I walked through the world with a huge lack of self-acceptance and self-love, and when I really dug in to identify where many of these walls came from, I realized much of it was based on the fear of rejection (and sometimes actual rejection) from *other women*.

Rejections create projections, and projections create rejections. This is what keeps us stuck in a feedback loop of separation.

The Light Work shows us that the woman standing across the food court longing to feel beautiful is our longing, that her desire to be seen is our desire, that her courage to self-express can inspire our courage, and her pain feels exactly like our pain (even if the circumstances that created it are different). Only then can we start to see ourselves and others with more compassion and, ultimately, expansiveness.

She's your mirror.

What you see in her is what you possess yourself; otherwise, you wouldn't be able to see it. (Read that twice.)

When you start to see how one and the same we truly are, and stop pitting yourself against and projecting onto other women, true *Sisterhood* can finally form.

SISTERHOOD WITH A CAPITAL *S*

There is a common conversation happening among the modern-day collective of women. At the time of writing this book, #WomenEmpowerment has been hashtagged more than 25 million times on Instagram and 11 billion times on TikTok—and is growing by the minute. There are over 400 million worldwide businesses that are either women-owned or women-operated, 42 percent of US-based businesses are owned by women, and the percentage of female entrepreneurs has increased by 114 percent in the last 20 years.[2] In the corporate world, the share of women who hold executive level positions has grown significantly at 31.7 percent, up five points since 2015 at 27.1 percent, according to the US Census Bureau.[3] Terms like "community over competition," "girl gangs," and my personal favorite, "sisterhood," are touted everywhere.

I'm here for it all. In many ways, this conversation has been the catalyst for my entire career.

Now, if we look a layer deeper, this is a sisterhood with a small *s*.

Much of the time, we're talking the talk, not walking the walk. We are still easily seduced by gossip, we default to unconscious competition, and we allow our insecurities to breed in the shadow of another woman's radiance. To *want* sisterhood versus being truly *available* for Sisterhood requires a dissolution of some of our most unconscious beliefs about other women and ourselves. It requires us naming, claiming, reframing, and integrating not only our self-limiting beliefs about our very best friends but about all women, everywhere.

This can be some really painful work, as it requires us to unearth where we do not feel whole, where the gaps of our own unconditional self-love can be filled, and where we must take radical responsibility for our own projections. Only then can we truly give and receive the full power of Sisterhood.

This lack of wholeness can stem from the parenting (or lack thereof) we received, our schooling, the communities we grew up in, cliques we were either a part of or got cast out of, our religious upbringings, grudges we hold, and every facet of our culture and society. Just open up Instagram, check the covers of magazines as you stand in line at the grocery store, take stock of the bombardment of ads women receive to improve themselves, pay attention to the watercooler chatter at the office, or just turn on the fucking news. We are bombarded with fear, reactiveness, comparison, and never-enough-ness.

Our specific stories might be different, but we are all being fed the same lie: that we cannot all shine, thrive, and expand at the same time. This ultimately holds us back from intimately, vulnerably, and authentically connecting with other women, with full trust and faith, in order to become each other's truest allies.

Imagine a world where all women, despite age, race, weight, socio-economic status, family origin, aesthetics, kids or no kids, career, and dreams were on the same team. Where we embodied the truth that we are *already* a Sisterhood because we are women. Not only would we heal some of our deepest wounds, we would heal Gaia, our Mother Earth. This is all she wants for us: to *remember* that we are all her daughters, which makes us all Sisters.

A Sisterhood with a capital *S* is unshakable. Among the insanity of our society, the roller coaster of romantic relationships, the instability we face in our careers, the challenges of motherhood, and the childhood traumas we've endured, Sisterhood can be the truest, steadiest thing in a woman's life.

When I close my eyes and picture a Sisterhood manifested, I see the image of an infinite Tree of Life, as big as the planet. Our Sisters will, without a fraction of a doubt, catch us when we fall. They will give us a hand up as we climb that tree and cheer for us when we've reached our own summits. Because Sisterhood realizes that we're *all* the tree, and more so, we are each an intrinsic and needed branch, colored with our own unique leaves, extending out to touch our own unique corners of the universe.

Whether it's a woman you see on a dance floor, a chick you follow on Instagram, a work colleague, your very best friend, or a stranger you observe at the mall, the Light Work is here to unlock the Information that each leaf on the Sisterhood tree is beautiful and needed, and that means yours is, too.

I'm willing to bet, like me, you haven't always felt needed. You've always felt a bit like an outcast, or a little lonely. The longing for Sisterhood runs deep for most of us.

Life, however, can get in the way.

A NEVER-ENDING LONGING FOR SISTERS

I grew up in the North Shore suburbs of Chicago, in one of the most notably affluent areas outside the city. Growing up around extreme wealth with modest self-made parents was a cornerstone of my starseed upbringing. Read: I never felt like I belonged.

At my school, it was normal for girls to get nose jobs and rock Chanel bags at thirteen. Most of the cars in the student high school parking lot were nicer than the cars in the teacher's lot. Cliques were very much a thing.

With my frizzy hair, systemic acne, and insistent baby fat, combined with my outfits from T.J. Maxx, bolstered by the instability I was experiencing at home, the experience of nonbelonging was a sensation that followed me through the majority of my middle school, high school, and even college years.

In middle school, I experienced my first bout of female friendship rejection, when all of my elementary school friends were deemed "popular" overnight by some unspoken code of adolescent approval, and I wasn't. Within the first few weeks of sixth grade, I experienced social loneliness for the very first time. Further into seventh and eighth grade, the bullying began.

By freshman year of high school, being the outsider I had become, I made friends with a group of rebellious, pot-smoking, curfew-breaking sophomores. By sophomore year, I had outgrown them (or at least my parents had disciplined me enough to quit trying to keep up) and I turned to a small group of nerdy, homebody seniors. In junior year, those seniors graduated and I was left friendless again, only to find a home in the theater department alongside the other misfits. It wasn't until senior year that I had solidified a new gay male best friend, who, in truth, was my only friend.

When I went to college to study acting, I found a small tribe of girlfriends through my program. The bummer was that we would have to compete against each other every semester for the same lead roles in the plays. Most of the time, they got cast and I didn't. When that happened, I vividly remember never feeling jealous of them. I was, of course, sad for me, but I was genuinely excited and happy for them. My friendships with them were always more important than the lead role in *The Taming of the Shrew*. So they went on to shine, and I watched.

It wasn't until my mid-to-late twenties that I was even able to articulate the longing and the yearning I had for a true Sisterhood. It's the root reason why, on a conscious (and at times subconscious) level, I have created businesses that have allowed me to connect more deeply with other women. This part of my career didn't *manifest* itself as much as I had to *manufacture* it throughout my thirties.

Today in my forties, I still long for Sisters. The remnants of these lifelong yearnings remain, and they are so very real. As we get older, finding Sisters actually gets harder, not easier. That's because our lives get busier and in the go-go-going, everything else aside from our sisterly nourishment seems to take priority. I'm talking about parenting our kids, tending to our families, growing our careers, building businesses, trying to stay fit, and honestly just keeping it the fuck together on a daily basis. Add in the fact that 90 percent of our communication exists using technology and social media, not to mention the global isolation we all got so used to in the COVID-19 pandemic years, being in a deep, consistent community with a Sisterhood can become nearly impossible.

Sisterhood is what I want more than anything. I believe most of us do.

From the outside in, I am aware my life looks adventurous, social, and full. With my wonderful husband and thriving career, I've been told that I look like "I have it all." The truth is, I am terribly lonely a lot of the time. I still get FOMO if I don't get an invite to an event that everyone else seemed to get. I am still practicing the concept of quality over quantity, reminding myself that I don't need tons of friends to feel full but rather just a few deep ones. I am still embracing the fact that there are friends who come into our lives for a reason, a season, or a lifetime, and that if I'm really lucky, I'll get one (or two) who check all of those boxes. I still have to schedule months in advance for dinner dates with longtime friends because my schedule as an entrepreneur is ludicrously intense. I will meet a supercool woman at an event or yoga class, feel an instant connection, only to never see her again, because neither one of us has *time* to reconnect.

How does our Tree of Life grow if we don't have the space or capacity to even water it?

In order to cultivate a real Sisterhood, we have to first *name* our longing for one, *claim* it as a void only we can fill, *reframe* our perspectives to believe there is an abundance of friendships available to us, and if we want to manifest a Sisterhood, we must *integrate* new practices rooted in the Divine Laws of Light, like *courage* in making new connections, speaking with *authenticity* in conflict, opening ourselves to more *connection*, and changing our perception that we are alone to a perception of *Oneness*.

I know I am not alone in the complex but beautiful experience of forging, cultivating, and maintaining authentic female friendships, both with women I call my best friends or brand-new connections. However, if there's anything I have learned when it comes to Sisterhood, quality over quantity is the finest form of a community. This is in large part why I host my global "Claim Your Light" retreats, to go deeper with women who are living their Light. Over five days, I, of course, teach business, branding, and spirituality, but it's this newfound Sisterhood that is the most invaluable. It is in sacred containers such as these that we come to find "narrow and deep" is far more nourishing than "shallow and wide." This understanding has been a profound healer within my never-ending longing for a Sisterhood and for so many women in my community.

Let's explore where in our lives we can create space for more authentic female friendship (its highest form), and also female allyship (Gaia's greatest wish).

As we claim our longings, name our projections, recognize that we are all each other's mirrors, and embrace Sisterhood's Tree of Life, we enter one of the greatest transformational portals of Light, a portal in which we embody one luminous Truth:

We are all longing for *each other*.

YOUR TURN

By now, you've come to understand not only why Sisterhood is one of our greatest medicines (and that of Gaia's) but that we have opportunities to go deeper into our healing, and therefore our wholeness and ultimately our Light.

It's time to honestly consider your relationships with women. Examine whom you follow on social media, your work colleagues, your entire friendship network, or a singular relationship. It's all entirely up to you.

Use the following worksheet to start by naming your self-limiting beliefs, behaviors, and *stories,* and let the Light inside you lead the way as you claim, reframe, and integrate new ways of being in relationship with our collective Sisterhood.

As you do, remember this: the roots of this tree run deep into the earth, and its branches reach toward the infinite sky. Learn to trust the innate connection we have to each other as the women of this planet. We are the ones who hold each other when we fall and, more importantly, lift each other up as we rise. Rewrite the old stories, reclaim new beliefs, and *believe.* Profound healing is waiting for you on the other side, Sister.

The Invitation: Strengthen Your Sisterhood Tree

- What women in your life do you admire?
- What women do you admire who aren't in your direct social circle?
- What about them inspires you?
- How can you open up your life and find more space for female friendship connections?
- What actions can you take to "walk the walk" of women empowerment at your job, in your community, in your neighborhood, or online?
- What new *Information* do you possess about the power of sisterhood?

The Key: Claim Radical Responsibility for Your Stories, Judgments, and Projections About Other Women

▽	**Example:** If she succeeds, there's less room for me to succeed, too.	Name it:
▽▽	**Example:** This is an old-school belief rooted in societal constructs that women have to compete, and this has unconsciously informed how I show up with other women.	Claim it:
▽▽▽	**Example:** There's enough to go around, and in fact, her success creates more space for my success, and all our success. When I support other women, my heart opens, opportunities expand for all, and I am able to receive more of what's coming for me.	Reframe it:
▽▽▽	**Example:** Take stock of how and where you can truly walk the walk of supporting other women: show up to her event, comment on her latest Instagram post with some love, buy her book, share her event on social media, refer her a client, introduce her to your friend to date. (Watch how not only your heart but your whole life expands).	Integrate it:

Please visit jessicazweig.com/unlock to access all the Invitations and Keys.

8

MONEY

REWIRING YOUR ABUNDANCE CODES

Your true nature is abundance. Everything else is a lie.
—ANONYMOUS

My evolutionary journey with money, worth, and abundance has been far from easy. Perhaps you feel me?

After building my first start-up and failing to scale it, I went belly-up broke. I was in my early thirties, swimming in a sea of credit card debt, with literally net-negative bank balances in both my personal and professional bank accounts. My feelings of guilt, shame, and grief were more insurmountable than the financial ruin itself. This experience of true, *actual* scarcity was a traumatic event in my life, and one that went on to live within my body as much as my psyche.

Years later, after paying down the debt and taking space from the loss, I got enough courage to start my second business. With new entrepreneurial lessons in tow after my first failure, I quickly scaled it to a multi-seven-figure business within a few short years. "*I'm in abundance!*" I could finally tell myself. It was that same business, the one that made me finally feel abundant, that left me burned out to my core with physical depletion and diagnosed depression from the excessive, all-consuming, toxic-masculine hustle.

I didn't have to look that hard to realize I wasn't actually "in abundance," but rather "running from scarcity." I wasn't designing a career so I could thrive. I had created a business to ensure I could survive.

When it comes to wealth, survival is the biggest program—or trap—of them all.

I'm here to let you in on the biggest money manifestation secret: cultivating safety in the body is the ultimate antidote.

MONEY MEDICINE

For the past few years, I've been working with an incredible medicine healer. In our spiritual work together, she introduced me to a healing power previously unbeknownst to me, MDMA.* Before this meeting, MDMA was a party drug, and one I dabbled in a few times at concerts and music festivals. However, in working with this true healer, who possesses the utmost love, integrity, and servitude to her clients' transformations, I've learned this medicine doesn't just raise my serotonin levels, get me into my heart space, or make me want to dance it out. This medicine has the ability to support astral travel to past and future lives, open up cosmic doorways, connect me with spirit guides from various dimensions, and restructure my DNA. (Yes, really.)

Cosmic doorways and restructured DNA might sound too good to be true, but stay with me. As we have covered, most bodies on Gaia right now are vibrating at lower densities and are cast under a series of "spells." This is not only due to the inherent fear-based constructs of modern society (the toxic media, our poisoned water, pharmaceuticals, excessive alcohol consumption, processed food, government, and the like), but in large part due to our unprocessed, unhealed childhood and ancestral traumas.

In these lower vibrations, our bodies cannot access light codes, release

---

* As I've stated, I highly encourage you to use discretion in partaking in healing medicines of any kind. This has become a trendy, overglorified topic, and as a result, the world of these medicines and the "healers" that serve them can at times sway more dark than light. Please be discerning, do your research, spend earnest time getting to know your facilitators, and always follow your gut.

shock, transmute trauma, or drain what is clogged in our energetic bodies. As a result, we unconsciously repeat negative programs of scarcity, fear, competition, hustle, and survival, over and over. This prevents us from consciously co-creating our own realities. MDMA opens the heart, activating the emotional and energetic body, significantly raising its vibration. Every person is different, based on their starting point, but the medicine allows bodies to access old codes, which in and of itself enables us to release them. By getting in touch with the old programming, we not only have the power to complete it but to rewrite, and ultimately rewire, a new energetic blueprint in our bodies entirely.

This is precisely what happened to me.

In one of my first journeys with my healer, as soon as the medicine hit, I immediately felt something physically arise in my Sacral Chakra. The more the medicine came on, the clearer that "something" became. It was a woman, *literally living inside my womb.* My healer asked me if I could decipher her name, where she was from, and in what year she existed. I tuned in deeper to the sensations in my body, and once the picture of this woman became clearer, I could feel the affirmative truth of what I was seeing in my heart, my soul, and my cognitive mind.

"Her name is Marguerite," I said with conviction. As soon as I said her name, I accessed her entire story and began downloading information.

She was a part of my lineage, an ancient ancestor, located in Eastern Europe in the 1500s. She was young, possibly twenty-five, but was so worn and haggard, she looked like she could be in her fifties. She was wet, freezing, and starving. Her black eyes were sunken into her face, her pale translucent gray skin as thin as paper, and her dark hair sopping wet from being outside in the cold, freezing rain. She had been abused and abandoned, living on the street, with nothing to her name. It was impossible for her to get warm, and she shook uncontrollably from the cold and hunger. What stuck out to me the most was her hands. They were skinny, spindly, with knobby knuckles that looked like they were gripping for literal life, although she was holding nothing.

As soon as the download came into my mind's eye, I could feel in my *body* the primitive, primal, physical feelings of hunger, anxiety, shame, fear, and, above all, Marguerite's desperation to survive.

I viscerally understood Marguerite's fears because they had unconsciously become *my* fears. She had been right there, lodged in my womb all along, like a stuck piece of matter, as her DNA reprinted like a carbon copy on mine, which I could see had been carried over for generations of all the women before me. Specifically, her *gripping survival* had been living inside my *womb*—my ultimate source of creative freedom and expression—which had been the undercurrent driving my whole entire fucking life. It was the root cause of what caused me to go broke: devaluing my worth, chasing checks, begging for scraps, and shaming myself for having nothing. It was also the root cause of my unintegrated creation of "abundance," which is what eventually led to my burnout: hustling 24–7, being a "yes" woman to every opportunity, spreading myself thin because I had not yet learned to trust that making money could actually be effortless.

I realized then that the real "upgrade" in becoming a cosmic manifester was to rewire this deep programming, and it had to start with one foundational physical embodiment: *safety.*

BECOMING A SPIRITUAL HUSTLER

My story isn't unique. (Okay, maybe the MDMA is.) We all stem from generational and ancestral lineages predicated on survival. This isn't exclusive to women. This is how humanity evolved, and the fittest have always won. Because what really drives survival? *Fear.* Fear is the literal antithesis of Love. It is the opposite of Light. Fear is what drives the darkest forces on the planet and within the entire universe. We don't need to take a medicine journey to know this, see this, and feel this. Turn on the news. Talk to your friends. Strike up a conversation with your Uber driver. Flip open TikTok. Fear is the vibrational baseline at which most of the world is living right now, and it's so deeply etched into our own unconscious programming and ancestral DNA that we don't even realize it's there. How can this incessant vibration *not* impact our relationship with money?

For what it's worth, I give the collective a ton of credit for trying to move our way through this, especially when it comes to money. How to make more money more easily has flooded the mainstream spiritual narrative. Throw a stone and you'll hit a podcast, book, social media account, teacher, or guru talking about money, manifestation, and the laws of attraction. It's safe to say that "abundance" is a modern-day obsession.

However, much of this approach is *cognitive,* using the tools of visualization, affirmations, expanded consciousness, neuroplasticity, and psychology. While these are beautiful and powerful practices (and true to the Pleiadian teachings of *thought is, thought creates*), this is the content, not the *context.* We are trying to rewire our minds (the content) by skipping over the context: the physical state of our nervous systems, our ancestral trauma, and the DNA of our lineages, which have been driving our need for survival for generations.

Together, we're going to rework the context by transmuting the darkest parts of our unconscious beliefs and behaviors around money so that you can embody a new energetic, physical and emotional *vibration.* This is the greatest unlock toward manifesting the wealth we so deeply desire.

We manifest wealth by, yes, *seeing* what is possible, *feeling* we deserve it, changing our thoughts and therefore our language, and *owning* our worthiness. We also must experience *physical* safety, trust and receptivity by releasing old stories, lower densities, and past programming. When we do, the "hustle" is no longer what drives us, and instead allowance becomes our guide. This upgrade lives inside our cells, where our light codes live.

Today, I no longer hustle. I *spiritually* hustle. And by that I mean I don't hustle for money. I hustle for meaning. I don't hustle *from* lack. I hustle *for* love. I don't hustle from fear and survival. I hustle for mine (and humanity's) thriving. I hustle toward healing the ancestral programming of fear, and in its place has come a knowing that I am safe and provided for *always.* This shift has not just helped me move through life with more ease, receptivity, and effortlessness: I have unlocked my *abundance codes* by reaching a new energetic set point of safety to receive, manifest, and prosper. As such, I've become softer and subsequently wealthier than I've ever been. It was within this new peaceful state that I got the clarity I was ready to sell my business, the SimplyBe. Agency. Since exiting, I started my own personal platform serving female entrepreneurs through my business, branding, and spirituality coaching programs, masterminds, and retreats. It's still a lot of work, but it is soul-aligned and I am not killing myself to make it all possible. This evolution was a revelation for me at first, but I have learned to trust it. In this new space, I have launched new creative endeavors, merely as experiments, which have now become multi-seven-figure creative projects, and I have taught my coaching clients how to do the same. I have shed the identity of a hustler and stepped into being a spiritual hustler. The spiritual hustler knows that safety is her vibrational path to true, *effortlessness* wealth, and I am so excited to teach you how to tap into this.

Once you tap in, you become an effortless co-creator. You become a spiritual hustler, also known as a Divine Feminine goddess living her Light in *actual* abundance.

It's time to rewire the programming so we can lead the New Earth.

FEMININE FINANCIAL LEADERS OF THE NEW EARTH

There is a new consciousness birthing now on Earth. One that is rooted in the core of the Pleiadian teachings around abundance and wealth, or what they would call *the name of the game.* Working hard is a patriarchal paradigm. Hustling *can be* a toxic masculine construct. Most of us are playing out our parents' programs and their parents' parents' programs and the programs of the generations that came before them. We are literally *pro-*

grammed in our physical bodies and encoded in our DNA to believe that *only* if we work really, really hard will we get what we deserve. This is erroneous. When we are in a state of sheer trust and allowance, it is only then that the Light can move through us and the universe can compensate us in immeasurable and unexpected ways.

When it comes to money, it is vital to remember there is no limitation. Our ability to manifest all the wealth and abundance we desire is truly infinite. To unlock it, we must come to realize that manifesting wealth is actually *intended* to be effortless. It comes down to our state of mind *and* our frequency. **Change your thoughts about money, and you will change your relationship with money. Shift the frequency of your body and therefore your DNA, and you will shift your reality with money.**

All right, you might read the above statements and scoff. Trust me, I get it. What I'm talking about is quite literally an otherworldly perspective and one that we have been hardwired to disbelieve. We Lightworkers are part of a collective awakening right now, learning to unlock a multitude of infinite possibilities inside of every aspect of our lives. By now, you're starting to unlock some of your most deeply stored self-limiting beliefs around your body, your emotions, your power, your family, your friendships, and your romantic relationships, and transmuting them into the Light, into more Information, into Truth.

Money is funny, isn't it? Unlearning what we've been conditioned to believe around work, worth, deservingness, and, most of all, *safety with money* can take years and years of evolution.

When my Light body activated within Hathor's music chamber inside Dendera in Egypt, the Seven Sisters of Pleiades shared with me just how critical a role women are playing on the planet right now, shifting it back into the feminine frequency. Part of that shift requires women to step into their financial power and thereby become leaders of the New Earth. **Because when women have money, women have power, and when women have power, this world will become a better place.**

Yet women—more than men—question our worth, our abilities, and our deservingness. This is more than just our internal, subconscious programming. This is the patriarchal construct, one that was designed by and for men. Despite considerable progress since the 1980s, when women were paid sixty-five cents for every dollar a man made, today we've only risen to eighty-two cents for every dollar.[1] It's still *less than*. It's quantitatively inferior. This energetically impacts the subtle realms of the collective consciousness. While women are no doubt rising on the spectrum of wealth creation (most of my female friends are the breadwinners in their families, which never ceases to amaze and delight me), we still have a huge opportunity to evolve beyond the current construct to amass *incredible* wealth, but this time, on different terms—the terms of a Lightworker, living within and operating from the feminine frequency.

We are here to embody the Goddess because we *are the Goddess,* as Hathor and the Pleiadians shared with us. How do we do this? Through the *Embodiments of Divine Feminine Wealth.* Notice how they are not cognitive "principles" or "rules" or "laws" or "practices." They are *embodiments.* This is when the true rewiring of our abundance codes can be found: when we release our respective "Marguerites" from our energetic bodies, shift our beliefs, and step forward in a new paradigm using the embodiments of *frequency, equanimity, service, reciprocity, self-sovereignty, trust, generosity,* and *receptivity.*

When we orient ourselves to our innate worth, know our intrinsic value, and operate from light-filled intentions for what we shall do with our money, *effortless manifestation* becomes our inherent way of being. This is the Light Work made manifest as your money.

These eight Embodiments of Divine Feminine Wealth comprise your ultimate *remembrance* of your true abundant nature and financial power, and it's about damn time that you reclaim it.

THE EIGHT EMBODIMENTS OF
DIVINE FEMININE WEALTH

Frequency is the first embodiment, as it encapsulates all the embodiments unto itself. Money is a frequency, as much as any other force or matter in the universe. Our own personal frequencies must attune to the frequency of the quality, level, and amount of money we wish to create in order to more effortlessly attract it. This starts with declaring, owning, and embodying our *value*.

A couple of years ago, I was standing in my backyard in Nashville, playing with my dogs when I got a very clear download. Like a spark of Information shooting through my Crown Chakra, I heard, "*Host a retreat in Nashville.*" I had hosted retreats before in Bali, Costa Rica, and Italy, but it had been over two years since my last one. I had no real strategy, specific time, location, or target number of women I would call in. I just got the message from Spirit, and I decided to act. First, I felt into the image of whom I wanted to be there (highly conscious, successful, empowered, warm, and loving women) and witnessed how it made my body feel: alive, connected, and *grateful.* Then I tuned in to *how I wanted to feel* in hosting it: confident, of service, nourished, and *abundant.* From this aligned vibration, it was time to pick the date, location, and ultimately the fee. A typical all-inclusive retreat costs around $5,000, but due to the venue I would choose, that wouldn't leave much profit for me and my team. In my mind, I went up to $10,000, which would provide more financial upside, but I tuned in further. It didn't feel entirely right, either, as there was a slight heaviness in my body, knowing how much work would go into it, and I didn't want to bring that energy to this project. I felt the frequency of abundance in my *body,* and the price was clear: $15,000. That's how much *I decided I was worth.* In that embodiment, my frequency shifted. I launched the retreat to my community, and within less than one month, seventeen women registered and I made $255,000 *effortlessly*, all from a single product. I didn't hustle by wanting abundance and striving for it. I *spiritually* hustled by embodying abundance and allowing it.

Many of us are familiar with the term "valuation," which means the monetary worth of something, as estimated by an appraiser. The embodiment of frequency is realizing that you choose your own value, no outside validation needed.

No one is you. No one knows what you know, has seen what you've seen, has healed from what you have healed from, has done what you have done in the exact way you've done it, and that innately, intrinsically has a value.

You were born, and therefore you matter. You breathe, therefore you are important. You exist, therefore you are worthy of having, achieving, and creating anything you could ever desire.

This is a Divine Law of the universe as much as it is an embodiment of Divine Feminine Wealth. I encourage you to dream up a program, offering, product, service, retreat, or experience and price it at what intuitively feels right. Tune in to how that price makes you *feel*. It's not the product or price itself that manifests abundance: it's the frequency you emanate. Believe in the core of your soul that you inherently *possess* value. This decision shifted my frequency, and as a result, it shifted my entire financial life. It can shift yours, too. This is the first step toward embodying abundance.

Equanimity is the second embodiment. In order for your relationship with money to be at a high frequency, and thereby of the Light, it must possess equanimity, which can also be defined as a balanced, equal exchange of value. We have all been in professional situations where we *knew* we were giving too much and getting underpaid for it. How did that make you feel in your body? Describe it. Maybe it made you feel heavy, resentful, or angry. For the first few years of running my branding agency, we were overservicing our clients and constantly allowing for "scope creep" (when clients ask for more work outside their set retainer without paying overages, ultimately losing the business money). During that time, there was a sense of chaos in the day-to-day, a heaviness in my culture, and an unspoken entitlement with my clients. Sure, we were making money, but it didn't always *feel* good. As a company, we weren't *embodying* abundance but rather grinding for it.

On the flip side, perhaps you were in a situation where you were giving too little but getting too much? How did *that* make you feel? Maybe a bit guilty, shameful, or anxious?

When there is a lack of equanimity, we carry these dark and dense energies in our bodies. In order to clear these lower vibrations out of our systems and thereby create more calm in our nervous systems and more money in our lives, equanimity must be at play in *every single financial transaction* we co-create. Today, there is equanimity in my agency (which allowed me to ultimately sell it), my retreat experiences, my coaching programs, and my digital products, and the entire energy of my financial life has changed, and so has my peace of mind. When you witness a lack of equanimity in your business, career, or financial relationships, the first step is to simply become conscious of it. From this place, you can make different choices, set clear expectations, define better terms, have stronger contracts, and use your voice to speak up and out. This takes courage, confidence, and humility, but it's always worth it.

Service is the third embodiment. A few years ago, I was embarking on launching a free webinar, after which, at the end of the session, I was going to sell a new product. I was nervous, not wanting to turn off my audience by coming off sleazy and sales-y. I was lamenting to a wise friend about it, who reflected, saying, "Do you believe that what you're offering can help people?" My response was yes. "Then don't call it an 'upsell.' It's an 'up-serve.' They are lucky to be served by you, and you are lucky to be able to serve them."

This concept of "selling as a service" is not new and seems like a no-brainer. That's the rub. Selling and serving your clients cannot come from your brain. It has to be a true act from the heart. To feel the vibration of true service is the experience of Divine Love, and this is one of the purest, most purposeful, and joyful embodiments that exists. It is the cornerstone currency of the New Earth. My scarcest times were the chapters of my career when I sold the hardest. I was not thinking of serving anyone but myself. Not only did my energy body reflect low vibrations, so did my bank account.

Where in your business, career, and therefore *body* can you feel a true sense of service? Connect to your gifts and to the sensation you *physically* feel when another human benefits from them. Cultivate that authentic, physical feeling in every "sell" and watch your abundance expand.

Reciprocity is not only an Embodiment of Divine Feminine Wealth, it is the ultimate code of Gaia. (We will spend more time exploring Gaia's codes in the final section of the book, so stay tuned.) For the purposes of how it relates to money, it's critical to understand that your financial well-being can only be Divinely *Feminine* if there is financial well-being for all. To focus only on how much *you* can manifest, how rich and financially free *you* can become, how much luxury and ease *you* experience is, at its core, a low-vibrational embodiment and one rooted in unconscious survival. Amassing wealth isn't the aim, nor is hoarding it when we do. Roughly 4 billion people, that's nearly *half the world's population,* live on less than $5.50 per day.[2] I don't know about you, but that not only makes me feel profoundly grateful for everything I have in life but motivated to *give.* No one person can change the world and erase all its poverty. (Actually, a few people could: Jeff Bezos, Bill Gates, and Elon Musk just decide not to.) Lightworkers cannot depend on the nonaction of the toxic masculine, which the aforementioned men are simply personifications of. We can only turn to our own conscious reciprocation in every interaction we financially participate in. Reciprocity works like an infinity symbol, on a loop. What you give, you get. What you get, you give.

If someone buys you a coffee in line ahead of you at Starbucks, buy a coffee for the person behind you. If you sell out your workshop that had a no-refund policy, send back the money to the people who had to cancel due to personal circumstances. Pay people back when they loan you money, and do so in as timely a manner as possible. If your friend treats you to lunch, treat her next time. When you see a person on the street experiencing homelessness, give them the extra money in your wallet. If you don't have the cash, buy them a warm meal at the closest to-go spot. If you don't have time to do that, look them in their eyes, smile, and bless them.

Will these actions save world hunger? No. However, they will shift your body, your energy, and your frequency to call more abundance into your life so that as you receive more, you can ultimately give more. This is how we *really* heal our planet.

Self-sovereignty is the embodiment of setting boundaries, saying no, and actually cutting cords with clients, jobs, projects, and opportunities that no longer align with your frequency of value. It's about cutting the proverbial fat from things in your business or career that weigh you down and feel heavy. This comes to life in what you charge for your services, the salary you desire, what clients you take on, and whom you turn away. It can feel really scary to, for example, double your rates, ask for a raise, or say "no" to a huge opportunity that just doesn't feel right. This is the edge of fear we are being called to move through as women, to more fully step into our authentic vibration of power. This is about transmuting the lower energetic experience of survival, trusting that others will value you, and above all, that you are safe in stepping into this power.

When you let go of clients or financial opportunities that are not in alignment, you will begin to financially fly. Don't be afraid to say no. Create a set of qualifications for what you are looking for, just as much as a client would for a vendor, or a company would for an employee. It's a fascinating frequency shift and the ultimate safety game. Make it clear to the universe that you are in fact the prize, and be precious and intentional with how you spend your time, exert your gifts, share your talents, expend your energy, make your magic, and open your offerings to the world. Your presence is your finest form of currency. You hold sovereignty over all of it. It's yours to decide when, where, to whom, and how much you want to give it away for.

In the earlier years of building my agency, we consistently raised our rates every six months, and every time, I felt a tinge of fear. Yes, my team was growing, our services were expanding, and our clients were seeing incredible results. I was once told that when clients keep buying your services quickly, it's time to raise your rates. Our frequency as a business had an increased value, and the market was responding well. It was scary at first, but I had to embody self-sovereignty, which is accepting that not everyone can afford you. This might mean letting go of some clients and opportunities. It's staking a holy Light-filled wand into the ground and declaring to the world, "*This is my value, take it or leave it.*" Pay attention to the type of clients and opportunities you attract when you come from self-sovereignty, while noticing who and what you repel. When you step into this Divine Feminine Embodiment, the clients you attract will be the best clients you ever have because they know your value. The opportunities you manifest will be the most lucrative opportunities. Because it's a frequency match. Self-sovereignty is the ultimate referee.

Trust is the embodied knowing that when a door closes, a million windows open. The real flex on the path to abundance is nonattachment. The gripping Marguerite-like hands do not belong anywhere in your financial life. A proposal to a client, for example, might take weeks or months to close. You might put all your eggs into a single job opportunity. You then might find out the client doesn't have the budget, the company went with another candidate, or the client is moving plans for their initiative to next year. Trusting that all outcomes are in the highest good of all, even if you feel defeated in the moment, is one of the highest orders of the Divine Feminine frequency. This sense of trust, which is *rooted in safety in the body,* has been the biggest activator of abundance in my life. When we truly surrender to a door closing, floodgates can open. No more gripping, clenching, squeezing onto this one little tiny thread of a singular possibility when there's a whole spindle of *infinite* possibilities that exists beyond our awareness waiting to be unraveled in your direction. Trust is the way. Abundance is more than a mindset. It is a safety that lives in your body, that emanates based on your energetic frequency into every single area of your life.

Then there's **generosity.** If you want to make money like a goddess, you have to spend money like a goddess. Invest your money in people, the planet, your programs, and your causes. This reverberates back to you in subtle and immeasurable ways. Generosity is different from reciprocity. Unlike reciprocity's infinity loop of giving and getting, generosity is a one-way street of pure giving. No returns needed or expected.

One habit I've never given up from my single days is taking myself out on dates and sitting at the bar solo at fun new haunts. Just a few years ago, I took myself out to the hottest new restaurant in Chicago. At 4:55 P.M., there was already a line around the corner, anticipating the 5 P.M. opening. By the time I got to the host stand, all the bar seats were full. "Table for one?" the hostess offered, as I nodded my head, mildly relenting. My server that night was a young woman named Leigh, who reminded me of, well, me. Before I became a struggling entrepreneur turned successful one, I was a struggling actress/waitress for a decade. My heart will always be in the service industry. Leigh took such good care of me that night as I got to know a little of her story and how grateful she was to be back on the floor after being quarantined for the previous year. The service industry did indeed get hit the hardest, as we know. After Leigh dropped off my $90 check, I decided to leave her a 100 percent tip. It felt so good to be sitting there as a woman, once young like Leigh, who came from nothing, because for a time she believed she *was* nothing, who hustled her way through credit card debt *and* a multimillion business she built from scratch. It was the best $180 I have honestly ever spent.

The next day I received a text from Leigh, who had tracked down my number. Her gratitude was palpable and overflowing. She offered to hook me up with a table at this hot-spot restaurant anytime I wanted, and I've since entertained clients there, taken my friends for girls' nights out, and celebrated my family on their birthdays. Here's the truth: I could have never talked to Leigh again, and I still would have been grateful she was my server that night. As I said, there is no better feeling, or *embodiment,* in the world than being of service. When we give to give, with absolutely no expectation to receive anything in return, that, my friends, is a *quantum leap* into abundance.

So next time, put all your spare bills into the donation jar at the community center. Round up and donate an extra dollar (or fifty) to animal welfare when you check out at the pet store. Give your Uber Eats driver a ten-dollar tip instead of two dollars. Consistently tip more than 20 percent at restaurants. This shifts your frequency into the abundant queen that you are, and like an infinite fountain of Light, shifts the frequency of abundance in the world at large.

Receptivity is our final embodiment for a reason. Receiving is the ultimate expression of abundance. When we grow the muscle of receiving, we decrease contraction in every area of our lives and open up the floodgates to more money (as well as more love, peace, connection, joy, opportunity, luck, impact, and whatever it is you're calling in). However, women are naturally givers. While this is an inherently beautiful quality, we have a tendency to overextend, expend, exert, and do and do and do. There is no judgment here. It is a powerful thing (and one of the eight embodiments) to be in service of our clients, our communities, our teams, our families, and friends. It is hardwired into us that it is selfish to take, and as a result we deflect and shut down opportunities to receive, without even realizing it.

Most of us cannot even accept a compliment. Our knee-jerk reaction when someone tells us we are beautiful: *"Oh stop! I look like shit today!"* When someone tells us how much they admire our work, we deflect: *"Oh my gosh, stop! I love your work, too!"* When someone tells us we did a great job at a task, we question it by saying, *"Really? I didn't think it was anything special."* One of the simplest but most profound life-changing practices I adopted years ago was, when someone compliments me, to stop, look the person in the eye, put my hand on my heart, and simply say, *"Thank you. I receive that."* Try it every single time someone says something kind to you, and it will change your life.

If we block ourselves from receiving a kind word, how can we expect to receive millions of dollars in the bank, our next perfect home, an incredible new client win, that dream speaking engagement, the six-figure book deal? Begin by practicing this one action and watch how it changes your ability to receive. Don't just stop with compliments. Begin to look at the universe as one big love letter of giving back to you. Whether someone opens up the door for you, the waiter offers your table an extra side of fries, or you get randomly upgraded to a nicer room when you check in to your hotel, perceive it as one big affirmation that you deserve to receive. Receiving is different from taking.

The primary message I received from Hathor in the Dendera Temple: *it is a gift to be in a female body.* Our bodies are designed to be receiving portals and to experience all the joy and pleasure we possibly can in this life. Receptivity is the ultimate expression of the Divine Feminine. Recall the inverted triangle, which represents the chalice, the womb, the void. The Divine Feminine is in an unwavering state of nondoing, operating as a metaphorical and literal receptacle. From this place she *creates life.*

From this place she creates whatever she wants.

From this place she magnetizes.

From this place, she manifests . . . *effortlessly.*

Abundance literally lives within you, encoded in your body and being; but to access it, you may first need to do a little rewiring.

REWIRING YOUR ABUNDANCE CODES

The paradox of abundance is in the Pleiadian point of view itself. If *state of mind is the name of the game,* but manifesting money should be effortless, how does one get out of the logical mind while tapping into an energetic new frequency of trust, flow, and ease?

You don't tap out, but tap *in.* Rewiring your abundance codes is a both/ and. We must start with choosing new thought patterns and beliefs around our value, our worthiness, and our deservingness. Expanding our own *capacities* to receive more requires a frequency shift in our bodies. Remember, Light is Information, and your unique light codes are stored in your body.

I know, like me and like Marguerite, we all want to feel not only abundant but safe to *be* abundant in the first place. What are you willing to shift? The bigger question is . . . what are you willing to embody?

How can you apply the Embodiments of Divine Feminine Wealth to your business or career *right now*? How can you step out of the low-vibration hustle and into the higher frequency of *spiritual hustle*? Know that when you do, you set a new energetic tone in the world around you. You are reverberating the feminine frequency and creating new resonance on Gaia. Money is energy, money is power, and therefore money is to be held sacred, shared with reciprocity, and used with intention.

These codes of abundance are your birthright.

You are worthy enough to unlock them all.

You are safe enough to have it all.

The Invitation: Rewire Your Abundance Codes

- Where in your life do you feel like you're just trying to survive?
- Where have you felt the most disempowered about money?
- What makes you feel the most empowered about money?
- What does it mean to you to be spiritual hustler?
- What does it mean to you to be a feminine financial leader of a New Earth?
- Which of the eight embodiment principles do you feel the most comfortable with, and why?
- Which of the eight embodiment principles do you feel the least comfortable with, and why?
- What new *Information* can you teach to your clients, your team, your community, and the world about money?

The Key: Effortless Abundance Visualization

When it comes to money, there is no limitation. Our ability to manifest all the wealth and abundance we desire is truly infinite. And to unlock it, we must come to realize that manifesting wealth is actually *intended* to be effortless. It comes down to our state of mind. Change your thoughts about money, and you will change your reality about money. This is what the Pleiadians want us to know more than anything. This knowing needs to imprint into our bodies.

When you're ready, find yourself in a comfortable seated position, close your eyes, and take three deep cleansing breaths in and out. Reflect on where your relationship with money, savings, investments, charging what you want, getting paid on time, or asking for a raise feels heavy and difficult. Let yourself feel the contraction in your body, acknowledging this discomfort and not bypassing it. Now begin to rewrite this scenario in your mind's eye, imagining the ideal circumstances falling into place with ease and joy. *Your new client pays you triple your rate with pure gratitude and zero resistance. Your boss delivers you the news you're getting a 25-percent raise. You launch your new program on social media, and the transactions roll in as you watch your bank account rise and rise. Someone pays you a compliment; you say, "Thank you, I receive that," and the next day, you receive the cash you've been waiting for.* See it. Feel it. Allow it to move through your body. Melt into the sensation of *effortlessness*. Open your eyes and record what you experienced in your Light Work journal.

Please visit jessicazweig.com/unlock to access all the Invitations and Keys.

PART III

FUTURE LIGHT

There is a Knower who experiences everything.
There is a Presence dancing everywhere.
There is a Lover who embraces us all.
I am one with that Light.
I am one with that Power.
I am one with that Love.

—THE RADIANCE SUTRAS

9

MISSION

YOUR CREATION, YOUR CALLING, YOUR CAUSE

*Humanity creates the sacred bridge between Earth and sky, which
some have called the rainbow bridge. The Bringers of the Dawn
allow these energies to merge, so that the dawn, or the light, is
awakened within them. They then bring that light to civilizations.
This is who you are. This is what you are doing.*

—BARBARA MARCINIAK

Toward the middle of my fifteen-day spiritual pilgrimage to Egypt, we visited the Temple of Karnak in Luxor, also where the Temple of Ptah, of the lioness goddess Sekhmet, is located. Karnak is a massive property, spanning two hundred acres. It is considered one of the most important in all of Egypt due to its size, various temples, chapels, and chambers on the property, and events recorded on its walls. It is believed to be a place where all of creation began. Within its walls is a great mystery of the Pharaohs, the Holy Lake, whose level has not changed in three thousand years, despite its distance from the Nile River.

As our bus pulled into the parking lot, before we descended to get our tickets and explore, our guide got on the microphone and shared, "Karnak is known to be the temple of *purpose*. Many find that they traverse these walls pondering their purpose and walk out with a renewed clarity of what theirs is. . . . *Enjoy!*"

My immediate thought to myself was this: *Purpose-shmurpose. I have built a huge brand, a huge business, have written a bestselling book, have a number-one-ranked podcast, and have created so much abundance. Clearly, I'm already "on purpose." Not gonna find anything new here.*

I smugly hopped off the bus with my group, eager to get myself to Sekhmet, who had visited me in my dreams my first night in Cairo; she had chewed me up and spit me out with her lioness powers of war and healing. It was there in her chamber, as I have shared, where I felt my Root and Sacral Chakras begin to tingle and I received Sekhmet's wisdom that all my power lives within these centers of my body. Getting that opportunity to step into Sekhmet's chamber made my visit to Karnak complete, but only up to that moment.

Walking through those sacred sites alone was always my favorite part of each visit, and after the Temple of Ptah, that's just what I did. In my wandering, I came across an obscure structure, located near the Temple of Amun, dedicated to the god Amun-Ra, the supreme god, or "Invisible One." Step-by-step, as if being drawn by an invisible force indeed, I made my way into an inconspicuous alcove that was nearly pitch-black, with only a small stream of sunlight piercing through a small opening in the worn ceiling. I leaned my back against the wall, closed my eyes, and took several deep breaths. There in the dark, something in me stirred, as if something truly invisible was making itself known to me.

Descending back outside, through the doors, I tilted my head up toward the sun to adjust my eyes. In that exact moment, a tiny white feather floated directly in front of me, inches from my nose. Instinctively, I held out my right hand and opened my palm as the feather landed right there. Feathers, specifically *white feathers,* have long been my symbol from the universe that I am on the right path. I could hear the universe lovingly, ironically laugh at me.

"Your purpose is not what you thought it was, Jessica," it said. *Your purpose is to learn how to live as light as a feather. To come to know, understand,*

and embody that you can be powerful and free at the same time. Your mission is to teach other women to do the same."

So here I am, humbled and teaching. Stepping into the belief that my mission, our mission, is greater than any of us can imagine.

WHAT AN EXCITING TIME TO BE ALIVE

You know you did not pick up this book by sheer coincidence. You were called to it for a very specific reason: because you are a member of the Family of Light. A renegade on assignment to help return the planet to its original state of harmony, reciprocity, reverence, interdependence, Oneness, and Love. These are the Divine Laws of Light and the highest frequencies of Gaia. This reason for your being, otherwise known as your *mission,* is not meant to be easy. It is an awesome task to carry light, and there's a reason we are otherwise called Light Warriors. We have been chosen to be here as much as we have self-selected to be here at this time. As members of this great family, it is up to us to bust paradigms, liberate ourselves, and move beyond the limiting constructs of identity placed upon us on a planet vibrating with fear and control. *This is our mission.*

Doing the Light Work is about so much more than what it gives you. We've all come here on our unique timelines, but also the same timeline. Can you consider how absolutely *wild* it is to be here at this exact inflection point in the history of all humanity? We are amid a true planetary shift and revolutionary uprising, where the polarities between light and dark have never been stronger. For the last four thousand years, we've been living in a patriarchal paradigm, where control, supremacy, and colonization have dominated our planet, all in an attempt for power. This has been spearheaded by major religions, big government, and corporate capitalism, resulting in a collective consciousness of fear. As a Lightworker, this is precisely the fear you came here to transcend.

In the last few very short decades (which, when compared to the past thousands of years of patriarchy and four billion years of Earth's existence, is a true drop in the bucket of the infinite), we have experienced unprecedented times. Within the past thirty years alone, we have lived through 9/11, the birth of the internet, the turning of the Mayan calendar, the COVID-19 pandemic, Black Lives Matter, the explosion of the Information Age, the dawn of social media, the development of artificial intelligence, the heightened conflicts in the Middle East, discoveries of billions of other galaxies by NASA's technology, the #MeToo movement, the evolution of the trans community, Donald Trump as president of the United States—to simply name a few. What an absolutely, extraordinarily, wildly phenomenal time it is to be alive at this exact moment of humanity!

Many of these aforementioned earthly anomalies and global events have in many ways been designed to divide the human race and create even more duality and polarity. Do not be fooled and, most of all, do not be discouraged. You did not incarnate here in this life, at this precise time, in your exact body, with your exact soul's assignment to live a life of your own personal contentment. You certainly didn't come here, as a member of the Family of Light, to play it small or safe. You, renegade, are here to live out a critical human experiment: one that is dictated not by fear but by Love and Light. Your expression of that Light, based on your own unique DNA, is indeed your *mission*. **Your assignment is to carry Information and to evolve yourself to the highest capability within the human form.** When you do this, as the Pleiadians say, you cannot help but affect multitudes.[1]

Thus far we've covered how to connect to source, honor our emotions, revere our bodies, find our personal power, circuit-break the traumas of our family lineage, find even deeper self-love through romantic love, establish a Sisterhood, heal through the power of friendship, and manifest limitless abundance in a Divine Feminine way. These are not simply things we "get to do." **These are the things we *must do* in order to ensure this planet heals and thrives.** Sojourning our dark inner terrains, unpacking shadows we outwardly cast, and transmuting our unconscious beliefs, thoughts, and behaviors into Light is no small feat. That's some Light Warrior shit. Now we must take this newfound, integrated Information, connection to our Truth, and an even deeper understanding of the power of Love and bring them into the future.

Who are you not to be *that* exceptional? Women especially have kept themselves disempowered by the programmed belief that we are arrogant to feel we are destined for worldly recognition or global impact.

The programming stops here. We are the stewards, the way-showers, the literal trailblazers for the next generation and the generations and generations beyond them. They will be directly and indirectly impacted by how we show up, who we become, and what we do with our current lives in this new moment in time. *What you do with your Light* and therefore *how you design your life* is literal history in the fucking making.

Knowing this, let's unpack how we become conscious co-creators of our own unique missions and leave a legacy of Future Light.

The key word? *Remembering.*

MEMORY RETRIEVAL

Since you've been called to this book and you've made it this far, I am going to make some safe assumptions: you believe that you were born for big things; that your life, no matter what you do with it, must make a difference in the world; that **you were *destined* to be you.**

This single through line of Truth, the blueprint of who we are meant to be and what we came here to fully express, can get clouded, frayed, and most of all *forgotten*. It is our dualistic 3-D reality itself that creates this programming of amnesia. Where we literally forget just how powerful, needed, loving, and connected to each other we all really are. How do you think our memory gets lost?

Just look around and you will see this dualistic hologram of purported "better or worse," "opposing forces," and ultimate supremacy reflected everywhere: Democrat or Republican, Black or white, rich or poor, queer or straight, boss or employee, influencer or fan, spiritual or atheist, Jewish or Christian or Muslim (and the distinctive sects within each), or any other religion, vegan or carnivore, vaxxed or unvaxxed, Gen X or millennial, millennial or Gen Z, breastfed or bottle fed, royal or common, free or enslaved . . . and the list goes on.

Remember, *when millions of people focus their attention upon listening to the same words, seeing the same pictures, and hearing the same descriptions, tremendous energy is generated and mass thought forms are created,* the Pleiadians warn.[2] These are literal vibrational blueprints that are creating reality, and the power of this programming is so strong and so alluring that our creative drive to manifest our own realities gets suppressed and ultimately dissolved under the global weight of this polarity programming.

When we attach to these deeply programmed beliefs (and it can feel impossible not to), we block our ascension as Lightworkers, as we get hooked into an endless cycle of unconscious judgment, self-judgment, and fear. When we judge, we separate. When we separate, we don't just shut down our Light, we shut it off. This drags us deeper into more of this patterned low-vibrational frequency, where we lose sight of who we really are, the Light we came here to express, and the responsibility, let alone the courage, to fully live out our true missions.

As a Lightworker, you are awakening. It's time for a reclamation. A *re-membering.* You are reevaluating your purpose, or your *mission.* You are dissolving and disrupting the visible and invisible forces of the Matrix. You are resurrecting the light codes of consciousness, or Information, stored within your being. You are reclaiming who you are with the power of your own thoughts and, above all, you are *re-membering who you really are.* When you do, you ascend, transform, and transmute not only your own life but the lives of others on the planet, based on the frequency shift in your own being.

I cannot encourage you enough to *not* take for granted your own lifetime. What you dedicate your life to will impact the frequency of the future generations. Do you want your children, your children's children, and your children's children's children to live in the same separate, dualistic, oppressive, and judgmental world we experience today? Or do you want them to be empowered to live in and lead a more harmonic, interdependent, compassionate, and safe world for all? We are literally co-creating what they are going to inherit. What you do with your lifetime and timeline impacts future lifetimes and timelines more than you have allowed yourself to recognize.

There's nothing wrong with going through the 3-D motions of getting a college degree, working a job, raising a family, taking a couple vacations a year, and calling it a day. However, you did not incarnate here to live in a tunnel vision of self-servitude.

You, Lightworker, came here to activate a new frequency. You came here to live your cosmic truth. When you remember this, you are then able to accomplish your mission.

THE ANATOMY OF A LIGHTWORKER'S MISSION

In order for us to authentically embody our missions, we first must define what a mission is. Perhaps you've already pondered your "purpose." This concept of "finding your purpose" has in it a subtle innuendo of absolutism. Like, what if you don't actually find it in this lifetime? Are you fucked? The concept of purpose is just that, a *concept*. One we've read about in endless self-help books, heard dozens of podcasts about, and most likely have hired a few coaches to help us find. Purpose is beautiful and necessary, as it helps us to connect more deeply with our professional work, our lives as parents, our time as public servants, our dedication to our communities, and our inner voices on our own unique platforms. We usually equate purpose with a set of tasks, a doingness, or outward expression of our value. Living a "purposeful" life connotes an expected output.

Purpose is connected to *what you do*. Mission is *who you are* and *why you are*.

Mission is stored in your DNA. It's something you already came here with, have been encoded with, and it is your literal job to activate it. It's critical you understand your very important role here on Gaia. Light, which carries Information, rearranges every single vibrational frequency it touches. Light expands new systems so that old systems dissolve, birthing something new in their place. *A brand-new order is formed* when we live our Light. You have been birthing a new version of yourself since you opened this book. You have come to understand Light's impact in your own personal life, from the inside out. It's now time to carry your Light, which is your true mission, out into the world around you.

The first step to living your mission is getting clear what yours uniquely is and defining it with alignment.

The anatomy of a Lightworker's mission, like the sacred Divine Feminine inverted triangle itself, is composed of three holy parts: your *creation,* your *calling,* and your *cause.* It's where your human's purpose and your higher self's mission merge. These multidimensional aspects of your mission can live out in linear form one at a time, bridge into each other, or coexist separately as one all at once. Our creations are traditionally our businesses, careers, and creative projects; our callings are what our souls ultimately, truly want; and our causes are what we are here to leave behind—our legacies of Light. Combining them into one expression becomes our mission.

Let's break this down into some real-life examples of women Lightworkers whom I deeply admire, who are living their missions in the world.

I'll start with my dear friend Alyssa. One of the most celebrated and recognized architectural and interior photographers in the country, with over nine hundred features in the world's most renowned design magazines, Alyssa has a multi-six-figure creative career that is nothing less than aspirational. Her photography business is more than just a business: it's her literal *creation,* made manifest by her unique gifts, talents, point of view, tenacity, and style, based on her own unique DNA.

However, her *calling* is more than photography: it's *using creativity as a tool for healing.* Alyssa is a survivor of thyroid cancer, a condition she developed in her early thirties while working a grueling corporate job and not taking a vacation for six years because of her own Marguerite-like desires for survival. During her recovery at thirty-three years old, Alyssa picked up a camera for the first time in her life. It taught her stillness, introspection, and discernment. While Western medicine helped heal her physical body, it was creativity that really saved her life. Healing through creativity, regardless of specific ailments or creative modalities, is what Alyssa ultimately brings to the world through her work. This has been the root of not only her success as a businesswoman but her impact in her community.

Her *cause* is bigger than her beautiful photos or even her thriving social media community of creatives. Rather, she utilizes her message, her platform, her own bestselling books, and ultimately her *existence here on Gaia* for something far, far greater: to unite people from all walks of life, humanize our differences, and build bridges across race, religion, sexual orientation, creed, and gender, using the power of courage and creativity. Her cause focuses on the inequities that exist for these groups, specifically within the Jewish community and in the American South. These three interdependent aspects make up Alyssa's mission. She is a woman living her Light.

Another Lightworker soul sister of mine is Dana, a multihyphenate woman of color who has various *creations.* She is a working actress, published poet, marketing agency owner, yoga teacher, fitness instructor, film director, and producer. She is a woman who has uniquely crafted all her creations from the seed of her soul, designing a truly one-of-a-kind career, and is thriving in all aspects of it.

Her calling is deeper than making art, elevating brands, and helping her clients stay in shape. Dana's *calling* is to blaze a path for rising Black artists, creatives, and entrepreneurs to build financially successful careers and to know (and demand) their worth. She knows that her success only matters in the grand scheme of her lifetime if she's creating a more equitable world, beyond her own personal success. Dana has made a commitment to share her journey via her personal platform, social media channels, artistic communities, and the professional industries she moves through. She takes her communities with her in an open, honest, generous, consistent, and authentic way to cultivate not only more financial well-being but Black empowerment.

Unlike anything to do with her creation or calling, Dana's *cause* is clear. As a single mother, it's her daughter who will be the ultimate manifestation of the light and the legacy of Black excellence she will leave behind. Dana named her daughter Phoenix, inspired by its metaphorical legend of fire, flight, overcoming, and rebirth. Phoenix has lived up to every bit of her name through her own life experience and what she continues to teach Dana. Being a mother is Dana's truest legacy: the gift of a new generation to cultivate more abundance, break barriers, and heal the traumas—past, present, *and* future. At the intersection of her work, her community, and her own daughter, Dana is living her mission.

Similar to Alyssa's and Dana's missions, the three aspects of my mission's anatomy intersect and build upon each other, although unlike theirs, they stand alone in their own rights. Yet they are all intrinsically connected, because it is my soul, body, and DNA that collectively expresses them.

My greatest *creation* (thus far) has been starting and ultimately selling my company, the SimplyBe. Agency. As a serial entrepreneur who has started and failed quite a few times, SimplyBe.'s success has been rooted in a sense of clarity, conviction, alignment, and purpose that inspired me to literally create it in the first place. From day one, I didn't want to just help people with their personal brands, although marketing, branding, social media, and PR are some of my strongest professional skills. Branding yourself means knowing how to magnetically communicate your value, your worth, and your importance in the world, and I have helped thousands of clients do just that. Today, the business lives on under a new entity, but it will always be one of my most sacred creations.

My *calling* is unique to my creation. The book you are holding in your hand right now is my *calling*. Empowering women to know, own, and share their Light, manifest effortless abundance, make a major impact, all while living light as a feather while they do it, is what connects me to my heart more than anything. I have been able to take my creation and meld it with my calling, supporting professionally driven but spiritually ready women through my sold-out global retreats; my virtual programs;

my VIP coaching clients; my podcast, "The Spiritual Hustler"; and my online community of Lightworkers. Teaching women how to build massively financially successful brands, businesses, and careers in the world the Divine Feminine way literally *calls my soul*. Because as I said, when women have money, women have power, and when women have power, this world will be a better place, and that is a critical component to my work, my mission, in the world.

Speaking of making the world a better place, my *cause* expands beyond both my creation and calling, which is to (quite literally) save the planet, specifically the animals and wildlife that exist on Gaia. I dedicate time, resources, and energy each month to organizations that are helping to protect animals. My favorites include the Humane Society International; the Animal Love Rescue Center, a dog and cat sanctuary in Costa Rica; and Inti Wara Yassi, a rescue, rehabilitation, and care center for trafficked wildlife in Bolivia. One day, I plan to start my own philanthropic initiative dedicated toward saving, rehabilitating, and caring for the animals of this Earth. Until then, I have committed a percentage of proceeds of my coaching business to tithing to these organizations, walking the walk of the Divine Feminine Embodiment of reciprocity. Having a clear and focused vision of a mission is equally as potent as living it out. The key is to get clear and bring your creation, calling, and cause into the world every day, in some way, small or large.

What has been your creation? Perhaps it's a singular effort or a collective trajectory of accomplishments. Maybe it's a professional project you've been cultivating for years, a recent entrepreneurial endeavor, a series of corporate jobs you have accrued, a particular partnership you sealed, a book you wrote, or a massive event you produced. Your creation doesn't have to be a fixed thing. Many of us are consistently birthing new businesses, projects, creative endeavors, professional partnerships, campaigns, and experiences of all kinds. Ask yourself, at this current juncture of your life, what are you most proud of? To go a layer deeper, what do you think you have been put here to create, and for what reason? Maybe you're a bit overworked, overwhelmed, or simply "over" what you currently do for a living. We can all relate to being out of alignment with our work at some point. Can you look soulfully to see how your past and current *creations* have served your evolution? How has it served the people you've touched, and therefore humanity? It's critical to remember that exploring and experimenting with our creations—and getting them wrong sometimes—is a necessary part of the journey. Every seemingly "wrong" choice leads us to a clearer understanding of what is right, and this creates a depth, a wholeness, and an authenticity that our ultimate creations require of us.

Is your *creation* the same thing as your *calling*? Maybe it overlaps, like Alyssa's, or is a bridge from one to the next, like mine. Or maybe the two are completely mutually exclusive. Your creation is no doubt an expression of your unique DNA and light codes, but we did have to use our logical minds to create such professional accomplishments in the world. When it comes to your calling, tap into your heart. Ask your soul what it came here to do. Get really still and quiet as you wait for the answer. Another way to connect to your calling is by reflecting on what doesn't feel like work. What would you do every single day even if you didn't get paid for it?

Maybe your creation and calling are completely independent, like those of my friend Lauren, a TV news anchor (her creation), but her calling is astrology, mysticism, and all things "woo." She keeps these parts of her life deliberately separate, and both are equally fulfilling. If you're like my friend Rachel, whose creation is her corporate career as a rock-star executive in the spirits industry, her calling is creating lifetime memories and unforgettable moments through the power of experience. Her creation and calling are directly intertwined, which is why she loves her career so much. Simply getting clear on your calling is an activation in and of itself. It provides clarity, power, and freedom in the heart and the body.

Your cause has nothing to do with the money you make, the résumé you build, the awards you win, or the audience you reach, but is the true essence of Light, of healing, of elevated frequency you leave behind when you die. We are all mortal in these human bodies, but our Light is immortal. When your physical body dies and your soul passes on to the next incarnation, what is the true legacy you will leave behind? This is a legacy that the future inherits.

You, and all of humanity, are destined to evolve.

When looking at your mission through this lens, you find your internal compass. We can access a new blueprint and understand what we are being guided to. Your mission exists in the deepest parts of your body. By naming and claiming our reasons for being, defining our mission, and boldly stepping forward to live a life rooted in Light—beyond our own personal contentment and instead for the collective awakening—you activate.

When you activate, you will not be the only one who remembers your mission.

By being an example of Light, the world will remember, too.

When you emanate Light, you will *attract* Light. You'll attract the people who are meant to receive and reflect the unique Light you bring to the world.

FIND YOUR PEOPLE

Your *mission* transcends beyond this lifetime and into the multidimensional reason for your being. You were sent here to live it out, fully. You know this in the deepest parts of your being, and yet it can still feel scary to fully flex the Truth of who you are.

Do not be afraid, for the more you live your Light, the more you will broadcast out a new frequency that acts like a transmitter to call back that frequency toward itself. Like attracts like. This is simply quantum science as much as it is a spiritual belief. Being a part of the Family of Light is no small task. You cannot play small or stay quiet. We have been conditioned to fear everything, from something as trite as ridicule to something as severe as death for speaking our Truths, for attempting to live out our missions. This has been the programming of control for centuries.

Many of us allow ourselves to share our innate beliefs in intimate circles, but in our workplaces, on social media, and even in our family systems, we do not give ourselves permission to speak our Truths, let alone live them. You have been chosen, Lightworker. There are multitudes upon multitudes waiting for your activation and your voice. We have all come here for a massive task, and that task is at hand. The time is now.

The Family of Light comes from the same place within the universe. When we activate our missions, this acts as "a broadcast system." The more you transmit your frequency, the faster we will find each other. This ultimately strengthens our missions, because there is power in numbers. We call upon more strength when we are in a tribe, a piece of a bigger whole, and in a true like-minded community.

I have been telling my friends, my clients, and communities for years that there are more people in the world who need their voices heard, but they don't know it yet. When we embody our missions, we not only magnetize the people who are directly needing our unique message and medicine in the world, but we attract like-minded Lightworkers on their respective missions, too. Together we grow. Together we burn brighter than we could alone. Together we shift the planet back to its original frequency of Light. It is going to take many of us to come together. We can only find each other, and this shift is only possible, when we live our Light.

When I first started my entrepreneurial journey, my creation started calling in clients immediately. In those early days, I struggled supporting them. They weren't fully clear on their objectives, they were a bit needy, a tad jealous, a touch insecure, and a little all over the place. They were . . . me. They directly matched the frequency I was projecting into the world. I believe our business and careers can only grow (in abundance, service, and impact) to the extent that we grow as human beings. The more evolved, clear, and unapologetically Light-driven my message became in the world, that's whom I began attracting.

Today, I host retreats, lead a digital community, and coach women from all over the world, from all walks of life, with all different professional backgrounds. I am always amazed at how eclectic and different they are. Women of all religions; mothers; nonmothers; entrepreneurs; executives; women in their thirties; women in their fifties; women who are single, married, divorced, gay, straight, Black, white, Asian, Middle-Eastern, Latina—they all show up with their differences. There are always common threads: *kindness, compassion, drive, maturity,* and *radical self-responsibility.*

Light attracts Light.

Step up and use your voice. Share yourself in service of a mission, and magnetize more and more like-minded Lightworkers. Move through the conditioned fears, and trust that you are not alone. Make a commitment to yourself and to the world around you that you will not keep your Light locked away. You came here to anchor a new frequency on this planet by anchoring that new frequency inside yourself. The evolution of a new species starts with the evolution of a few. So find your few, and let the collective Light compound.

It starts with you, it starts with me, it starts with every member of the Family of Light.

As we vibrate higher, we find each other.

Remember: the world needs us.

THE TIME IS NOW, RENEGADE

Your job here on Gaia is to *live your Light.* For when you do, you become a living example of Light. Don't stand on a soapbox, but do not be afraid to stand up and be seen. This requires a level of courage that you might not yet have accessed. Missions are for the brave, Light Warrior. Commit to your own evolution first. We can only heal the world if we do our own healing first. We can only raise the frequency of the planet if we raise our own first. We can only be way-showers of Light if we are willing to take the risk of stepping through new and uncharted territory first.

There is an urgency here. Having an aligned creation, a heart-centered calling, and a conviction-driven cause is a critical part of understanding your mission, but this can of course take time to understand. It is meant to be an unfolding evolutionary process toward your highest Light. Sometimes activating our DNA can happen in a literal flash, as it did for me in the Dendera Temple in Egypt. Sometimes it takes years of suffering and loss, gaining new Information as lessons, and transmuting dark into Light. I am asking you, dear Lightworker, to not wait. To use this newfound understanding of what the collective is up against and live your Truth, speak your Truth, and share your Truth in even the smallest of ways.

Use your voices. Stop being so afraid of disagreeing with common opinion. Call out injustice, harm, programming, supremacy, and control when you see it. Accept that there may be (and most likely *will* be) people who are repelled by your Truth, your Light. *This is part of the mission.* The women I have mentioned in this chapter have faced great hardship and opposition in their plights to live their Light. It comes with the territory, in this great revolutionary moment on Gaia, that you will be misunderstood and even silenced for sharing your Light. Keep shining it anyway. Keep your mission clear and well-defined at all times. It will help you to maintain an unapologetic authentic frequency of Light. Consistency is key in busting the paradigms that have been instilled in our *collective unconsciousness* for centuries.

If you struggle seeing yourself as *this powerful, this needed,* and *this important* to the future of our planet, ask yourself: *If my inner renegade had a name, what would it be? What does she look like? Where in the universe is she from? What does she want me to know about her mission? How does she want me to help her complete it?*

Take a look around what's happened in the last thirty years, once more. The Light *and* the dark are rising. For the first time on the planet, the Light is winning (even though it might not feel this way), and the dark knows it, as it fights back even harder. It's exactly *why* the polarity continues to get more intense and the world seems to get scarier by the minute. The planet is awakening, and you are a part of this moment. There is urgency to this time. We cannot delay. The Light can only win if you think the highest thoughts, feel the deepest of emotions, keep your vessel clear, claim responsibility, and stay focused. Because what you create is just as important as what you think, as thought is, and therefore thought creates. What you are called to do is connected to how you *feel*, as our emotions are the key to ascending into multidimensional realities. Embody your cause, as your body stores DNA ready to be recoded and thereby to heal, activate, and re-code the planet one Lightworker, one mission at a time.

That time is now, renegade.

The Invitation: Design Your Mission

Your Creation	Your Calling	Your Cause
• What's your greatest accomplishment, personal, professional or otherwise? • What is your highest hope for this creation?	• If resources or time were not a factor, how would you spend your days? • If you were to give the fiery passion in your soul a voice, what would it say right now?	• What lesson are you here to learn and teach others in this lifetime? • When this life ends, death arrives, and your soul passes on to the next lifetime, what legacy are you leaving behind?

- Studying your above answers, what aspect of your creation, calling, or cause lights you up the most?
- Do your creation, calling, and cause intersect? If so, where?
- Can you carve a path toward defining your creation, living your calling, and expressing your cause more clearly?
- How can you start living your mission more boldly into the world?

The Key: Your Galactic Renegade Visualization

There are two steps to this visualization exercise. The first step is to give your inner renegade a name. She is the version of you that came here as a member of the Family of Light to rebalance this planet with Information, Truth, and Love. When we "dress up" or play a character, we find a little more courage to fully embody a new but equally legitimate side of ourselves. My renegade's name is Queen Esther Sheba of the Feathers. (Esther is my Hebrew name, feathers are my spirit totem, and Sheba came to me in this very visualization.) Let's begin.

When you're ready, find yourself in a comfortable seated position, close your eyes, and take three deep, cleansing breaths in and out. Begin to picture your galactic self. What is her skin tone, her hair color, her eye color? How tall or short is she? What is she wearing? Is she wearing any kind of crown or headpiece? Is she carrying any tool, sword, or wand? Does she have any kind of spirit animal by her side? Once you have fully tuned in to her physical and energetic appearance, ask either silently or out loud, "What is your name?" Wait for the answer. Once you hear it, you will know it to be true. Open your eyes. Write her name in your Light Work journal.

Now close your eyes again. Envision your renegade living out every aspect of her creation, calling, and cause in her fullest Light and to her fullest capacity. Imagine a world with your mission fulfilled. Envision how people live in that world versus the world today. How does it make you feel? What does it activate inside you? How are you already living this galactic avatar? What impact are you *already* creating with your mission? Open your eyes and record in your Light Work journal what you saw, felt, and experienced.

Please visit jessicazweig.com/unlock to access all the Invitations and Keys.

10

MENTORSHIP

YOUR FUTURE YOU NEEDS YOU

*On the other side of this jungle is a new and glorious day on earth,
when our daughters will not be judged wrong for their passions
or held back because they are bursting with such power,
strength, and love.*

—MARIANNE WILLIAMSON

When I was sixteen, I ran away.

After one particularly heavy night, I had reached my limit in dealing with my parents' fighting. The dysfunction between my mom and dad had reached an apex, and I was done being caught in the crossfire.

In my teenage rebellion, I literally ran from my house in the midst of the fray and made a beeline to the closest grocery store in my downtown neighborhood—the only place I knew had a pay phone. I called my best friend at the time, Bradley, a fellow thespian in the acting department. I was hysterical, and there wasn't much else he needed to know. He was on his way.

For two weeks, I stayed with Bradley and his single mom, Pat, and during that time, something profound shifted and opened inside me.

Together, they lived in a small but lovely townhouse, decorated with Pat's eclectic colorful art from Santa Fe and sculptures by Brian Andreas, with quotes that said things like *"In my dream, the angel shrugged & said, If we fail this time, it will be a failure of imagination & then she placed the world gently in the palm of my hand."* Pat would say things like, "You can be your own best friend or your own worst enemy—you *choose.*"

Pat ran her own small stationery company, with an impeccable eye for designing wedding invitations and Bar and Bat Mitzvah place cards. Her small, colorful, and immaculate office on the first floor was adorned with photographs of the international trips she'd taken with her girlfriends: to Bali, Portugal, Kenya, and Brazil. She had a lover named Barry, who came by often, had a gentle and kind spirit, and clearly had been a hippie in his younger days. Pat spoke openly and with pride about her gay son Bradley's talent as an actor, the freedom she felt from her divorce, her vast dreams of growing her business, and, despite her clearly passionate relationship with Barry, how much she loved being on her own at this stage in her life. She was the first empowered, independent, entrepreneurial woman I'd ever met.

My own mom, as I have shared, is the sweetest woman I know. She really did nurture me with tender loving care as mommies do, and I'm grateful I incarnated as her daughter, as the lessons my soul came to learn in this life-time were designed for our ultimate mother-daughter relationship. While my mom was a beautiful model of love, she was not the greatest model of personal empowerment. You could say the reason I felt inspired to leave my home that night was because I was searching for guidance as much as I was looking for an escape.

Witchy, spiritual, and living life on her own terms, Pat was a guide in ways I never could have imagined. For those two weeks, her home became more than a safe haven. It became a portal. She introduced me to cosmic books by Wayne Dyer and Louise Hay, crystals, and most significantly, the runes.

One night during dinner between just me, Bradley, and Pat, I broke down crying. My parents wanted me to come home, but I didn't feel ready yet. Pat stood up from the dinner table and escorted me into her bedroom. It was a part of her house I hadn't been in yet. Walking into the dimly lit, cozy master bedroom, I inhaled a soft mix of rose and sandalwood as I took in her dresser, which she had turned into an altar, adorned with crystals, sacred totems, and artifacts of goddesses I didn't recognize.

She sat me down on her bed, walked to her bedside table, and grabbed a small velvet pouch along with a tiny companion book engraved with gold lettering. In her hand, she held the runes, stones etched with an ancient symbolic alphabet from the Germanic peoples of Northern Europe, Iceland, Scandinavia, and Britain from the third to the seventeenth centuries. Each runic letter carries an activated symbolic meaning and holds wisdom from other realms. As I wiped away my remaining tears, Pat instructed me to close my eyes and take a deep breath. She told me to ask the runes for guidance on what I was struggling with, and when I felt ready, to reach in and pull out a stone. As my fingers swirled inside the small green velvet pouch, images of what was happening back at home flooded me, and I questioned what I would need to do when I eventually would have to go back. I opened my eyes to see the tiny stone sitting in my palm. The rune I pulled was *courage*. Something about that stone, that moment, and that message *activated* me. I don't know if I would be writing this book today if it weren't for that pivotal moment, and that's the truth.

I took all that *courage* indeed and ended up moving back home to my parents' house a few days later. When I walked in the door, I could tell I wasn't the same young woman who had hysterically run out of it a few weeks earlier. Sure, I was stepping into the same house, but I was a new version of myself, a version who possessed a newfound understanding of how to see the world, how to see myself, and who I could *choose* to be: my own best friend.

Most of all, I had discovered a beautiful and brand-new kind of relationship: a *mentor*.

AN EXPANDED APERTURE

When you think of "mentorship," what comes up for you?

Maybe when you hear the word "mentor," you feel a sense of longing, which would reflect the fact that 63 percent of women have never had a formal, professional mentor.[1]

Maybe you feel a tinge of anxiety if you don't yet have a mentor, as having a mentor in your career can help strengthen your personal confidence, expand your professional network, help you to grow your salary potential, and open up doors of opportunity. Mentorship programs inside of companies have been shown to improve retention and promotion rates for women and people of color, specifically 15–38 percent compared to nonmentored employees.[2]

Perhaps the idea of asking someone to be your mentor feels awkward. This requires humility on your part and time on theirs, which can bring about an inner shyness and make the search seem inauthentic.

While professional mentors certainly provide invaluable relationships as we grow our careers—because what we do professionally as Lightworker women will indeed dictate the future of this planet—looking at "mentorship" through strictly the professional lens has its limitations.

There are quantum possibilities in finding people of all walks of life, not just in your professional lane, who can support your expansion. When we loosen the grip of what we think a mentorship relationship needs to look like, while simultaneously living our Truths, mentors (who can come in the forms of angels, activators, and even ancestors) appear in our lives in the most serendipitous of ways. Allowance is key here, as 14 percent of mentor relationships started by asking someone to be their mentor, while 61 percent of relationships developed naturally.[3]

Meeting Pat at sixteen was an activation—not only into who I was becoming but a portal into a whole new world of relating to women at large. Up until that point in my life, I had only known to "look up to" the popular senior girls in high school, celebrities on TV, and, to the best of my ability at times, my own mom. Stepping outside my own bubble, I was able to viscerally understand that there was a whole world of women, from all different walks of life, women who had lived what I had yet to live, who knew what I had yet to know, who had healed what I had yet to heal, who stepped into their Light in a way I did not yet know was possible.

I don't even think Pat realized she was mentoring me at the time. She simply opened up her home, and thereby her heart, to me in a moment of need. It was there in that two-week portal, wherein she offered me nothing more than her Truth, her stories, her wisdom, and her life by simply, authentically living it as an example, that she completely helped me find my own power. I took a quantum leap into my Light.

We are going to open the quantum aperture of what "mentorship" really looks like and how to actualize more of who you are meant to be when we welcome mentors of various forms into our lives. We are also going to take a look at why it's so important to become a mentor yourself, a literal torchbearer of Future Light. Yes, we are the way-showers and renegades. But we need to be shown ourselves, by the torchbearers of Light who came before us. Imagine one torch of light, lighting up all the flames she touches beyond her, then lighting up all the torches beyond that, and so on. We have the power to light every woman's flame, in every direction, at every stage of our lives, by using our gifts, our knowledge, our presence. This is how we co-create the collective illumination of empowered women on Gaia.

So let's strike the match and step into a new quantum aperture of just how much Light we can create as one.

THE MAGIC OF MENTORSHIP

Mentors have the ability to help us grow professionally, personally, spiritually, and even cosmically. It just depends on how you look at them and how available you are to all the divine players who come through your life, whether they are in this dimension or beyond.

There are four main types of mentors you can call in and look out for: activator mentors, professional mentors, virtual mentors, and cosmic mentors.

Let's start with your **activator mentor**. Ask yourself who in your life lights you up, gives you new inspiration, new ideas, and new fire in your belly to activate your gifts? Who in your life helps fill in the gaps of your existing network of parents, friends, and coworkers? (Think outside the box on this one—this person may sit on the periphery of your "go-to" people and be someone you least expect.) Who is a person in your life who activated you into a new way of seeing yourself, your world, and others? This can be a woman or a man in your life—typically of a certain age that begets a level of wisdom beyond yours—who opened your eyes (and your heart) in ways that shaped your beliefs, your character, your ways of moving through the world. You have already learned about Pat, who happened to be my high school best friend's mom. Activator mentors can come from the most random or the most obvious parts of our lives. There is no wrong or right version of this. For you, this might be a grandparent, a professor, a life coach, a healer, or a slightly older friend. Ask yourself: Who has *activated* me in ways that have made me who I am? Tune in. The answer will appear in your heart.

Our **professional mentor** relationships are the most straightforward, of course, but these can be the trickiest to find. I met mine not at some fancy networking event or over a coffee date with a clear agenda, but at a yoga studio. I had joined a community yoga program, hosted by a local studio owner. We would meet every Saturday morning, do a ninety-minute power vinyasa class, and then sit in a sweaty circle talking about a New Age topic each week. On one particular weekend, we were unpacking the concept of *abundance,* and this was during the exact inflection point when I couldn't afford to pay my $200 phone bill. When we had gone around the circle and it was "my turn" to share, I spilled out my horrific, shameful truth with this group of mere strangers, with tears streaming down my face. I wasn't anywhere close to abundance that day. I was actually, factually, technically broke. I hadn't said it out loud until that moment. A woman with a slight Texan accent about fifteen years my senior was sitting directly across from me in that circle. She was staring at me dead in the eyes, and as soon as I paused long enough to stare back, she said with what felt like a billion tons of true empathy, "I'm going to help you."

Denise, it turns out, was a global marketing executive and had built a brilliant career as a C-suite world-class marketer. She and I started meeting for coffee every week thereafter, as she mentored me on how to turn my then-flailing start-up around to begin to earn revenue again. When I ended up walking away from that company, Denise offered me a role at a corporate company, where she was vice president of innovation. It was literally my lifeline. Years later, after I had gone on to start SimplyBe., I made Denise a board member. Our relationship has been a true full-circle journey, one in which we are not only mentor-mentee but colleagues and, most of all, friends. It started with Denise pulling me by my shoelaces out and up from my financial rock bottom and shined a light on my potential. I would not be the entrepreneurial leader I am today without her belief in me and her stead-fast mentorship. These relationships can enrich our lives, and our Light, in invaluable ways.

What environments do you commonly move through where a profes-sional mentor could exist? How can you show up even more authentically to magnetize new relationships?

Perhaps you're coming up dry when identifying an activator mentor, or simply cannot connect with a professional mentor. Then ask yourself, *Who are the authors, speakers, podcasters, thought leaders, and teachers who in-spire me? Who motivates me to my best self?* I call these our **virtual mentors**. Sure, they might not be able to provide introductions and personalized feedback, but they can nonetheless be people who activate you, who hold up mirrors to your power, who open up new perspectives in seeing yourself, your business, and the world. These mentors indeed shape our Light as much as activator mentors and professional mentors can.

While I have loved following the work of Brené Brown, Michael Beckwith,

Danielle LaPorte, Esther Perel, and Sara Blakely, my most significant virtual mentor of all time is Marianne Williamson. She is one of the few women in the world who I could point to and genuinely say: *that woman changed my life.* Her books, her talks, her social media accounts, and her overarching message of love in the world transformed me. I did not need to know her personally for that to be true.

It just so happens, however, that during the week of my fortieth birthday, I took one of my "alonemoons" to Ojai, California. On that trip, I brought along Williamson's copy of *A Woman's Worth.* I had made the very conscious decision to delete all my social media apps, as well as my email and texts from my phone. I wanted to be fully present to Gaia on that trip, and to myself, as I celebrated this sacred milestone birthday. Occasionally, I would snap pictures of the beautiful landscapes or beautiful food I was trying, and at one point, I took a photo of the cover of *A Woman's Worth.* That trip was one of the few times in my life I can say I completely tapped into Divine Feminine flow. I had no agenda, no concern of linear time, and felt completely tapped into the 5-D frequency of harmonic beauty and aliveness of Gaia.

When I arrived at LAX to fly home, I reinstalled Instagram on my phone and began sharing some of the photos of my trip as I waited at the gate. One of the photos I shared was the photo of Marianne's book, and I tagged @mariannewilliamson's account, simply expressing how much I had loved reading it. Within less than thirty minutes, I received a direct message from the Marianne Williamson Instagram account. It was her assistant, who excitedly introduced herself, thanked me for the tag, acknowledged that I hosted a podcast, and asked me if I'd like to have Marianne on as a guest. A part of me was shell-shocked; however, my higher self knew in my being that I had called in the Divine Feminine frequency, for, as I stated in chapter 8, it is when we are in that vibration that we can magnetize effortless manifestations.

Today, Marianne checks all three boxes of activator, professional, and virtual mentor. Most of all, she is my Sister on the Sisterhood tree with a capital *S.*

We cannot forget about our **cosmic mentors**, who come into our awareness to support us when we don't even realize we need their unique medicines. A cosmic mentor comes in the form of an angel, spirit guide, ascended master, galactic being, or ancestor. Have there been angels, spirits, and/or deities that you have felt a strong connection to in your life? Maybe you have had a recent spiritual experience that created a newfound connection to this cosmic being in your life.

Flashback to my broke-as-a-joke days: I had scrubbed two pennies together to hire a life coach, Gina, who had given me a massive discount and offered a very generous, extended payment plan to even afford her. Gina has become one of my greatest activator mentors in my adult life, but it was she who introduced me to my first cosmic mentor: Lakshmi, the Hindu goddess of wealth and abundance. From the moment I first heard of her, I became so enthralled (okay, fine, a little desperate) to cultivate Lakshmi's medicine in my life, that I went on Amazon and bought a small fifteen-dollar statue of her that same day.

The day she arrived, I put her in the corner of my apartment, which, according to the feng shui grid I had googled, was the "abundance" section of my home. With gratitude, intention, and reverence, I sat her on my delicate shelf and put out a small bouquet of flowers to honor her and welcome her, and went about my day. That night, the very first night she was in my home, I had one of my most unforgettable, lucid dreams. Lakshmi and I met in the inky, endless sky of the whole universe, adorned with billions of diamond clusters of endless stars. She and I were dancing together, as I experienced a feeling of sheer, unfathomable, infinite *bliss*. I had never felt this way in my human life and, to be honest, have never touched this feeling since. I knew when I awoke that it was a visitation from Lakshmi and that she had indeed come into my life in not only physical form sitting in my apartment but in a quantum, multidimensional capacity. Within just a few weeks, my entire financial life started to turn around. I started making more money than I ever had in my life up until that point, received unexpected lucrative projects, and began to pay off my credit card debt with effortless ease. Today, that tiny statue of Lakshmi sits next to my bed, and I commune with her daily. Her cosmic medicine healed me, and she will be forever one of my most treasured cosmic mentors.

I share these stories of Pat, Denise, Marianne, and Lakshmi to showcase different ways of thinking about mentorship and how it can shape, direct, and change our lives—mostly to demonstrate all the ways we can call them in. It is not by trying, searching, or even seeking, but by *trusting* that when the student is ready, the teacher appears. Sometimes we don't even know we're ready. Sometimes it just takes us showing up, one day at a time, in our messes, in our Truth, in our authenticity and our Light, to call in exactly who we need when we need it.

That is the real magic of mentorship.

At some point, however, the student must become the teacher, too.

PASS THE TORCH AND LET THEM FLY

In living our Light, by activating our cellular memory of Information, Truth, and Love, we are without question the trailblazers, the renegades, and the way-showers on this planet right now. We can do even more good if we know which paths to follow and can walk in the footsteps of those who have come before us.

We are each other's way-showers.

Mentorship is a critical component of the Future Light I speak of. We are all flames of fire in our own right, burning through transmutations and transformations of our own unique healing. As we heal ourselves, we heal the world. The only way to ensure the future continues to heal is when we proverbially reach forward *and* reach back. While each of us can no doubt greatly benefit from being mentored, the *world* can greatly benefit when we find our own *Sacred Light mentees.*

Part of running a women-owned business focused on women empowerment means attracting a lot of young, empowered female talent seeking that kind of work environment. Part of that also means that after a certain amount of time, those talented, blossoming, empowered women spread their wings and fly away. To be honest, growing a team of young women has been the best part of running my business, *and* the hardest. There is nothing I love more than mentoring them, giving them the permission to shine with confidence, and literally witnessing their evolution in front of my eyes. Some of these young women are still with me, and some of them have flown away. Mostly, every time they do, my heart breaks a little.

After one particular young protégé I loved decided to fly away, she looked at me and said, "*These past two years being at your company and working for you have changed my life.*" I realized at that moment that I didn't need her to work for me for five more years for that to be true. Time is an illusion. What a gift she gave me; what a gift I gave her; and because we knew each other, regardless of how long we were in each other's lives, we gifted the world with more feminine frequency by forming that mentor-to-mentee relationship in the first place. Best of all, today we are true friends.

Let us all mentor those of the next generation with no attachments or expectations for what they "owe" us. They owe us nothing. The only thing we should expect from them is that they continue to fly. If our fingerprints can be a small part of their *becoming*, what a gift it is to have touched their lives and for them to have touched ours. This is what makes them our *Sacred Light* mentees.

If we are lucky, our Sacred Light mentees stay by our sides for years, creating a symbiotic return of support, cheerleading, and partnership. My two founding members of SimplyBe. Agency, Aleksa and Nora, to whom this book is dedicated, started as my employees, became my mentees, and transformed into friends who became family and eventually business partners. Witnessing them become true female bosses in the world has been my life's greatest work—not the money I have earned, books I've sold, or awards I've won. They would tell you that their lives are forever changed because they met me, but I would say the same thing. I would not be who I am, where I am, creating what I've created without them. It has been an equal exchange of love, of Light, of growth. Are our relationships perfect? No, but it's honestly pretty close to being so. That's because we truly honor each other's areas of genius, dreams, and ambitions; we don't step on toes; we respect the one-to-one dynamics that exist within our trinity; have learned how to give each other open and honest feedback (even if it sucks in the moment); root for each other; and allow one another to fly. Mentorship, at its highest expression, can turn into Sisterhood.

Together we rise.

Mentors of all stages of life, I encourage you to hold with integrity and intention your words, your wisdom, your presence, and how they are impacting the future generations of women who will one day become leaders, officials, and decision-makers on the world stage. It is critical we become conscious of our influence, and that we direct our Light knowing that nothing is ever imparted in vain. As Hathor shared with me at Dendera, the planet is shifting into a feminine frequency, and it is going to require women to step up and lead in a Divinely Feminine way. This is loving *and* fierce. Compassionate *and* discerning. Inclusive *and* reverent. Empathy *with* boundaries. Humble *and* confident. Every single relationship, every interaction, every chance to speak with younger women—it doesn't matter how old you are—is a micro chance to impact the macro of this New Earth.

It begins with you, Goddess. (Hathor told me to tell you so.)

If you don't have younger women in your immediate circles, how can you seek out Sacred Light mentorship? Stepping up as a volunteer at local organizations, colleges, summer camps; committing to be someone's godmother; or playing a larger role in the lives of your nieces, nephews, and neighbor's children all count.

It's not only Hathor that wants us to remember our importance in the feminine frequency, but it's Gaia, too, who is calling out for our return to her and to each other. She needs us to always remember that yes, we are all *her* daughters, making us all Sisters and part of her great Sisterhood tree. We are all each other's mothers and daughters, too. It doesn't matter if we bear biological children of our own or not. We each play a role as women Lightworkers of this time, creating a continuum of empowerment, support, activation, and love from one moment to the next, one relationship after the next, one generation after the next. As we enter the Age of Aquarius, the women, as daughters of the Earth, will be the most needed players on the world stage of forward evolution. This has already been set into motion, and we are responsible for driving its momentum.

We light this torch and pass the flame, not only in our professional settings but in our families, organizations, communities, and our societies at large. May our desires be for the daughters of Light to burn bolder and shine brighter than we already have.

This reminds me of the words of Grant Achatz, founder of and chef at Alinea. Achatz is one of the world's most celebrated and top-ranked chefs in the world. He was interviewed in the Netflix movie *For Grace,* which was about the journey of Curtis Duffy, Grant Achatz's former chef de cuisine at Alinea. Duffy had recently left to start his own restaurant called Grace and was aspiring to be awarded three Michelin stars, an accolade that would put him on par with Alinea, the only restaurant in the city at the time with that badge of honor. The interviewer of the documentary asked Achatz how he would feel if Duffy's new restaurant dethroned Alinea from being the only three-starred Michelin restaurant in town. Achatz's response moved me to my core. His words constantly ring in my heart. He responded by saying, "If the protégé doesn't outdo the mentor, then the mentor didn't do a very good job, did they?"

We must do more than a good job.

We must do *our job.*

We must continue to pass on the Light.

We must continue to keep it burning bright.

Your future "you" needs you to do so.

The Invitation: Calling In Your Cosmic Mentors and Sacred Light Mentees

Activator mentor: an influential person who "activates" our gifts and sense of self	• Who in your life lights you up, gives you new inspiration, new ideas, and new fire in your belly to activate your gifts? • Who in your life helps fill in the gaps of your existing network of parents, friends, and coworkers? (Think outside the box on this one—this person may sit on the periphery of your 'go-to' people and be someone you least expect.)
Professional mentor: an influential person in our career who supports our professional development	• Who in your professional world—either a peer or a leader—genuinely supports your growth via resources, conversations, personal challenges, introductions, etc.? • Who at work gives you consistent feedback—genuine, painful-at-first-but-you-know-it's-good-for-you feedback that allows you to grow?
Virtual mentor: a person (or people) we don't personally know but who has impacted our lives with their work from afar (i.e., authors, thought leaders, public figures)	• What thought leaders do you support and consistently learn from (think: you're the first one to pre-order their next book when it's announced)? • What public figures do you follow on social media that consistently light you up and encourage you to put down the phone and take action?

Cosmic mentor: an angel, deity, Ascended Master, spirit guide, galactic being or ancestor who comes into our awareness to support us when we don't even realize we need their unique medicines	• Is there an angel, deity, spirit guide or otherworldly being or energy you have a strong relationship with? • How did this being come into your life and can you name a specific situation where their wisdom, medicine, or presence helped you get through? How is your life different because they are in it?
Sacred Light mentees: the young women we mentor who carry on the Light	• Who in your life can you impart wisdom upon and share this work? • Who fits the mold of your younger self? How can you give back to that community of future Lightworkers?

The Key: Keep the Torch of Light Burning Bright—a Written Code

Bring out some of your finest stationery and grab your favorite pen. Send an unprompted thank-you to one of your mentors. Share with her specifically how she touched your life, who you have become because of her influence, and how grateful you are that she empowered, activated, and showed you your Light. Then send an unprompted word of praise or encouragement to a Sacred Light mentee. Share with her the vision you see for how she will carry the torch of Light. Remind her just how brave, strong, and capable she is, and that she is the future. Pop these two letters in the mail at the same time, and when you do, visualize a bright white fire of Light expanding into the world. Seal this visualization with the mantra "Together as one, we co-create the New Earth. Together, we rise."

Please visit jessicazweig.com/unlock to access all the Invitations and Keys.

11

GAIA

THE REASON FOR YOUR (LIGHT) BEING

Nature isn't just a place out there—it's also a place in here.
You are related to the elk and deer, butterfly, gazelle and tiger.
The mountains live in your bones, the river in your veins,
wildflowers grow along the chambers of your heart.

—ANGI SULLINS

Years ago, I took a trip to the Napo Wildlife Center located in the Yasuni National Park within the Ecuadorian Amazon Basin in the Amazon jungle. While it spans across nearly 2.5 million acres of lush rainforest, there are more living organisms in 2.5 acres of this part of the world than the entire European continent.[1] Over a third of the Amazonian mammals inhabit this region.

The journey to get there was a wild adventure itself. What was supposed to be a thirty-minute flight from Quito, the capital of Ecuador, to a small town called Coca, instead took us three hours because our flight was delayed. (For the entirety of this trip, surrendering to "South American time" had become a growth edge for my hypervigilant, type-A, deeply American, Virgo-rising, control-freak tendencies.) From Coca's airport, we hopped onto a two-hour bus ride that took us to a motorboat on the "white water," the faster moving opening of the Amazon River. After forty-five minutes on the white water, we came to a small clearing in the jungle, where we had to get out and walk for thirty minutes on foot to a tiny canoe on the "black water," the lowland tropical waters of the Amazon. We rowed another *three* hours on the black water until we arrived at our destination, a bit worn, extremely hungry, and . . . in complete and utter *awe*.

Deep inside untapped, unbridled Mother Nature, completely disconnected from the "real world," I connected to the *real world*. The vegetation, the insects (much to my horrific dismay), the birds, the sounds, and the smells were so new, so different, so unlike anything I had ever known to exist that it was hard to comprehend this new reality. Caimans (terrifying-looking black alligators), spotted frogs, howling monkeys, and enigmatic jaguars made it subtly clear that I, a mere mortal and quite vulnerable human, was on *their* turf. "Mother trees" (which had trunks with a circumference as big as ten grown men holding hands in a circle) had roots the size of logs busted through the rich soil, connecting to a vast webbed network of deeply embedded roots stretching underground for miles, feeding all the surrounding trees with their vital nectar. At night, the sky was jet-black with not a single photon of artificial light in sight. You could see the entire Milky Way lit up like an electric circuit board on full blast.

My most significant observation, however, was the Indigenous people deep in the heart of Ecuador, the Kichwa Añangu community. While these lands are considered to be the most biodiverse in the world, it is the original lineages of human inhabitants that have allowed them to remain so. The Kichwa Añangu people are responsible for the conservation of a select fifty-three thousand acres out of the 2.5 million of the Yasuni National Park, and they have been recognized, both domestically and internationally, for their work to protect the environment and the ecology. This community neither hunts nor fishes nor cuts trees to sell lumber.[2] No activities that could threaten the mission to protect their sacred land are allowed. This reverence stems from a primitive, sovereign culture dating back thousands of years, wherein the natural resources and biodiversity were always used sustainably, honorably, and harmonically, without ever depleting them.

What I found to be the most fascinating was that at the eco-lodge, the entire staff (from the concierge, to the waitstaff, to the chefs in the kitchen, to the cleaners who tidied our rooms) were all men. There was not one single woman who worked on the property. The workers' village was a two-hour canoe ride away, and we were told they worked in three-week shifts, going home for one week to be with their families each month. There was a softness, a gentleness, and, dare I say, a maternal energy, to these men and the way they took care of us as their guests with pure, earnest love. It was strikingly different from any other masculine energy I had ever encountered.

One of our excursions included taking that two-hour canoe ride to their village, to visit their cultural center, which was managed by the women of the community. Along with managing the center, the women cooked meals, raised families, and tended to the land. As tourists, we were brought there to pay homage by watching their tribal dance ceremonies, visiting their naturally made homes, learning about their culture, and contributing to their economic well-being by purchasing their handmade crafts and jewelry. I remember thinking to myself how *powerful, strong,* and noticeably masculine these women were.

There was an energetic difference in the men and women of this community than any male-to-female dynamic I had ever witnessed at home in the States. Their Divinely Masculine and Divinely Feminine ways of being were so distinct and created a symbiotic connection of yin (the feminine) and yang (the masculine), which worked together intuitively, instinctually, and effortlessly.

It was there in that village, deep inside this Indigenous, untouched world, that I tapped into the pure, palpable vibration of harmony for the first time in my entire life. *This is the frequency of Gaia*: a harmonic intelligence within an ecologically holistic, biodiverse, Divinely Masculine and Divinely Feminine balanced society that honors all living things within its realm. This frequency was something I could never unsee, something I could never unfeel.

It was there that my heart expanded and broke all at once.

The "frequency of Gaia" should not be a rare, once-in-a-lifetime anomaly of an experience that takes a full day of planes, buses, hiking, boating and canoeing to get to, but rather an everyday humanistic baseline experience. Humanity has grown so far away from this vibration, not only in physical distance but in our evolution, that the notion of returning to and restoring our resonant, *original* planetary harmony seems almost impossible. To many, it's not even desirable.

We have turned away from tribal communities and now live in isolated, metropolitan apartments made of concrete, and single-family suburban homes with literal and metaphorical fences. We don't live off the land, but instead off of mass-produced food packed with preservatives that line the aisles of mega grocery stores, while we sip toxic tap water and scroll our phones and numb our brains with TV for an average *three hours* of waking life every single day.[3] Gone are the values of reciprocity, reverence, respect, harmony, and Oneness from the original vibration of Mother Earth's people. In their place, we have evolved toward the modern-day societal "norms" of consumption, destruction, possession, hoarding, greed, numbing, pillaging, and materialism.

The ramifications of this are costing us more than heartbreak: they are costing us our physical health, mental sanity, and the future of this planet. Worldwide, air pollution has become the biggest threat to human health, instigating 7 million premature deaths per year.[4] Factory farming accounts for 37 percent of methane emissions, which has more than twenty times the global warming potential of CO_2.[5] An estimated 8 million tons of plastic gets dumped into our oceans annually, destroying our delicate oceanic ecosystems and poisoning our fish.[6] In the last forty years, the Brazilian Amazon has lost 18 percent of its rainforests due to illegal logging, soy farming, and cattle ranching,[7] which accounts for 80 percent of the destruction there, releasing 340 million tons of carbon per year.[8]

The fucking sheer wreckage of our planet's atmosphere, waters, forests, sentient animals, and living beings, let alone the crimes against humanity and our children, have become the rule to how this planet operates today, not the exception.

Sure, we could blame all of this on corporate capitalism, big government, the health-care system, factory farming, and the mass media. The everyday person is contributing to it as well. Not because we are malicious, but because we are *unconscious*. We are unconscious because we have become *disconnected*. In this disconnection, we have *disassociated*. In this disassociation, we are now experiencing endless *dis-ease*.

We don't need to take a trip into the middle of the jungle to realize we have lost our way. To see that we are far from living our truest nature within the authentic frequency of Gaia. As members of the Family of Light, Gaia is calling us home. She is asking for us to return to her, to restore her, to love her. She needs us to save her, to ensure the future of our planet carries forward with continued Light. She is the very reason for our Light being.

Before we can save her, we have to *remember* the gift, the responsibility, and above all, the magic it is to inhabit her in the first place.

When we remember our place on Gaia, we remember who we really are: Lightworkers, come to activate her frequency.

RETURNING HOME

For a long time, I couldn't stand being here.

By "here," I mean on Gaia.

Sure, in my earlier spiritual discoveries I had learned to revere the wisdom of Mother Earth. Yet, growing up in a dysfunctional family while being brutally bullied at school, only to then graduate into adulthood to experience more pain in getting my heart shattered in romantic relationships, feeling lost professionally, and living in scarcity (not to mention the collective pain of the world motivated by division, separatism, illusion, and fear), inspired my own special kind of avoidance. All this suffering was too much for my starseed soul to bear, and so I began to find ways to *leave*.

For a while, "leaving" looked like a lot of different things. It started with an intense meditation practice, humming mantras, eyes rolled up into my third eye, where I mastered ascending out of my body through my Crown

Chakra. Here, I learned how to connect with cosmic energy, spirit guides, angels, and aliens. These higher beings, the higher dimensions they came from, felt like a true home, and that's because it was. It was there on my meditation pillow that I found my relief, and this relief became my chase.

When I wasn't chilling in lotus position, I would go as far as traversing the world on big international trips, often targeting the most spiritually activated of destinations. On each and every adventure, I'd make a beeline to the temples—in Bali, Thailand, Israel, and Egypt—sit within their walls, and download messages as I hitched a ride into higher and higher dimensions.

If I couldn't leave my city, I found ways to leave my body through psychedelics and plant-medicine ceremonies, anything to help me fly faster out of this realm. And when the chanting, traveling, or tripping would come to any kind of stop, I'd fill my free time consuming as many metaphysical books, podcasts, and videos as I could get my hands on. I searched for *anything* that would help me ascend, transcend, and basically get the fuck out of here.

Truth be told, my dedication to departing Gaia has served me in many ways. These consistent practices and lifestyle choices honed my intuition, grew my clairaudient and clairsentient gifts, and I can now effortlessly tap into Source energy wherever and whenever I need to. The more I grew these abilities, the easier it became to *escape*.

I know I'm not the only one with this desire. We all have our own tendencies toward escapism, whether that be something as extreme as alcohol or drugs, to softer addictions and/or dissociative habits like workaholism, social media, sex, gambling, eating, shopping, gossiping, and, yes, even constant, conscious ascension. There are billions of everyday people, including me and you, trying to *understandably* escape the pain it is to be in a human body on Gaia. When I reflect on this version of myself, addicted to ascending as a means to avoid her reality, I send her so much love. I honor her dissociative, spiritual bypassing tendencies as a way of self-preservation.

The *root* of our habits, addictions, and escapism is *not* what we think it is. The traumas of our childhood, the trauma of our parents, their parents' parents, and the DNA of our lineage living inside our systems based on survival are the *symptoms,* not the cause. The root of our pain (and the world's pain) is hidden right there within the word itself: we have *unrooted* from Gaia herself. This manifests itself as a lack of respect for her resources, as much as it does our own disrespect toward our own bodies and each other.

Gaia is now asking us to remember that we are part of a bigger whole. We are her. In order to do so, she is asking us to come back into our bodies, not leave them. Our bodies are our path to understanding her laws and her principles. As members of the Family of Light, we are hearing this call stronger than ever, and more than most. We came here because Gaia called us here, and our bodies are the bridge between her and the cosmos. Rooting back down into her is a critical component to healing ourselves and fulfilling our missions, which is restoring the Light of Information on this planet at this time.

So how do we "root"?

For starters, we have to *stop being so obsessed with control.* Control is our Achilles' heel and one of the most deeply embedded psychological and metaphysical programs of the human race. Surrender is the ninja move to rooting into our bodies and therefore into Gaia, which means we must move at her pace. Another form of escapism is rushing. Seriously, why do all of us need to move so fucking fast? Where is everybody *going?* What's the *real* rush? Where is the hurry *really coming from?* Really be with that question for a second. (Or maybe a few hours.) As Isis said, Gaia's pace is slow enough to watch the seasons change, the flowers bloom, and hear the wings of the fairies flutter. Can you imagine moving, thinking, and operating that slowly? It probably brings up a whole fucking ton of fear, emotions, and panic. *Good.* Let yourself feel all of it. Feeling your feelings is part of the rooting. Start to become aware of just how fast you're moving and how much you attempt to control in your life. What comes up for you?

While you're at it, step away from your screens, turn off your headphones, and *get into nature.* Take off your shoes and put your bare feet into the earth, the sand, the soil. Breathe in the element of air; hear the natural sounds of birds chirping, the leaves rustling, the wind blowing; and feel the sun (or rain or humidity or coolness) on your skin. Feel the roots of your energetic body coming down through your feet, and imagine actual "roots" connecting down into the center of the Earth. Notice what happens in your body, to your anxiety and your mood at large. Make grounding a practice, and you will gradually develop a deeper ability to face your life versus avoid it. Let your heart break from being fully embodied in this exquisitely painful 3-D, dualistic reality, designed for you to experience bliss *and* pain. To be rooted means to fully surrender to all of Gaia's tumultuous and glorious seasons in tandem with your own. The constant cycles of death and rebirth are what we signed up for. It's the medicine we came for. We can no longer disassociate ourselves from it.

In addition to this, we must also come to *embrace that this planet we call Gaia is just as amazing as any other planet we could ever visit in the universe.* On Gaia, we have the ability to feel the full spectrum of the orgasmic, emotional human experience, journey across every type of ecological and geographical expression, and cohabitate with billions of other fascinating and sentient species, including our fellow human Lightworkers, who are activating codes of cosmic light intelligence and awakening a new dawn. As I rooted into this understanding, I had to ask myself: *Why would anyone want to leave such a wondrous world?* Gaia is the place to be! Today, all I want to do is be here, fully present to the gift of life. All I want to do is root.

When we focus more on levitating up and out (using our preferred versions of escapism) versus rooting down and in (using the vehicles of our bodies, our emotional strength, and the pure power of our Light), we don't just suffer from hijacked nervous systems, depression, anxiety, autoimmune issues, loneliness, scarcity, and survival.

We miss the magic of the Mother.

She doesn't want us to escape her, avoid her, or leave her at all. She wants us to stay, to ground, to root so that she can mother us with her Divine Love. She is craving for us to love her back in equal measure.

For it is only in this union of "right relationship" that we can fully and finally heal.

For us to rebuild our right relationship with Gaia, we have to recall her Truth, *our Truth.*

We have to reclaim our inner Goddess.

RECLAIMING OUR INNER GODDESS

Based on patriarchal programming over the last four thousand years, there has been a mass distortion of Gaia's place in our world from a religious, metaphysical, and historical perspective.

When reflecting on the "history of time," specifically within the last four thousand years, most of our modern-day historical teachings and understandings have been written through the lens of the patriarchal masculine, depicting the forming of the world as we know it today: one that was formed based on religion, recorded war, and the declarations over land and territory. So much emphasis has been put upon the historical recollection of 2000 BC to AD 2000. Look objectively at historical texts recounting the thousands of marquee events that took place during these ages, and you will repeatedly see words like "civil war," "domination," "assassination," "conquest," "defeat," "victory," "attack," "persecution," "construction," "destruction," "succession," "reign," and "rulership." Examining these words, one can easily see that they don't only characterize history, but our present-day reality.

You'll be hard-pressed to find much historical material within this window that discusses, let alone validates, the Goddess. Forget validation. For the past four millennia, which some historians have classified as the "all-encompassing timeline,"[9] the Goddess has been repressed, oppressed, and eradicated. Um, well, if Gaia is scientifically proven to be 4.543 *billion years old,* the math doesn't math. We must ask ourselves what has really taken place before the beginning of the "beginning"? How were civilizations pre-

2000 BC constructed? How did we live *far beyond* this tiny drop in the bucket of four thousand years compared to eons? Who did we worship? How did we coexist with the earth, the seas, the skies, and above all with each other?

Scientist James DeMeo has described part of the answer: "There's no clear and unambiguous evidence for the existence of warfare, sadism, traumatization of babies, subordination of women, nor any of the trappings of patriotism anywhere in the world prior to around 4000 BCE. None!"[10]

Additionally, in their iconic work *The Great Cosmic Mother,* Barbara Mor and Monica Sjöö state, "It is important to grasp the time dimensions involved: *God was female for at least the first 200,000 years of human life on earth* . . . The Great Mother everywhere was the active and autonomous creatrix of the world."[11]

For the hundreds of thousands of years prior to "history," as we commonly know it, matriarchal goddess cultures led civilizations. As Tricia McCannon describes in *Return of the Divine Sophia,* these cultures "were always associated with the cultivation of food, agricultural knowledge of herbs, roots, healing and other medical aids, as well as the invention of writing, arts, weaving, textiles, and the very foundations of civilization itself."[12] These feminine societies honored and domesticated animals, advanced the understandings behind astronomy, led sacred rites and ensured they were recorded, and above all, revered all living things as sacred. (Maybe you see yourself in the original female creators of society? I certainly do!) In these communities, "no weapons have been unearthed, no defensive earthworks [found], no evidence of an oppressive ruling hierarchy or of social conflict."[13]

This is not folklore. This is our DNA. Simply, objectively, look at the timeline. What do you think holds more biological weight in how humans evolved: four thousand years versus three hundred thousand years versus four billion years? What defines our true nature: historical and religious books written by men, or the civilizations of eons who lived in harmony with the planet? Yet the idea that "God" was in fact female since the dawn of civilization might still seem impossible to fathom for many of us. To believe this may challenge our deepest psychological *and* physiological programming, which, when you look at the history books, stems from the patriarchal system of control, supremacy, linear time, separatism, and power. It's so woven into our conditioned consciousness, like vitamin C in orange juice, we don't even notice it's there.

Part of activating and *living* our Light (which, remember, is *Information*) requires us to recall the Goddess within as much as without. She lives in our cells. She lives in the trees, the birds, the ants, and the dolphins. She lives in the people who pass us on the street. She is us. She is everything. Spend a moment taking that in.

"There will be a return and an awakening to Mother Goddess energy," Barbara Marciniak writes in her Pleiadian-channeled book *Earth.* "You will find . . . that all of your religions are based on a false ideal. They are all based on a controlling, cold-hearted, patriarchal movement, when in actuality it is the Mother Goddess who is behind all things."[14]

Today we are living within cultural and societal constructs that do not honor this at all. It is a world designed for men, by men, with literal man-made principles, values, laws, and beliefs. This has been the *uprooting.* On the macro level, all we have to do is turn on the news to see the repercussions of this by the outer pillaging and destroying of our Great Mother Gaia. On a micro level, this repression of the Divine Feminine has contributed to the pillaging and destroying of our own inner feminine.

So how do we embody the Goddess? The first practical step is recognizing that we are playing by man-made rules. In the depths of my burnout while running my agency, I was struggling to maintain a quarter of a half-million-dollar monthly payroll, aiming to "crush" my monthly revenue goals, grow quarter over quarter to show to my board, and demonstrate a year-over-year profitability mostly for my own ego. Hooked on toxic hustle and drowning in scarcity, I took a session with one of my most trusted astrologers to find some answers. Lying on her sofa, I unraveled all my anxieties, and she matter-of-factly responded, "All things are nature, and this includes your business. It has cycles and rhythms. Deaths and rebirths. It will go through seasons of expansion and retraction. To believe it must always operate in straight lines ascending upwards is nothing more than a construct. It's a lie."

We are still all living our lives according to a literally man-made Gregorian calendar established by Pope Gregory XIII in 1582. Can you reflect on where and how you exist within a construct of linear time? Monday through Friday, nine to five, Q1, Q2, Q3, and Q4 (fiscal quarters), 365 days, 24–7. Just thinking about it all makes me spin with anxiety.

As I look around, I see a new collective consciousness arising. We are *re-membering* Gaia's principles and bringing them back into our ways of being.

However, a warning to the awakened: doing the Light Work of restoring the Great Mother isn't a trend. There is much buzz about the rise of "Divine Feminine" today. Throw a stone and you'll hit a spiritually awakened woman touting the magic of the moon, with feathers in her hair, exalting the powers of the archetypal goddesses, potentially steeped in a salt bath with oils and herbs, surrounded in crystals. She's doing *all the things*. I'm here for it all, but the true frequency of Gaia does not reemerge based on what we read, what we buy, how we dress, or what we preach on social media. *It is who we are.* Gaia is asking us to design our lives, careers, families, and platforms completely differently than what we've been conditioned to believe. *To simply be.* We cannot bring the same energy that has contributed to our uprooting (dominance, control, proving, and hierarchy) to reclaim the Goddess and heal her and thereby heal ourselves.

As I wrote this book, cranking away at my word count, in the Costa Rican province of Puntarenas on a writing sabbatical, a white butterfly flew into my purview. I stopped my fingers from typing and followed this delicate, floating manifestation of life with my gaze. For just a few short minutes, I took in her beauty, her freedom, her levity. Watching her fly, I felt my heart open like a flower, and a tingling vibration moved through my body. This was the Gaia frequency pulsing through me: pure love, pure peace, pure presence. It didn't come in action but nonaction. It was right there in front of me and within me, with a single breath.

Our reclamation is right here, right now. When we step outside of the patriarchal constructs, root down into Gaia, and activate her frequency through our Divine Feminine presence, we are doing more than the Light Work. We are setting the stage for not just what the *next* four thousand years will be, but the next four hundred thousand and the next four billion.

We, the feminine leaders of this time, write history. We bring a new dawn. Gaia is our guide.

She knows best how we can heal her. She holds the codes to her restoration, and we must be ready to receive them.

THE GAIA CODES

On Earth Day, April 22, 2023, I was deep in meditation, sitting outside on a sunny spring day in Nashville. As I attuned to the energy of Mother Gaia, I waited for a message. Within a matter of moments, a spirit guide appeared. She was an ancient Indigenous woman who had lived centuries ago on the land my house now sits on. Her face was worn as leather, etched with cavernous wrinkles and deep, wide, wise eyes. She looked as though she could have been one hundred years old. She told me her name was White Eagle and that we, the daughters of Gaia, are the white feathers, here to spread our wings of Light as part of Gaia's restoration.

Right before White Eagle's death, the European settlers had invaded her land, severing and uprooting her people from their homes, their safety, and their freedoms. She knew that this trauma would reverberate far beyond her own lifetime and into generations to come. White Eagle shared with me the infinite sadness she felt for the legacy of her people. Despite my lack of understanding of her people's lived experience through my own whiteness, I asked her what it was she wanted me to do to help heal her sorrows.

Her message reminded me of something that the Pleiadians have shared: *Whenever a people are separated, and they focus on what they do not have in common or label themselves different from others, it is a perfect disguise to*

*keep them from discovering what they do have in common. This separation
keeps people from banding together and becoming very strong.*[15]

On Earth Day, we are encouraged to celebrate and honor the planet—to
recycle, compost, and eat organic. What Gaia and White Eagle shared with
me that day is that Earth Day is not only about honoring the planet but honoring each other, because *we are all her.*

In his classic text, *The Hero with a Thousand Faces*, Joseph Campbell
characterized the Goddess this way: "The goddess is red with fire of life; the
earth, the solar system, the galaxies of far-extending space, all swell within
her womb. For she is the world creatrix, ever mother, ever virgin. She en-
compasses the encompassing, nourishes the nourishing, and is the life of
everything that lives. She is also the death of everything that dies. . . . She is
the womb and the tomb. . . . Thus she unites 'good' and the 'bad,' exhibit-
ing the two modes of the remembered mother, not only as personal, but as
universal."[16]

That day on Earth Day, sitting on the rich soil, with White Eagle in my
field and the frequency of Gaia pulsing with me, I viscerally understood
Campbell's words.

As I sat there, the codes of Gaia came through. The words *"reverence"*
and *"reciprocity"* downloaded into my consciousness and began to reor-
ganize my cellular memory. I began to pulse with the deep and profound
knowing of what she was asking of me.

Reverence is deeper than respect. It is a deep bow of humility and awe.
We must have reverence for all things. Not just what we find beautiful and
interesting, like a butterfly or a sunset. Those are things we can easily feel
reverence for—mostly for things that are unlike us, unfamiliar, or even uncomfortable, specifically people and cultures who are different from us. Age,
race, religion, sexuality, gender, and every single multifaceted expression of
Gaia in human form imaginable requires our deep bow of humility and awe.
As do, of course, our hills, our valleys, our mountains, our trees, our sentient
animals, the Indigenous people of our lands . . . they require our reverence.
This is the bare minimum, Gaia told me.

Reciprocity is her highest principle, the most holy Gaia code of all and our biggest opportunity as a species to heal. We must integrate equanimity in our communities, our families, our bodies, and our lives. One reciprocal act at a time creates a spiraled continuum of harmony. Where there is a cause, there is an effect. Do not take more than you can give, and should you do so, ask yourself how you can restore, return, and reciprocate in equal measure. This is her highest order.

To know the truth of her codes not just in your mind but experientially in your body changes your frequency to that of Light. We carry these codes in our body, and we have been programmed to forget. It has been written out of history, while society has moved into parts of the world miles and miles away from her untapped, Amazonian-level vibration. We have been cut off from our roots, causing escapism, addiction, trauma, and self-serving agendas for survival. We are hooked on a patriarchal man-made system founded upon the values of conquest and rulership, guided by linear timelines, constructed to keep us controlled. As we keep getting sicker, more fearful, and more destructive, we fall further away from the essence, the frequency of Gaia.

Reverence and reciprocity are the codes Gaia holds to return us back into the right relationship with her and, therefore, the entire web of humanity. This is our reason for our Light being.

You have been gifted a wild, wonderful, technologically advanced, light-encoded vehicle, your body, to experience this truly magical, epically vast place. **Your assignment has been to call back your cellular memory to literally *remember* just how powerful and sovereign you are.** Once that remembrance activates, you recall that you are a member of the Family of Light, here to be a sacred bridge between Gaia and the cosmos. When you deeply honor this assignment, you are able to redefine, redesign, and break the boundaries of humanity's amnesia and remember that we are Source, and Source is us. It is in everything, and we are in everything. Separation, division, and fear are illusions. So is disempowerment. We have stepped into the grand experiment in the third dimension to experience this illusion so that we can wake up. And when we do, we become tuning forks, broadcasting a new frequency.

By activating your Gaia codes, you are literally creating this awakening, this rebalancing, this healing, as you read these words. Soon you will put the book down, and your *work* will be to live these words.

This is part of your assignment, Lightworker. The future of Light on this planet depends on you, on all of us. Let's not let her down.

The Invitation: A Return to Gaia

- What's your preferred method of escape?
- Where do you find yourself rushing the most in your daily, weekly, monthly life?
- How are you, consciously or unconsciously, playing by man-made rules in your life?
- What do you seek to control most in life?
- What would happen if you trusted that Gaia is on your side in this?
- What's your favorite space to be in nature? Go there in your mind's eye. How does it make you feel?
- What do you find the most reverence for?
- Where are you living with reciprocity? Where are you not?
- What new *Information* do you possess now that you understand the Gaia codes?

The Key: Daily Rooting Crystal Meditation

If we want to live our Light, rooting to Gaia cannot be an anomaly but our everyday baseline way of being. When we tap into her codes, we recalibrate our nervous systems and well-being into her frequency of harmony. This is why I am going to recommend you do your best to make this rooting meditation a daily practice.

As often as you can, get into nature. Take off your shoes, put away any technology such as your phones, headphones, or smartwatch. Find a stretch of soil, sand, or grass—as unobstructed a piece of Gaia as you can find. Let your bare feet soak in the elements beneath your feet. Breathe in the air, hear the natural sounds of birds chirping, the leaves rustling, the wind blowing, and feel the sun (or rain or humidity or coolness) on your skin. Imagine actual "roots" coming out of the soles of your feet, connecting down into the center of Gaia. When you get to her center, imagine a crystal of your choosing. This can be a clear quartz, ruby, emerald, citrine, amethyst, or any crystal of your choice. Feel the energy of this crystal charging the roots as you draw up that energy through the roots from the center of Gaia back into your feet and into your whole body. Allow yourself to be with this sensation for a few minutes and witness how your energy shifts. Do not be dismayed if you cannot feel a tangible shift. Surrender the control and the rushing. Know that by absorbing the frequencies of Gaia into your physical and energetic bodies on a daily basis, you *are* changing. Doing this daily will create a compound effect in your body, your life, and your spirit.

Please visit jessicazweig.com/unlock to access all the Invitations and Keys.

12

MIRACLES

GO LIGHT UP THE FUCKING WORLD

Above all, know that your DNA is a store of miracles
waiting to be tapped.
—RICHARD RUDD

On the closing morning of my spiritual pilgrimage to Egypt, we finally reached the Great Pyramid.

Within less than an hour of rising from our last predawn wake-up call, I found myself climbing the tight, claustrophobic, narrow corridor steps to the King's Chamber. Upon entering, I was overwhelmed by pitch-blackness. The humid heat caused my body to bead with sweat within a few short minutes, as the smell of musty sudation and the remnants of thousands of people *and* thousands of years wafted up my nose. Our group of seventeen spread out in a circle, looping around the king's granite sarcophagus. I steadied my feet, fixed my gaze into the dark center of the chamber, and allowed the intensity of the climb, my exhaustion, and my discomfort to move through me.

It was a rare opportunity to be in the King's Chamber this early, exclusively with our own group, let alone be granted the permission to chant. We all stood in that circle, "*om*"-ing in cascades for over an hour. After the crescendoing days of light-body activations, lucid dreams, 5-meO-DMT explosions in my pineal gland, and catching white feathers, I thought there could be no greater climax to my trip to Egpyt.

I was wrong.

The Great Pyramid is said to be located on a direct line to one of the most active cosmic portals on Gaia—a galactic gateway where the original civilizations of humanity came through. Here I was, eons later, standing in this very doorway, my own humble human experience of this country now behind me. What came through in that chamber can only be described as the deepest, cosmic experience of pure Love that I had ever felt in my life.

This feeling wasn't an explosion, a dissolution, a becoming.

It was an engulfing.

I cried so hard. My tears came from the understanding of just how much I had denied that endless Love, how much I had pushed it away: from other people, from myself, from the world. How little I had trusted that *that* Love is always ever-present and available to me and within me. Even more, I cried because it felt so *profoundly* safe to be loved that endlessly. To know that I am *always* loved that endlessly.

I came home from Egypt new. Everyone and everything else wasn't. It was the same. My integration caused a lot of conflict, stress, and strife in my life for months to follow. When we go into any kind of transmutative, alchemizing portals . . . we change. When we step back in, the world around us doesn't necessarily match our new frequency. Part of the walking of the walk of a Lightworker requires grace. May you remember that as you close this book.

On my darkest of days, of which I still have many, I go back to that final morning in the King's Chamber. In the pitch-black, smelly, compressing, uncomfortable darkness, I didn't find light. I found Love instead.

As the Pleiadians say, Light is Information, Love is creation. With Love, all possibilities exist.

My fellow Lightworker, we've almost come to the end. You know as much as I do that, just like the last stop of the Great Pyramid was for me, this is only the beginning.

You have activated the light codes inside your cellular memory and received new Information. You have recalled your authentic Truth in understanding that your own unique blueprint is *needed* on this planet. Most of all, you have reached new depths of Love (for yourself, for others, for the planet, and for future generations), unlocking a new 5-D consciousness in this reality with your very presence. You have integrated all three inside of yourself, and like the triangle expresses, you've done the Light Work.

(I'm not crying; you're crying.)

You are a living miracle.

A "miracle" is not what you might think. A miracle is simply a change in perception. A "holy instant" when it all changes, based on a choice you have made in your mind, your heart, your soul. You have made many choices here, you have had several "holy instants," and you have done more than change your perception here. You have accepted the invitation. *You have remembered.*

Each of the steps we have taken together has been a key. Each aspect of your Inner Light, Outer Light, and Future Light was the lock that only *you* could unlock to find your own unique message, lesson, and treasure.

You unlocked a new understanding of your connection to Source, the power of your emotions, the sacredness of your body, and the definition of true self-empowerment. You unlocked the *refinements* and soul upgrades you received from your family of origin, reclaimed the most passionate love affair you will ever have (the one with yourself), healed your deepest wounds through the power of friendship, and unlocked how to create wealth effortlessly through a new embodiment of frequency, worth, generosity, and trust. You unlocked your unique mission as a member of the Family of Light, rediscovered the importance of finding your way-showers and being one yourself through mentorship, reclaimed your reverence for Gaia, and committed to the reciprocity needed to bring all things back into right relationship, starting with how we honor the Great Mother, the original Goddess.

Most of all, you have remembered: you are the Goddess herself.

As Hathor shared with me in her temple, as light poured through every cell of my body and the voices of the Pleiadians rose in chorus with her: **you are a leader of the new feminine frequency on this planet at this time.**

That afternoon in Dendera, she was not talking to me. She was talking *through* me. I wrote this book as my own interpretation of their instructions through my own humble, imperfect, and human stories. I hope that they were nothing more than mirrors and that you saw pieces of yourself in them. As Hathor said, we are all pieces of the Goddess, and it is her guidance that stands above it all. Her words to me in Egypt are as true for me as they are for you: you are a leader of this time, Lightworker. Do not take this for granted.

Unlike Hathor, and despite the many frameworks, meditations, somatic practices, prompts and exercises, the Light Work is not intended to be an instruction. It is truly nothing more than my invitation. As the Pleiadians teach us, we are living in a free-will zone. There is nothing any of us *have to do*. Everything is a choice. We are all sovereign beings. With that sovereignty comes great responsibility.

Not everyone on Gaia will take responsibility. Not everyone remembers who they really are and why we all came here. They might be invited into opportunities for more Information, more Truth, more Love, and to activate their own Light through books, conversations, relationships, heartbreaks, polarity, and pain. Not everyone accepts the call. Some people choose, whether consciously or unconsciously, to stay asleep. That's okay. We are all on our own journeys, and we must honor everyone's human evolution without judgment.

The only way for us to bring Light back into this world is by being a walking example of it. Every single day. Whether that's greeting a stranger with more loving presence, being the first to take accountability for your side of an argument and apologize, or putting down the phone as you scramble to reach your astrologer (or coach or human-design expert or Reiki master, doctor, or therapist) and *remember* that you are the Source of your own power, your own joy, your own healing, your own Light. This is the biggest miracle of all: to remember that you are the Source. To stop, once and for all, the outsourcing. This *re-membering* is a putting back together, in every sense of the word, of who we really are as spiritual beings. This severing of our spiritual continuity, wholeness, and self-empowered, self-actualized, and self-generated Light has been intentional. There are dark forces on this planet, and your waking up to this fact is part of this miracle. As the Pleiadians say as channeled through Barbara Marciniak:

> "You take a very active role. There are many who say, 'Oh, no, here comes the light!' because light is known to alter every vibrational frequency that it encounters. Light carries information, and information expands systems so that old systems can no longer exist. So, as light moves to destroy, it also births new systems by what it leaves behind. A new order is formed."[1]

As you go on your way, I want you to continue to remember your power, yes, but I also want you to continue to remember your humanness. As much as you and I would like to be supernatural, galactic extraterrestrials (okay, maybe that's just me), it is precisely our 3-D, dualistic, polarizing human experience, riddled with dark, hard, sad, painful, angering aspects, that we incarnated to walk through. This walk is not meant to be linear. Unlike a book, there is no beginning, middle, and end to it. Like Gaia, the Light Work operates in cycles and rhythms, like the seasons. We experience a multitude of deaths and rebirths in all areas of our Inner and Outer Lights. And just when we think we've "completed" the Light Work and reached a point of conscious, ascended integration, there is a whole new path to walk, a new layer to unpack, an unseen depth to unravel.

I don't know about you, but this makes me so fucking excited. To know there's a whole network of cosmic intelligences stored inside my body and therefore my life, as I possess infinite *Information* yet to be *unlocked,* let alone *understood,* inspires me to live bigger, love harder, risk higher, dare more bravely, and allow the highs and the lows, the dark and the light to pulse through me as deeply as humanly possible.

This visceral dance with life and all its glorious, horrific, beautiful, and painfully exquisite experiences is what activates your *Truth*: your authenticity, your blueprint, your own unique expression. The more you dance, the more you heal yourself, your lineage, and the generations of starseeds beyond us to come.

This leads us to the key that sits in your soul that can truly unlock it all: Love. *Love is the master key*. **Love is the truth of the entire Universe. When one has Love, a New Earth is born. It starts, every day, with you.**

Keep unlocking the locks, my sweet friend. Keep asking yourself these questions: How can you connect more authentically with Source? Where can you claim even more responsibility for your power? Where can you embrace your curves even more? How can you tune in and *really listen* to your body when she speaks to you? Where can you forgive your father more completely or accept your siblings more fully? Where within your friendships can you get that much more vulnerable? Where can you open your heart to Love even more deeply? Where can you open your body to pleasure more unapologetically? Where can you raise your pricing in your business with more effortlessness and trust? Where can you create more time in your day-to-day life to pay it forward to other women? How can you stop avoiding the pain of being in your life and root down into it instead? Where can you find more reverence for Gaia, offer her reciprocity, and ensure you are moving into a right relationship with her? Where can you embody the elements of Information, Truth, and Love with that much more radical commitment? Keep asking the questions. Keep recalling your codes. Keep activating your cellular memory. Keep doing the work.

Just a few final words to the very wise woman you clearly are by now: Make play your ultimate *prayer*. Make *joy* your *job*.

Our darkness is our portal, our teacher, and so necessary for healing our trauma, transmuting our density, and alchemizing our pain into a purpose. It is meant to be a process, not a station. Don't stay in the questions. Don't remain in the pain. You don't have to make your shadow your story. What we focus on expands. Today, the real flex of a healed person is being a happy person. Doing the Light Work is not the ultimate aim. It is simply a pathway, one that guides you fully, completely, and unapologetically toward *living your Light.*

The word "light" can also be defined as *brilliant, luminous, rich, sunny, glowing, unobscured, lustrous, bright,* and *radiant.* Imagine the woman who embodies *that* frequency everywhere she goes? Who gets described that way when she's not in the room? Who has a sparkle in her eye and a smile that beams across the room when she is? The one you can't take your eyes off of? The one who makes you feel safe and championed to shine brightly in your Light because she's so clear and confident in hers? The woman who radiates a palpable sense of joy, magnetism, and *fun* that you feel in your own heart whenever you're around her? The one who makes this world a better place simply because she's in it?

This is not a woman who has had it easy. This is a woman who has done her work. She has done the Light Work.

She is a living *miracle.*

She is *you.*

That's because you have chosen to remember her.

In this remembrance, you've unlocked your Light and found your own key. You have found your Family of Light. We are forever by your side, and we have always got your back. You are safe to feel it all, to own it all, to claim it all, to be it all, to shine it all, and to have it all.

You deserve it, and you know it.

Because you have *worked* for it.

Because you came here to live your Light.

Now, from this miraculous state of *joyous* being, go light up the whole fucking world.

YOUR LIGHTWORKER RESOURCES

The Radiance Realm: Reader's Guide

As mentioned, it's most powerful to read *The Light Work* in a group of your favorite fellow Lightworkers, your very own *Radiance Realm.* You can gather in person or virtually and set aside at least one to two hours of time. Attempt to meet regularly at the same time and same day of the week or month. If you are in person, feel free to light a candle, spritz some aura clearing spray, burn some sage, and create a small altar with your favorite oracle deck and crystals. (If you are virtual, create your own sacred space with the same tools.) Don't forget your Light Work journal.

At the beginning of every Radiance Realm gathering, it is important to "open the portal" and create a conscious container. To do so, begin by playing the song "Ace of Cups" by LSDREAM from "The Lightworker's Playlist," found at jessicazweig.com/playlist. The full playlist is listed on page 242. Close your eyes, stay in silence, and simply listen to the recording as a group. Feel the music in your body and allow the lyrics to download into your field. When the song is finished, open your eyes. You are ready to begin.

Navigate the book together by selecting a new chapter (or a few) each time you gather. You can spend time journaling on "The Invitation" sections, found at the end of each chapter, and once you are finished, take turns going around to share what came up for you. You can also use these gatherings to activate "The Key" exercises by meditating, stargazing, rooting, moving your bodies, or practicing any of the rituals together to "unlock" as one.

When the time with your Radiance Realm comes to an end, consciously "close the portal" by reciting "The Lightworker's Invocation" (on the following page) out loud in unison. This not only seals the power of your intentions, it activates a potent vibration of magnetic Light for all you beautiful and needed renegades to carry with you into your lives and into the world.

The Lightworker's Invocation

Recite this invocation to activate your Inner, Outer, and Future Lights. This can be read aloud before you start your day, give a public speech or presentation, go into a difficult conversation, commence a retreat or workshop, recite to yourself before a big meeting, or simply at the beginning of any time you pick up this book to read. This invocation is also to be used at the closing of every Radiance Realm group gathering to seal your intentions.

I am here to unlock my power.

I am here to remember who I really am.

I am here to activate my authentic blueprint.

I am here to be a renegade and a way-shower to others.

I am here to live my Truth.

I am here to be my own greatest love.

I am here to experience bliss.

I am here to manifest abundance effortlessly and easily.

I am here to harness my thoughts and create my own reality.

I am here to reclaim my Light.

I am here to be the embodiment of Love.

With Light, all Information is available.

With Love, I hold the master key.

And so it is.

The Lightworker's Principles

These principles can be used in myriad ways. Write your favorites in your Light Work journal, and use them as prompts. Recite them out loud as affirmations, prayers, or chants. Print them out, frame them, and put them where you can see them. Make them a part of your daily life by incorporating your favorites into meditations; open up your yoga classes, retreats, or workshops with them; read them to your team as you start the work week; choose a few to unpack in your next therapy session; tattoo one on your body. Infuse them into the way you work, lead, live, and love.

THOUGHT IS, THOUGHT CREATES.
Therefore, my thoughts create my reality.
This is the name of the game.
I harness the power of my mind.
I am and always have been *that* powerful.
I take radical responsibility for my own precious life.

JOY IS MY BIRTHRIGHT.
Happiness is fleeting.
Joy is a choice.
Joy is my job.
Joy is the pathway to alignment and the lubricant to abundance.
Play is my ultimate prayer.
I choose to love my pleasure more than my suffering.

I AM THE LIGHT ITSELF.
My DNA is awakening.
My cellular memory is returning.
Light is Information.

Light expresses Truth.

Light amplifies Love.

These are the Divine Laws of Light.

I am co-creating a New Earth alongside my Family of Light.

EMOTIONS ARE MY ULTIMATE KEY.

The more I feel, the more I heal.

The more I heal, the more compassion I find.

The more compassion I find, the more I access 5-D consciousness.

The full spectrum of my emotions, from the dark to the Light, are
always welcome.

My emotions are my key to unlock my fully activated Truth.

What a gift it is to possess all my emotions!

The more I feel, the brighter my Light grows.

ABUNDANCE IS EFFORTLESS.

I am safe in my body to receive endless abundance.

I don't hustle from lack.

I spiritually hustle for love.

The spiritual hustler knows that making money is easy.

Wealth is the ultimate Divine Feminine Embodiment.

I am a feminine financial leader of the New Earth.

MY BODY IS A SACRED TECHNOLOGY.

The body is not flesh and bone.

It is a self-generating, deeply intelligent, light-encoded,
self-healing machine.

I am my own greatest healer.

My body is a vessel for Light.

I commit to honoring her.

I promise to listen to her.

I shall cherish her.

I AM ALWAYS MY GREATEST LOVE.

In my aloneness, I find my wholeness.

Whole people attract whole people.

Interdependence is the Goddess move.

Eternal life began with bliss.

My bliss is eternal.

WE BELONG TO THE SAME SISTERHOOD.

Women are my mirrors.

What I see in her I see in myself, or else I would not be able

    to see it.

Our friendships are our greatest medicine.

My mentors come in all quantum forms.

I am a torchbearer of Light for the future generations of women on

    this Earth.

THE GAIA CODES

Gaia is our Great Mother.

I honor her with my reverence.

I heal her with my reciprocity.

My body is the bridge between her and the cosmos.

I root down and I slow down.

Gaia is the most magical place to be right now.

*Please visit jessicazweig.com/unlock to access all the Invitations
and Keys, plus additional Lightworker resources.*

The Lightworker's Playlist

Music carries the frequencies that connect us more deeply to ourselves, while connecting us more deeply to humanity. This complete Lightworker's Playlist can be found at jessicazweig.com/playlist. You can also find the individual songs on Apple Music, Pandora, and YouTube.

TO ACTIVATE YOUR INNER RENEGADE

- **"Intro" by M83**—Start your day with this song. Listen while making coffee, showering, doing your makeup, or journaling. Turn it on full blast, let the whole song crescendo as you tap into your heart and allow your vibration to rise. When you're done listening, you will be ready to face the world as the Lightworker you are.

- **"Ace of Cups" by LSDREAM**—Use this short but potent song to open your Radiance Realm reading group. Listen and attune to the lyrics of this song as you activate your power as one group.

- **"Overnight" by Tensnake**—This is the perfect song to activate your galactic renegade avatar. Listen to this when working with "The Key" from chapter 9, "Your Galactic Renegade Visualization."

TO COMMUNE WITH THE GODDESSES OF EGYPT

- **"Hathor Frequency" by Elsa Field and J Rokka**—Use this *extremely* powerful song during any sacred ceremony, meditation, or journey. (This song contains Light Language similar to what I channeled in Egypt after my light-body activation at Hathor's temple.)

- **"The Goddess Isis" by Alana Fairchild**—I listened to this song as I walked into the Temple of Isis at Philae in Egypt, and it supported me reaching the expanded quantum state of consciousness and downloading her codes, mentioned in chapter 3. I recommend you meditate with this song in sacred solitude.

- **"Sekhmet (The Goddess Awakens)" by Elise Lebec**—Listen to this when you want to tap into your fiery, feminine, sexual, primal power and turn on your womb (sacral) and your yoni (root). Put on full blast, sashay, growl, scream, breathe fire, and shake your ass like the lioness queen herself.
- **"The Pleiadian Frequency" by Alana Fairchild**—This is a beautiful track that includes the Pleiadian vibration, Light Language, and the Ho'oponopono forgiveness prayer. It's a beautiful song to play in the background as you read this book and write in your Light Work journal, or to use in meditation or bath time.

TO ATTUNE TO GAIA

- **"Celeste" by Pete Kuzma**—this is the perfect song for a walk in nature. Pop in your ear buds and get lost on a hike, forest bath, or stroll down a beach at sunrise or sunset. Become a humble witness to Gaia. You can also listen to this as you journal on "The Invitation" questions from chapter 11.
- **"We Shall Be Known" by MaMuse**—Use this beautiful track to open or close any group ceremony, prayer group, ritual, or offering of reciprocity to Gaia (e.g., a fire ritual, a full-moon ceremony, a water blessing). The lyrics of this song signify the power in numbers, as it is sung in chorus. Gather your Sisterhood, Family of Light, or Radiance Realm members, and sing along to this together.
- **"Gaia Ma" by Mary Isis & Pathways of Transformation**—I love to play this song when I'm feeling disconnected to Gaia and need to root back into her. If you've been away from nature too long, live in a big city, have been on a lot of airplanes, or are just feeling

anxiety from the speed of your life, this is a great song to listen to with your eyes closed to drop back into Gaia's energy.

TO CONNECT TO YOURSELF

- **"Light of Truth" by East Forest, Formless, and Mooji**—Here is just the most perfect remembrance of the power of the present moment. Listen and instantly return to your heart, your body, your Truth.

- **"Heart Takes Flight" by Ram Dass and AWARÉ**—I listened to this song on repeat while I was in Egypt. This beautiful song is a portal into your soul, perfect to play while you meditate, walk in nature, or simply play in the background in your home, simply being.

- **"Hello from Earth" by Hyume (ft. Alex Serra)**—This is a perfect track to listen to if you're having a hard day and need to *remember* your Light, your beauty, your power, and your freedom. As you learn the lyrics, I recommend singing along to the chorus out loud. It will completely elevate your frequency.

- **"Presencia" by Danit**—Play this sexy, feminine, and romantic song as you get ready to "Take Yourself Out on a Date for One"—"The Key" from chapter 6.

- **"Dancing on My Own" by Robyn**—This is the ultimate "single girl" anthem. Blast it if you're in a relationship or not. Let the beat activate the paradox of loneliness and wholeness. Let the lyrics pierce through you as you feel the excruciating yearning for love and the sheer *power* of self-love. This song is alllllll the things. Dance your face off to it.

TO TRANSMUTE DENSE ENERGY IN YOUR BODY AND RAISE YOUR VIBE

- **"Steam" by Leon Bridges**—This song has such *soul*. It is the ultimate mood booster. I love to pop it into my earbuds during my morning walk and it inspires me to dance like a fool down the street in my neighborhood, regardless of who's watching. If you're looking to shake off projections of other people's energy and give less fucks about what people think of you, blast this on a walk, feel the beat and dance to this groove. It works like a charm.
- **"Junk" by Vivienne Chi**—The perfect song to reclaim your *thoughts.* The "junk" represents the self-limiting beliefs that can spin in all of our heads. When Vivienne Chi belts: "*Maybe you're missing something, but you're not missing anything,*" be reminded of who you really are. Turn up the volume and sing along.
- **"Bless Me" by Dombresky (with Discrete)**—the perfect ecstatic dance track, and it's especially powerful if you're feeling heavy, sad, overwhelmed, anxious or depressed. Put this on and just fucking dance. Shake, shimmy, jump, gyrate, flail, sway, spin or scream. Do not stop moving. You will feel better, I promise. This is a great song to play with in exploring "The Key" from chapter 2: "Emotional Alchemy Practices."
- **"1,175 Hz | Angelic Sound Healing for Light Body Activation" by Mei-lan Maurits**—Listen to this great song to clear the energetic body of fear and lower vibrations. I like to play this song during any sacred practice to clear my physical body, such as yoni steaming, coffee enemas, salt baths, meditation, or daily rooting into Gaia.

The Lightworker's Toolkit

LIGHTWORKER ESSENTIAL OILS

Essential oils are made with plants, flowers, and herbs, each holding their own unique vibrational frequency. When we smell or apply these oils to our bodies, our frequency rises to match the frequency of the oil. Additionally, we may feel emotional sensations aligned with the energy of that same plant, flower, or herb. For example, rose possesses one of the highest frequencies, vibrating at 320 MHz (megahertz). When you apply rose oil anywhere on your body (I recommend you place it on your heart), you will experience a palpable feeling of more love. Essential oils are a go-to in any Lightworker's Toolkit, as we know that our bodies are sacred vessels, and our frequencies, along with our emotions, are our most powerful tools to co-create our realities. Here are some of my recommended brands and oils, inspired by the light-code-activation chakra descriptions from chapter 3.

FAVORITE BRANDS AND RECOMMENDED OILS

- **Durga Interiors,** durgainteriors.com: The highest quality essential oils I have ever found, located in Vancouver and directly sourced from India.
    - ◊ blue lotus (third eye)
    - ◊ tuberose (sacral)
    - ◊ imperial blue jasmine (throat)
- **DoTerra,** doterra.com: A widely known, internationally selling brand, with one of the largest collections on the market.
    - ◊ melissa (crown)
    - ◊ bergamot (solar plexus)
    - ◊ geranium (heart)

- **Quantum Stones,** quantumstones.com: This retailer sells Gamal's Sacred Egyptian Essential Oils; Gamal is the healer I worked with directly in Cairo, mentioned in chapter 4.
  - ◊ rose (heart)
  - ◊ musk (sacral)
  - ◊ amber (root)

LIGHTWORKER MUST-READ BOOKS

These books can be some of your greatest teachers in helping you remember who you really are. They certainly have been for me. Activating your DNA, remembering your power, connecting to the spirit realm, embodying your Divine Feminine essence, and understanding your place in the greater picture of the universe are just a few of the lessons you will take away. Every Lightworker needs these on her bookshelf:

- *lifevisioning* by Michael Bernard Beckwith
- *DNA in the Sands of Time* by J. Justice
- *Bringers of the Dawn* by Barbara Marciniak
- *Earth* by Barbara Marciniak
- *Path of Empowerment* by Barbara Marciniak
- *The Ancient Secret of the Flower of Life,* volume 1, by Drunvalo Melchizedek
- *The Great Cosmic Mother* by Monica Sjöö and Barbara Mor
- *The Sophia Code* by Kaia Ra
- *The Gene Keys* by Richard Rudd
- *Guidebook for a Modern Priestess* by Ariel Spilsbury
- *A Return to Love* by Marianne Williamson

LIGHTWORKER MUST-LISTEN PODCASTS

When it comes to finding inspiration, education, and community today, there's no better place to look (and listen) than podcasts. Here are a few of my favorites, hosted by some of my favorite Lightworkers in the industry. Listen to mine, and the shows here, wherever you get your podcasts:

- *Take Back Your Mind* with Michael Beckwith
- *Ancient Wisdom* with Shaman Durek
- *The Spiritually Sassy Show* with Sah D'Simone
- *Gaia Speaks* with Pepper Lewis
- *Your Own Magic* with Raquelle Mantra
- *The Spiritual Hustler* with Jessica Zweig

LIGHTWORKER MUST-OWN ORACLE DECKS

Narrowing down the following oracle cards was tough, as I literally own a stack of fifty decks. I chose the following decks because they encapsulate what will no doubt be new and obscure Divine Feminine archetypes, the wisdom of Gaia, the Priestess (who is called the Keeper of Keys herself), as well as wisdom from higher dimensional and galactic beings. If you're looking to start a collection or add to yours, these decks are Lightworker essentials.

- "The 13 Moon Oracle" by Ariel Spilsbury
- "Divine Nature" by Angi Sullins, illustrated by Greg Spalenka
- "The Priestess of Light" by Sandra Anne Taylor, illustrated by Kimberly Webber
- "Keepers of the Light" by Kyle Gray, illustrated by Lily Moses
- "The Wild Unknown Alchemy" by Kim Krans, illustrated by Kim Krans
- "The Wild Unknown Archetypes" by Kim Krans, illustrated by Kim Krans and Su Barber

LIGHTWORKER MUST-HAVE CRYSTAL SELECTION

There is an endless array of crystals in the world, and the medicine, knowledge, wisdom, and expertise that come from this mineral kingdom is truly infinite. At this stage in my life, I own too many crystals to count. Here is the short list of my most favorite stones for practicing the Light Work. Place them in your home, carry them in your purse, wear them around your neck, or simply hold them when you meditate. The power is not in the crystal itself as much as the energy and intention you bring when using it.

- selenite—for space cleansing
- moonstone—for feminine healing and protection
- moldavite—for connecting with the higher chakras and accessing galactic frequencies
- Libyan desert glass—for emotional rebirth and reconnecting with interstellar energy
- pink opal—for self-compassion, self-love, and gentleness
- clear quartz—for general energy cleansing and upgrading your field

A FEW FINAL LIGHTWORKER RESOURCES, TOOLS, BRANDS

- LOTUSWEI Flower Essences—Packed with the chi of the flower and with close to one hundred varietals, these elixirs instantly up-grade your state of mind and energy (lotuswei.com/thelightwork).
- Daily breathwork meditation—*Guided Rhythmic Breathwork Meditation* with SHIVARASA is my favorite, which can be found on YouTube.
- yoni steam—Kitara Love has everything you need (kitaralove.com).
- salt baths—Keep it simple with Rose Petal Epsom Salt from 365 Whole Foods Market (wholefoods.com), or get a little boujie with Agent Nateur Holi (Bath) (agentnatuer.com).
- Gaia TV—My favorite network for conscious video content, and an amazing place to learn more about the Pleiadians. The shows *Open Mind, Deep Space,* and *Beyond Beliefs* all have episodes on the topic (gaia.com).

- Sage Smudge Spray—Infused with real quartz crystals and charged in the vortexes of Sedona, to clear your energetic aura or physical space (junipermist.com).
- Intention candles—From the Ruby Room (rubyroom.com).
- Nick Onken custom hats—The ultimate Lightworker crown (onkenmade.com).
- Rachel Lynn X Corri Lynn jewelry—Beautiful stackable bracelets, necklaces, anklets, and charms made of gemstones and crystals that go with any Lightworker vibe (rlbycl.com).
- Lightworker swag—Hoodies, hats, totes, journals, and more (jessicazweig.com).

Symbols of Light

 The Lightworker's Triangle—Each side represents Information, Truth, and Love, the Divine Laws of Light, culminating in the full expression of the Light Work.

 The Priestess Key—The Priestess is the Keeper of Keys. She is here to unlock the divinity in all.

 The Holy Trinity—The first of one of the naturally occurring patterns in Sacred Geometry represents the mind, body, and spirit.

 The Seed of Life—The universal symbol of all of creation sits at the center of the Flower of Life.

 The Flower of Life—A shape that is found across the world in ancient cultures and spiritual texts (Egypt, India, China, Ireland), it represents the unity of all life and the interconnectedness of all beings.

 The Merkaba—A three-dimensional Star of David, surrounding the energetic field of the body, is used as a vehicle for spiritual ascension, otherwise called the "Chariot."

Please visit jessicazweig.com/unlock to access all the Invitations and Keys, plus additional Lightworker resources.

ACKNOWLEDGMENTS

As I have shared countless times in this book, the human experience is equal parts exquisitely beautiful and exquisitely painful, and therefore a journey not meant to be taken alone. It's no coincidence that the Pleiadians refer to the collective of Lightworkers on this planet as a "family." And so, I'd like to officially thank mine.

First and foremost, thank you to Joel Fotinos, my incredible editor, and the publisher of St. Martin's Essentials. From our initial call, you saw me. "Tell me about the Pleiadians" was your very first request. Since the onset of our relationship, you have believed in my voice as a writer and my message as a teacher. You have mentored me, coached me, and guided me to step more fully into owning my Light. Thank you for taking this book to an entirely new level with your editorial magic. I will forever be grateful to call myself an author who was blessed enough to work with you.

To my entire St. Martin's Essentials team—Emily Anderson, Brant Janeway, Amelia Beckerman, and Sophia Lauriello: the spirit, enthusiasm, and passion you have had for this book was felt in my heart from the very beginning. Thank you for championing this experience for me in every way possible. To Tanya Khani, my soulful publicist indeed: working alongside you has been a dream come true.

Marilyn Allen, you make this ride *so much fun*. Our relationship is one of my most treasured in my career. Cheers to us, forever and into the infinite.

To Aleksa Narbutaitis and Nora Shepard, the other two pieces of the Holy Trinity. Only once in a billion lifetimes will you find the relationship, the connection, the synergy, the Sisterhood, and the undying support for one another's dreams, visions, and identities that the three of us have found in each other in this lifetime. This book would not be this book, nor would I be the woman who wrote it, without you two. From eons and for eons, let's continue to create the Light, share the Light, and be the Light.

To Megan Taylor, my twin flame, deepest laughter and cocaptain adventurer for life. Who knew #SilentGate would inspire a story for so many women to read and heal from? You are one of my biggest blessings, and the world's. I don't know what I would do without your technicolor frequency in my life, and it doesn't matter, because I know I'll never be without it. Thank you for amplifying who I am in the world, as only a best friend can do. I love you to the ends of the Universe. Merge.

To Tali Kogan, the woman who set my Light ablaze from the inside out: you activated something in me I didn't know I had, and that something led me here. Without you by my side, I would not burn as brightly, and that's the truth. Spirit told me that our friendship is as "old as stone," and I know we came together from ancient times to bring the Light to women everywhere today. Thank you for being my biggest cheerleader. I will always be yours.

To the incredible TeamBe: Building SimplyBe. Agency was one of the greatest rides of my life. Emily Oldfather, Aimee Schuster, Heather Redisch, Denise Senter, Julia Addis, Kristin Rohlwing, and the countless others who co-created its success and impact. Thank you for being the torchbearers of its bright yellow light. And to Shauna Nuckles. Thank you for holding a bigger vision for me than I ever held for myself. Our relationship has been nothing short of soul healing.

Stephanie Hand: you really are the greatest of all time. I will never be able to thank Spirit enough for the Divine timing that brought you into my life when I needed you the most. You are a living angel on this planet, and I am blessed beyond measure by your care, support, and oftentimes very needed ass-kicking in service of my highest good. I love you for it, and you are stuck with me. Let's keep helping women across the world claim their Light.

To Rea Frey: I would have never become an author if it weren't for you.

Much of my self-belief has stood on the pillars of you believing in me first. I will continue to believe in you, too.

To my Sisterhood Tree: Lori Harder, Danielle Paige, Danielle LaPorte, Marianne Williamson, Julie Solomon, Kate Northrup, Tara Stiles, Alyssa Rosenheck, Ophira Edut, Amy Porterfield, Heather Dubrow, Natalia Benson, Taylor Simpson, Scout Sobel, Breean Elyse, Hedy Dietzen, Dana Nicole Anderson, Gina Marotta, Christy Nault, Ashley Stahl, Kelli Tennant, Laura Holloway, Chellie Carlson, Katy Hanlon, Andrea Martinez, Dani Beinstein, and each and every woman who attended my Claim Your Light retreats in Nashville and Santa Fe. You are all the Divine Feminine Leaders of the New Earth, and it is my honor and privilege to ride beside you.

To the heart, soul, and quantum co-creators of my Family of Light, Michael Beckwith and Leigh Brown: the instant feeling of home when you came into my life was as real as when I met the Pleiadians themselves. Thank you for embracing who I am in the world, while giving me the gift to amplify who you are in return.

To my Dragon Sherpa, Lauryn Henley: you are my master teacher, and I am simply the master translator. Thank you for introducing me to my Galactic Taylor Swift. Hers and your wisdom is encoded into every page of this book.

To my father, Ron: I really believe my higher self wrote this book for us both to reclaim the pieces of each other we had been longing for. Thank you for your grace, your partnership, and your endless support. I know in my soul that your love is the most unconditional in my life and that the Universe gave me the most perfect father in you. My ten-year-old little girl is holding your hand forever and always, and never letting go.

To my mother, Suzanne, the soul I chose to mother me like no other woman could: your Light, humanity, and compassion is woven into every page of my life, and now this book. I'll never forget when you looked at me and said, "You're a writer, Jessica." As the woman who introduced me to the magic of books, I could not have asked for a more sacred and full-circle affirmation. Just like Baba said, *I love ya, love ya, love ya.*

To my brother, Doug: it's hard to find the words to describe how much I love you and cherish our relationship. You're not only the greatest brother and one of my best friends but one of the most extraordinary human beings walking this Earth. Our connection is like oxygen, and no matter how near or far we are, I promise to always breathe life into our bond. Thank you for enriching my life by choosing Naomi and for giving me my most coveted title of Aunt Jess. I hope to be the greatest role model of Light to Isaiah, Emmanuel, and Kaia.

To my community of Lightworkers on social media and through my podcast: I say all the time that while I don't know you individually, I feel you every day. It is *your* light, *your* authenticity, *your* brilliance, and *your* deep hearts that truly inspire me to keep making things. It's really all for you. Thank you for honoring me with the deep privilege it is to be your teacher, but most of all, your Sister.

To Sekhmet, Isis, Hathor, and the medicine of Egypt, and above all, to my star family, the Pleiadians: thank you for calling me home, for giving me the codes, and for activating my Truth with your Information. I hope that I did you proud.

And finally, to Brian, my lover, my best friend, my ninja, my partner in raising Don and Zooey, and without question my favorite person in the entire Universe: thank you for loving all my dark, all my light, and every shade in between. Our marriage has been my greatest container of spiritual evolution, and that's because you have been my most profound teacher. As the Pleiadians have taught me, the Universe is infinite and ever expanding. So are we, as is this epic adventure we call our life together. Our relationship continues to show me (okay, and Annie, too) that no matter what . . . I will always, always, always *remember*.

NOTES

1: SOURCE

1. Abdelrahman A. Amin, 2018. *Dendera, Land of the Goddess Hathor* (CreateSpace Independent Publishing Platform, 2018), 17.
2. Ananya Mandal, "What is Junk DNA?" *News-Medical Life Sciences*, November 29, 2022, https://www.news-medical.net/life-sciences/What-is-Junk-DNA.aspx.
3. Richard Rudd, *The Gene Keys: Embracing Your Higher Purpose* (London: Watkins Media, 2013), xxxii.

3: BODY

1. Tricia Cannon, *Return of the Divine Sophia: Healing the Earth Through the Lost Wisdom Teachings of Jesus, Isis, and Mary Magdalene* (Rochester: Bear & Company, 2015), 150–151.
2. Barbara Marciniak, *Path of Empowerment, Pleiadian Wisdom for a World in Chaos* (Novato California: New World Library, 2004), 143.
3. Carnivore Aurelius (@carnivoreaurelius), "What's changed in the last 30 years?" Instagram photo, May 2, 2023, https://www.instagram.com/p/CrwgB-buZy-/.

4: POWER

1. Marciniak, *Path of Empowerment*, 31.

6: ROMANTIC RELATIONSHIPS

1. Barbara Marciniak, *Bringers of the Dawn: Teachings from the Pleiadians* (Rochester: Bear & Company, 1992), 211.

7: FEMALE FRIENDSHIPS

1. Marciniak, *Bringers of the Dawn*, 211.
2. Sarah Hollenbeck, "47+ Women in Business Statistics," Bizee, accessed February 16, 2023, https://www.incfile.com/blog/women-in-business-statistics.
3. Sky Ariella, "25 Women in Leadership Statistics 2023—Facts on the Gender Gap in Corporate and Political Leadership," Zippia, November 9, 2022, https://www.zippia.com/advice/women-in-leadership-statistics/#:~:text=Women%20hold%2023%25%25%20of%20executive,of%20support%20staff%20positions%20globally.

8: MONEY

1. Rakesh Kochhar, Pew Research Center, March 1, 2023, https://www.pewresearch.org/social-trends/2023/03/01/the-enduring-grip-of-the-gender-pay-gap/.
2. Elizabeth Howton, "Nearly Half the World Lives on Less than $5.50 a Day," The World Bank, October 17, 2018, https://www.worldbank.org/en/news/press-release/2018/10/17/nearly-half-the-world-lives-on-less-than-550-a-day.

9: MISSION

1. Marciniak, *Bringers of the Dawn*, 140.
2. Marciniak, *Path of Empowerment*, 31.

10: MENTORSHIP

1. Stephanie Neal, Jazmine Boatman, and Linda Miller, "Mentoring Women in the Workplace," DDI, April 9, 2013, https://www.ddiworld.com/research/mentoring-women-in-the-workplace.
2. Naz Beheshti, "Improve Workplace Culture with a Strong Mentorship Program," *Forbes*, January 23, 2019, https://www.forbes.com/sites/nazbeheshti/2019/01/23/improve-workplace-culture-with-a-strong-mentoring-program/.
3. Christine Comaford, "76% of People think Mentors are Important, But Only 37% Have Them," *Forbes*, July 3, 2019, https://www.forbes.com/sites/christinecomaford/2019/07/03/new-study-76-of-people-think-mentors-are-important-but-only-37-have-one/?sh=348f195a4329.

11: GAIA

1. "Ecuador Votes to End Drilling in National Park," *News for Kids*, August 22, 2023, https://newsforkids.net/articles/2023/08/22/ecuador-votes-to-end-drilling-in-national-park/#:~:text=Yasuni%20National%20Park%20is%20reported,entire%20continent%20of%20North%20America.

2. "The Kichwa Añangu Community, A Sustainable Alternative in Yasuní," *Clave!*, https://www.clave.com.ec/the-kichwa-anangu-community-a-sustainable-alternative -in-yasuni/.

3. Rebecca Lake, "Television Statistics: 23 Mind Numbing Facts to Watch," February 26, 2023, CreditDonkey, https://www.creditdonkey.com/television-statistics.html #:~:text=On%20average%2C%20the%20typical%20American,or%201%2C692%20 hours%20per%20year.

4. "State of Global Air Quality Funding 2023," Clean Air Fund, September 28, 2023, https://www.cleanairfund.org/resource/state-of-global-air-quality-funding-2023/.

5. "Factory Farming Strains Natural Resources," *Poughkeepsie Journal*, February 26, 2015, https://www.poughkeepsiejournal.com/story/life/2015/02/26/factory-farming -strains-natural-resources/24059987/.

6. "Marine & Ocean Pollution—Facts 2020–2021," Condor Ferries, accessed January 12, 2024, https://www.condorferries.co.uk/marine-ocean-pollution-statistics -facts#:~:text=An%20estimated%208%20Million%20tons,15%25%20lands%20 on%20our%20beaches.

7. "Brazil and the Amazon Forest," *Greenpeace USA*, https://www.greenpeace.org/usa /issues/brazil-and-the-amazon-forest/.

8. Grace Hussien, "Amazon Deforestation," *Sentient Media*, October 13, 2023, https: //sentientmedia.org/amazon-deforestation/#:~:text=Cattle%20ranching%20is%20 a%20leading,tons%20of%20carbon%20per%20year.

9. Nick Routley, "Histomap—Visualizing the 4,000 Year History of Global Power," Visual Capitalist, August 25, 2021, https://www.visualcapitalist.com/histomap/.

10. James DeMeo, *Saharasia: The 4000 BCE Origins of Child Abuse, Sex-Repression, Warfare and Social Violence, In the Deserts of the Old World* (Natural Energy Works, 1998).

11. Barbara Mor and Monica Sjoo, *The Great Cosmic Mother: Rediscovering The Religion of Earth* (New York: HarperOne, 1987), 49.

12. Tricia Cannon, *Return of the Divine Sophia: Healing the Earth Through the Lost Wisdom Teachings of Jesus, Isis, and Mary Magdalene* (Rochester: Bear & Company, 2015), 147.

13. Victoria LePage, *Mysteries of the Bridechamber: The Initiation of Jesus and The Temple of Solomon* (Inner Traditions, 2007).

14. Barbara Marciniak, *Earth: Pleiadian Keys to the Living Library* (Rochester: Bear & Company, 1994), 90.

15. Marciniak, *Bringers of the Dawn*, 89–90.

16. Joseph Campbell, *The Hero with a Thousand Faces* (Princeton, NJ: Princeton University Press, 1949), 113.

12: MIRACLES

1. Marciniak, *Bringers of the Dawn*, 128.